Democratizing Biblical Studies

Toward an Emancipatory Educational Space

Elisabeth Schüssler Fiorenza

WESTMINSTER
JOHN KNOX PRESS
LOUISVILLE · KENTUCKY

© 2009 Elisabeth Schüssler Fiorenza

First edition
Published by Westminster John Knox Press
Louisville, Kentucky

09 10 11 12 13 14 15 16 17 18—10 9 8 7 6 5 4 3 2 1

Scripture quotations are from the New Revised Standard Version of the Bible and copyright © 1989 by the Division of Christian Education of the National Council of the Churches of Christ in the U.S.A. and are used by permission.

Book design by Drew Stevens
Cover design by Lisa Buckley
Cover art © 2009 Artists Rights Society (ARS), New York / ADAGP,
Paris / Franz Kupka, "Disks of Newton," 1912

Library of Congress Cataloging-in-Publication Data

Schüssler Fiorenza, Elisabeth, 1938–
  Democratizing biblical studies : toward an emancipatory educational space / Elisabeth Schüssler Fiorenza.
     p. cm.
  Includes bibliographical references and index.
  ISBN 978-0-664-23362-4 (cloth)
  ISBN 978-0-664-23509-3 (paper)
  (alk. paper)
  1. Theology—Study and teaching.   2. Bible—Criticism, interpretation, etc.   I. Title.
  BV4020.S38   2009
  230.071'1—dc22

                                                              2009011994

PRINTED IN THE UNITED STATES OF AMERICA

∞ The paper used in this publication meets the minimum requirements
of the American National Standard for Information Sciences—Permanence
of Paper for Printed Library Materials, ANSI Z39.48-1992.

Westminster John Knox Press advocates the responsible use of our natural resources.
The text paper of this book is made from 30% postconsumer waste.

Contents

Acknowledgments

This work owes its conception and development to the countless students who have enthusiastically participated over the years in my courses and seminars, trying to realize a radical democratic imaginary space of theological education. I am deeply grateful to them for many of the insights in this book. However, without the persistent prodding and encouragement of Philip Law, the former academic editor and UK/EU publishing director of Westminster John Knox Press, this book might never have been realized, since pedagogy is best done rather than written about.

I owe a great debt of gratitude to the Wabash Center for Teaching and Learning in Theology and Religion and its former director Lucinda Huffacker for a research grant in 2007–2008 that enabled me to take an unpaid study leave from Harvard Divinity School in order to complete my research and to draft the chapters of this book. I am grateful to Dean Graham for granting this unpaid leave.

This work has been enriched greatly by the contributions of the participants in my graduate seminar on Democratizing Biblical Studies in the fall semester 2008. Jason Bachand, Michelle Chaplin Sanchez, John Falcone, Arminta Fox, Elizabeth Jean Gish, Hannah Hofheinz, Roberto Mata, and Tyler Schwaller have sustained a radical democratic ethos and lively debates throughout the semester. The metalogue makes their voices and insights an essential part of the book in order to help readers to move from theory to practice. Their research papers, which will be published on the accompanying Web site, in turn critically expand the vision of this work. Their intellectual engagement and personal dedication promise a great future for emancipatory biblical studies. I owe a great debt to them.

It has been a great pleasure to work at Westminster John Knox Press with a wonderful team of experts. Stephanie Egnotovich, executive editor of Westminster John Knox Press, enthusiastically took over as editor of the book after Philip Law left the press. Her careful reading of the manuscript and wise counsel have immensely improved the work.

As so many of "her" authors I have been shocked and grieved by her untimely death but I am very grateful for the work she has done over the years to promote religious publishing, especially by women. We all will greatly miss her

I am also grateful to associate managing editor Daniel Braden for skillfully shepherding the book through the production process; to S. David Garber, who has meticulously copyedited the manuscript; to Teri Kays Vinson for her management of the cover design; to electronic marketing associate Andrew W. Yeager-Buckley for designing the accompanying Web site [http://www.wjkbooks.com/Democratizing BiblicalStudies/]; and last but not least to Jennifer K. Cox, the WJK marketing and production director, for all her work of coordinating the production and marketing endeavors.

I also thank my research assistants, Michelle Chaplin Sanchez, Elizabeth Jean Gish, and Tyler Schwaller, for their careful work in proofreading the book, especially for making suggestions for its improvement, as well as in proofing and standardizing the papers published on the Web site. I am also grateful to my office assistant, Cole Eliot Gustafson, for working on the two diagrams enclosed in the text.

Everything I write and do owes a great debt of gratitude to my life partner, Francis Schüssler Fiorenza, and our daughter, Chris Miryam Schüssler-Fiorenza. Without their unstinting support and friendship, I could not survive.

This work is dedicated to my colleagues and friends Regula Strobel, Renate Jost, and Jane Schaberg, who each in their own way have enriched my life. I hope that this token of my gratitude will indicate how much I appreciate their feminist commitment and work. It is also devoted to the memory of Stephanie Egnotovich to whom religious publishing in general and this work in particular owes an immense debt.

Introduction

Toward a Radical Democratic Self-Understanding
of Biblical Studies

This book continues my argument in *The Power of the Word*[1] that biblical scholarship has to become publicly accountable and to articulate biblical knowledge that sustains rather than undermines a radical democratic ethos.[2] Its main title, *Democratizing Biblical Studies*, is decidedly ambiguous. It can have "biblical studies" either as its subject or as its object of investigation. If biblical studies is understood as the subject of democratizing, it articulates the democratizing influence and impact of the Bible and biblical studies. If understood as its object, then the title points to the need for the pedagogical practices of graduate biblical education to be democratized. I understand the title in both senses and argue that we need to thoroughly consider and critically examine both possibilities.

The call for *Democratizing Biblical Studies* requires that biblical scholarship explore both the exclusionary spaces and the democratizing potentials of the Bible, that it becomes methodologically aware of its social

---

1. Elisabeth Schüssler Fiorenza, *The Power of the Word: Scripture and the Rhetoric of Empire* (Minneapolis: Fortress Press, 2007).

2. For the theoretical context of my argument, see for instance Seyla Benhabib, ed., *Democracy and Difference: Contesting the Boundaries of the Political* (Princeton, NJ: Princeton University Press, 1996); Chantal Mouffe, ed., *Dimensions of Radical Democracy* (London: Verso, 1992); Simone Chambers, *Reasonable Democracy: Jürgen Habermas and the Politics of Discourse* (Ithaca, NY: Cornell University Press, 1996); Jeffrey C. Isaaks, *Democracy in Dark Times* (Ithaca, NY: Cornell University Press, 1998); Anna Marie Smith, *Laclau and Mouffe: The Radical Democratic Imaginary* (New York: Routledge, 1998); Ewa Plonowska Ziarek, *An Ethics of Dissensus: Postmodernity, Feminism, and the Politics of Radical Democracy* (Stanford, CA: Stanford University Press, 2001); Sheldon S. Wolin, *Politics and Vision: Continuity and Innovation in Western Political Thought*, expanded ed. (Princeton, NJ: Princeton University Press, 2004).

location in a democratic society, and that it reflects on its democratic sociopolitical contexts.[3] In short, this work seeks to elaborate a view of democracy as a verb, as action oriented[4] rather than as a static political concept. It also seeks to elaborate an intellectual space where biblical education for global citizenship[5] can be engendered and practiced.

The subtitle *"Toward an Emancipatory Educational Space"* indicates the direction in which my arguments move. In postmodernity space has been rediscovered as an object of social discourse and as the possibility of an emancipatory critical practice. Spatiality as a social product and as a shaping force in life allows one to theoretically explore "how relations of power and discipline are inscribed into the apparently innocent spatiality of life, how human geographies become filled with politics and ideology."[6] Thinking of Biblical Studies in terms of educational space and historically constructed spatiality allows one to investigate the geographies of exclusion that shape the theoretical space of Biblical Studies. It allows one "to examine the assumptions about inclusions and exclusions which are implicit in the design of spaces"[7] such as the field of biblical studies or the cultural and political spaces constructed by Western democracy.

Since the Bible has had and still has enormous influence on the public political and educational spaces of the United States, it is necessary for American biblical scholarship to critically explore the impact of the Bible on American culture and life and to examine what it means for Scripture to have acted as both a conservative and a radical social force, to have provided a vocabulary for both traditional deference and innovative egalitarianism, and to have been a source for both stability in the face of anarchy and freedom in the face of tyranny.[8]

From its very beginnings the United States has understood itself as a biblical nation. Lawmakers assemble at the Capitol steps to sing "God Bless America," American flags grace churches and synagogues, and cit-

---

3. For a the*logical perspective, see John W. De Gruchy, *Christianity and Democracy: A Theology for a Just World Order* (Cambridge: Cambridge University Press, 1995); and Cornel West, *Democracy Matters: Winning the Fight against Imperialism* (New York: Penguin Books, 2004). See also my article "A Discipleship of Equals: Ekklesial Democracy and Patriarchy in Biblical Perspective," in *A Democratic Catholic Church*, ed. Eugene C. Bianch and Rosemary Radford Ruether (New York: Crossroad, 1992).

4. For such an understanding see also Morwenna Griffiths, *Action for Social Justice in Education* (Philadelphia: McGraw Hill, 2003).

5. See also the collection of essays by Nell Noddings, ed., *Educating Citizens for Global Awareness* (New York: Teachers College Press, 2005).

6. See Edward W. Soja, *Postmodern Geographies: The Reassertion of Space in Critical Social Theory* (New York: Verso, 1989), 6.

7. David Sibley, *Geographies of Exclusion: Society and Difference in the West* (New York: Routledge, 1995), x.

8. Nathan O. Hatch and Mark Noll, eds., *The Bible in America: Essays in Cultural History* (New York: Oxford University Press, 1982), 8.

izens acknowledge membership "in one nation under G*d.⁹" The U.S. presidents, be they Jefferson, Lincoln, Carter, or Clinton, have freely quoted the Bible. More recently a strident biblical rhetoric has been deployed by President George W. Bush in the interests of nationalism. For example, in his oft-quoted 9/11 anniversary speech in September 2002, Bush paraphrased John 1:4–5, saying, "This ideal of America is the hope of all mankind. . . . That hope still lights our way. And the light shines in the darkness, and the darkness will not overcome it."[10] This paraphrase substitutes "America" for "Jesus Christ, the incarnate Word of G*d," and thereby divinizes U.S. imperialism as "the light of the world."

The scriptural understanding of President Barack Obama is quite different. It is critically reflective, contextually aware, and understands the Bible as a "living word." In his book *The Audacity of Hope*, Obama explicates the hermeneutic of his reading of the Bible:

> When I read the Bible, I do so with the belief that it is not a static text but the Living Word and that I must be continually open to new revelations—whether they come from a lesbian friend or a doctor opposed to abortion. This is NOT to say that I am unanchored in my faith. There are some things that I'm absolutely sure about—the Golden Rule, the need to battle cruelty in all its forms, the value of love and charity, humility and grace.[11]

The Bible is a democratizing book. It is a collection of writings spanning the G*d-experience of many centuries, a book in which a rich plurality of "citizen" voices argue with each other, complement each other, and keep alive the vision of divine justice, care, and well-being.[12] These voices are democratically enriched by the many contexts in which they are heard and interpreted.[13] The word of G*d can only be heard as a Living Word by engaging creatively with this din of voices from very

---

9. To indicate the brokenness and inadequacy of human language for naming the Divine, in my book *Jesus: Miriam's Child, Sophia's Prophet: Critical Issues in Feminist Christology* (New York: Continuum, 1994) I have switched from the orthodox Jewish writing of G-d, which I had adopted in *But She Said* and *Discipleship of Equals*, to this spelling of G*d, which seeks to avoid the conservative malestream association that the writing of G-d provokes for Jewish feminists. For discussion of the term "God," see Francis Schüssler Fiorenza and Gordon Kaufman, "God," in *Critical Terms for Religious Studies*, ed. Mark C. Taylor (Chicago: University of Chicago Press, 1998), 136–59. Consequently, I write the*logy/the*logical which means speaking about the Divine in a similar way.

10. Jeffrey S. Siker, "President Bush, Biblical Faith, and the Politics of Religion," *SBL Forum* (n.p.: cited May 2006), http://www.sbl-site.org/publications/article.aspx?articleId=151 (accessed April 4, 2009).

11. Barack Obama, *The Audacity of Hope: Thoughts on Reclaiming the American Dream* (New York: Vintage Books, 2008), 265.

12. See Jaroslav Pelikan, *Whose Bible Is It? A Short History of the Scriptures* (New York: Penguin Books, 2005).

13. For the understanding and use of the Bible in the African American community, see Allen Dwight Callahan, *The Talking Book: African Americans and the Bible* (New Haven, CT: Yale University Press, 2006).

different political contexts, voices searching for freedom, equality, justice, and well-being in times of violence and empire. Such a radical democratic understanding of the Bible requires an equally far-reaching democratizing of biblical studies.

A similar point is made by the editors of *The Bible in the Public Square*. However, they argue not with reference to the struggles around the world for radical democracy, but with reference to the biblical call for "reading the signs of the times":

> To read the Bible in the public square in these times is to take on a challenging task. Issues of hunger, poverty, and violence are urgent and call for our response. . . . It follows that Biblical scholars can and do have a role to play in the public square, an ecumenical, plural, democratic space that is neither the church sanctuary nor the classroom. They carry out this obligation in different ways depending on what model they employ, their own location, their audience, and their area of expertise. For all of them, however, responsible Biblical scholarship requires reading "the signs of the times."[14]

In other words, rather than just learning how to interpret texts, study history, or reflect on the Bible theologically, future biblical scholars need also to learn how to read "the signs of the times" (Matt. 16:3). To do so, biblical scholars must become schooled in societal, ecclesial, and cultural analysis capable of naming powers of injustice and dehumanization. Such analysis must be careful, though, not to limit but rather to keep open its conception of the public.

In his book *Democracy and Tradition*, Jeffrey Stout has drawn attention to the problematic meaning of "the public square" if it is understood statically as a place. Instead, Stout proposes that the "public square" be understood as a dynamic "public" sphere characterized by a compelling religious vision of how citizens can reason with each other and hold each other accountable.

> One is addressing the public whenever one addresses people as citizens. In a modern democracy, this is not something one does in one place or at once. Wherever two or three citizens are gathered whom one might address as citizens, as persons jointly responsible for the common good, one is in a potentially public setting. . . . If you express theological commitments in a reflective and sustained way,

---

14. Cynthia Briggs Kittredge, Ellen Bradshaw Aitken, and Jonathan A. Draper, eds., *The Bible in the Public Square: Reading the Signs of the Times* (Minneapolis: Fortress Press, 2008), 1.

while addressing fellow citizens as citizens, you are "doing theology" publicly—and in that sense doing public theology.[15]

Wherever two or three citizens are gathered to study the Bible, its democratizing power as the Living Word can be experienced. This requires an understanding that biblical studies has the function of enabling citizens to recognize that their coming together constitutes a public in which they are responsible for articulating the Living Word in their different sociopolitical religious contexts. Democratizing graduate biblical education would then mean that scholars recognize and elaborate as the "home spaces" of biblical studies not only the academy and the church but also democratic society, with its variegated citizenship. The emerging fourth paradigm—an *intercultural/interreligious–emancipatory-radical democratic paradigm*—of biblical studies, I argue, is in the process of articulating such a radical democratic space of biblical interpretation.

However, as indicated by Dale Martin's recent study of the discipline, which is based on interviews at ten theological schools and surveys of the Web sites of others, the discipline is still engaged in the modern turf war between historical-critical and theological-doctrinal studies. Martin points out that "the dominant method of interpretation students are taught, just about everywhere, is traditional historical criticism."[16] Michael Joseph Brown's primer *What They Don't Tell You: A Survivor's Guide to Biblical Studies*[17] confirms Martin's observation of the dominance of historical criticism in graduate education: again and again he stresses that biblical studies does not mean "Bible study" and warns his readers not to engage in eisegesis. His "Rules of Thumb" include the following, for example: "Be careful not to read your modern assumptions into ancient texts. A translation is only as good as its translator. An overactive imagination can get you into trouble." These rules seek to explicate the survival skills necessary for students who want to pursue biblical studies, while making it clear that the discipline is understood primarily in terms of historical-critical scholarship.

Neither Brown nor Martin seems to be concerned with educating graduate students to "read the signs of the times" by learning how to critically analyze their own sociopolitical cultural-contextual locations and the function of the Bible in these contexts. In line with the "new

15. Jeffrey Stout, *Democracy and Tradition* (Princeton, NJ: Princeton University Press, 2004), 113.
16. Dale B. Martin, *Pedagogy of the Bible: An Analysis and Proposal* (Louisville, KY: Westminster John Knox Press, 2008), 12.
17. Michael Joseph Brown, *What They Don't Tell You: A Survivor's Guide to Biblical Studies* (Louisville, KY: Westminster John Knox Press, 2000).

traditionalists,"[18] Martin argues for a curriculum of biblical studies that values the theological and doctrinal function of Scripture in the church and places it at the center of theological education. He argues that graduate education, now almost universally focused on the historical-critical method, needs to foster the study of premodern biblical hermeneutics and postmodern theories of text.[19]

While I agree with the insistence of Dale Martin that a critical theological education and sophistication is absolutely necessary for biblical ministry education, I do not think that "the new traditionalism" in theology will solve the problem. Nor do I think that theological literacy should be restricted to Master of Divinity (MDiv) students. Rather, I am concerned here with theological education in general and the education of future biblical scholars and leaders in theories of interpretation, hermeneutics, and ideology critique. Unlike Michael J. Brown, I am not concerned primarily with articulating ideas for surviving historical-critical biblical scholarship. Rather than trying to persuade students to adopt the dominant historical paradigm, I seek to marshal arguments for changing graduate biblical education into a radical democratic space of critical inquiry, sociopolitical ethical exploration, and creative religious re-visioning.

To those knowing how difficult it is to change entrenched institutional habits, such a transformative vision might sound like an impossible pipe dream that cannot be realized. However, as a radical democratic dreamer, I do not envision that change is going to take place from the top down but only from the bottom up. Whether we are contemplating entering into biblical studies, whether we are studying for ministry in the church or for working in the media or schools, whether we are undertaking doctoral studies or are professors teaching these students, whether we are administrators of theological schools or recruitment officers—each one of us can contribute to this radical democratic transformation. To do so, we must turn away from positivist scientistic scholarship, functionalist skills orientation, or fundamentalist anxiety; instead, we must envision and claim a radical democratic ethos and pedagogical space.[20] This book's metalogue and the student

---

18. Jeffrey Stout, who has coined this term, counts among them Stanley Hauerwas, Alasdair MacIntyre, and John Milbank, who proclaim "radical orthodoxy" (cf. *Democracy and Tradition*, 92–179).

19. Dale Martin, *Pedagogy of the Bible*, 29–70.

20. Stephen Protero, *Religious Literacy: What Every American Needs to Know—and Doesn't* (New York: Harper One, 2008), points out that American college students are more religious than Europeans but also much more ignorant about religion. Hence, he has developed a "Dictionary of Religious Literacy" in order to answer the question, What does a U.S. citizen need to know "to understand and participate in religiously inflected public debates?" (185).

papers on the accompanying Web site are examples of such a pedagogy and research.[21]

CONTEXTUALIZING ARGUMENTS FOR A RADICAL DEMOCRATIC EDUCATIONAL SPACE

Such a *radical* (from Latin *radix* = *root*), that is, *grassroots*, democratic space is carved out today by social movements for change. I suggest that biblical scholars must learn from them. Grassroots movements for justice have initiated processes of democratization around the globe that allow people to determine their lives, to participate in decision making, and to contribute to the creation of a just civil society and religious community. In my usage, however, democracy does not denote representative formal democracy. Neither am I concerned with governance. Rather, I envision a profoundly egalitarian space where citizen interpreters of the Bible are accountable to a global citizenry.[22]

Three broad understandings of democracy[23] and democratization can be distinguished: liberal democracy, Marxist/socialist democracy, and direct participatory democracy. *Liberal democracy* entails a shift from the direct rule of the people to representative government, which protects individual rights, equal opportunity, constitutional government, and separation of powers. *Marxist/socialist democracy* argues that effective participation of citizens in the political process is prevented by class and other inequalities. Human emancipation is only possible with the overthrow of the capitalist system. However, socialist democrats increasingly seek to incorporate pluralism and multiculturalism into a Marxist theory of democratization.

Participatory democracy insists on a literal understanding of democracy as the "power of the people." It distinguishes itself from other forms of democracy by the conviction that such a "people democracy"

21. See also the important and path-breaking collection of student essays *The Bible and the American Myth: A Symposium on the Bible and Constructions of Meaning*, ed. Vincent L. Wimbush (Macon, GA: Mercer University Press, 1999), which is a paradigmatic example for what I envision.

22. See David Held, *Democracy and the Global Order: From the Modern State to Cosmopolitan Governance* (Stanford, CA: Stanford University Press, 1995); Seyla Benhabib, ed., *Democracy and Difference: Contesting the Boundaries of the Political* (Princeton, NJ: Princeton University Press, 1996); and the important argument of Kwame Anthony Appiah, *Cosmopolitanism: Ethics in a World of Strangers* (New York: W. W. Norton, 2006), for an ethical space that enables a flourishing of cosmopolitanism in which people can give expression to a multiplicity of identities while also creating a radical democratic community through discovery and dialogue.

23. For an overview, see Alex Demirovic, *Demokratie und Herrschaft: Aspekte kritischer Gesellschaftstheorie* (Münster: Verlag Westfälisches Dampfboot, 1997); Robert A. Dahl, *On Democracy* (New Haven, CT: Yale University Press, 1998); Josiah Ober and Charles Hedrick, eds., *Dēmokratia: A Conversation on Democracies, Ancient and Modern* (Princeton, NJ: Princeton University Press, 1996).

is *actually realizable*. It entails equal opportunities for all to take part in decision making for matters affecting not only the political realm but also the workplace, the community, and interpersonal relations. Participatory democracy also encourages people to take control over the course of their lives and supports structural arrangements that motivate citizens to exercise self-determination, to respect the rights of others, to take part in debates about the "common good," and to create new institutions that are truly participatory and egalitarian. This participatory understanding of democracy recognizes that

> democracy needs to continue to undergo a process of re-creation and that a more active and substantial participation can only take place as a result of experimentation with new and different ways that seek to enhance citizen involvement and discussion. In a sense, democracy can never be achieved in any final form—it has to be continually re-created and renegotiated.[24]

Democratic grassroots movements are the embodiment of such ongoing democratization processes. These community-based initiatives, base groups, or people's organizations address practical everyday problems; they are committed to improving living conditions in a particular location and to promoting values associated with local radical democratic politics. Such movements work toward a transformed, more just society by seeking to create and to expand spaces for democratic decision making, consciousness raising, individual self-development, group solidarity, and more effective public participation. Wo/men[25] are and have been at the forefront in creating and shaping such global processes of democratization.

---

24. Jill M. Bystydzienski and Joti Sekhon, eds., *Democratization and Women's Grassroots Movements* (Bloomington: Indiana University Press, 1999), 9. This book analyzes the variety of ways in which wo/men from sixteen different countries struggle "for more control over their daily lives while simultaneously creating and extending opportunities for greater participation" (18).

25. To lift into consciousness the linguistic violence of so-called generic male-centered language, I use the term "wo/men" and not "men" in an inclusive way. I suggest that whenever you hear "wo/men," you understand it in the generic sense. Wo/men includes men, s/he includes he, and fe/male includes male. Feminist studies of language have shown that Western, kyriocentric—that is, master, lord, father, male-centered—language systems understand language as both generic and as gender specific. Wo/men always must think at least twice, if not three times, and adjudicate whether or not we are meant by so-called generic terms such as "men, humans, Americans, citizens." To use "wo/men" as an inclusive generic term invites men in the audience to learn how to "think twice" and to experience what it means not to be addressed explicitly. Since wo/men always must arbitrate whether we are meant or not, I consider it a good spiritual exercise for men to acquire the same sophistication. Men must learn how to engage in the same hermeneutical process of "thinking twice" and of asking whether they are meant when I speak of wo/men. Since, according to the philosopher Wittgenstein, the limits of our language are the limits of our world, such a change of language patterns is a very important step toward the realization of a new feminist consciousness.

In modernity most of the social movements for change have been inspired by the dream of radical democratic equality and equal human rights. The Western democratic ideal has promised equal participation and equal rights to all, but in implementation has restricted power and rights to a small group of elite propertied gentlemen; hence, those who have been deprived of their human rights and dignity have struggled to transform their situations of oppression and exclusion. However, it must not be overlooked that radical grassroots democratic struggles are not just a product of modernity. Neither is their ethos and vision of radical democracy restricted to the West.

The role and contributions of intellectuals in radically democratic social movements is greatly debated. Cornel West has responded by calling for intellectuals who understand themselves as cultural critics to become involved in a "cultural politics of difference."

> The new cultural politics of difference are neither simply opposi-tional in contesting the mainstream (or *malestream*) for inclusion, nor transgressive in the avant-gardist sense of shocking conventional bourgeois audiences. Rather, they are distinct articulations of tal-ented (and usually privileged) contributors to culture who desire to align themselves with demoralized, demobilized, depoliticized, and disorganized people in order to empower and enable social action. . . . This perspective impels these cultural critics and artists to reveal, as an integral component of their production, the very opera-tions of power within their immediate work contexts (i.e., academy, museums, gallery, mass media).[26]

West acknowledges the feminist roots of the cultural politics of dif-ference and observes that the decisive push toward it has come not from male intellectuals of the left, but from black wo/men of the African diaspora. Cultural critics have the task to align themselves in solidarity with those who are dehumanized by the relations of domination and to spell out the operations of power in such relations. However, I won-der whether the responsibility of such intellectuals is best characterized as "empowering and enabling social action." In my view, intellectuals will be able to articulate knowledges and visions that engender and empower sociopolitical action and the change of relations of domina-tion only if and when we as participants in a sociopolitical movement

---

26. Cornel West, "The New Cultural Politics of Difference," in *The Cultural Studies Reader*, ed. S. During (New York: Routledge, 1993), 204.

for justice attempt to "hear into speech"[27] the theoretical problems and challenges of people involved in grassroots democratic struggles.

I do not want to be misunderstood. I do not propose an emphasis on theorizing and vision above social action. Rather than continuing to question the "role" of intellectuals in social movements, I propose refocusing our attention on what these movements themselves contribute theoretically to the articulation of what is considered as knowledge. Such a shift underscores the significance, creativity, and initiative of grassroots movements for articulating emancipatory knowledges and wisdom over and above that of the talented intellectual and privileged advocate. Instead of seeking to empower and enable people at the grassroots level, public intellectuals must first *learn from* the politics and values of grassroots movements for justice and well-being.

The abolitionist movements of the nineteenth century and the liberation movements of the 1960s—the antislavery, workers' rights, civil rights, anticolonialist, gay, antiwar, and radical democratic student movements, and last but not least, the wo/men's liberation movement—constitute the social location of, and have provided the language and discourses for, a radical democratic biblical interpretation. These movements have impacted biblical studies so as to initiate the emergence of a new fourth emancipatory paradigm of interpretation in the academy.

A critical emancipatory pedagogy and ethos not only has to critically focus on the dehumanizing power of oppression and its effects as "power over," but also to hold open the possibility of transformation. Far from reinscribing the binary dualism between oppressor and oppressed, emancipatory discourses insist that the humanity of both oppressor and oppressed is severely deformed and damaged by the powers of domination, which liberation theologians have named as structural sin. Emancipatory theory is an account of the oppressive workings of power whereby oppressive power or domination is seen as the ability of one person or a group to dominate and exploit the other. Further, emancipatory theory and theology distinguish between two modalities of power: power as "power over" or as "domination" on the one hand, and power as "power for" or as energy and creativity on the other hand. Hence, the transformation of unjust situations is central for emancipatory theory and theology. It presupposes a principled opposition to domination and exploitation in the name of justice.

27. Nell Morton, *The Journey Is Home* (Boston: Beacon Press, 1985).

Emancipatory theory articulates biblical interpretation in terms of an ethics or morality of radical equality and justice. This ethics of the irreducible value of human beings who are wo/men is the central moral truth in emancipatory studies. One's self-worth and dignity depend on oneself and are not derived in competition with others. There is something absolute about the value of human beings, who are all equal before G*d. This moral truth is completely at odds with the ways our societies and communities are organized and structured around marginal status and relations of domination. It also rejects all arbitrary privilege and relations of dependence, which generate all kinds of repression, equivocation, and uneasiness.

The kyriarchal[28] discourses of domination in turn engender an ethics of inequality that requires relations of superiority and inferiority between human beings. Some people are held to be more important and valuable than others. In the ethics of domination, one's sense of importance, goodness, and worth depends on the negation of such qualities of someone else, who must therefore be in some way comparatively insignificant and inferior. Discourses of domination not only socialize us into the ethos of superiority/inferiority but also pressure us into identifying and colluding with those who have status and power. A pedagogy of domination compels us to recognize the importance of those in power and to disassociate and distance ourselves from those who are "unacceptable" and without power. The economic, psychological, social, and political costs are high if one refuses to collude in this pedagogical ethos of domination. Students lose their initiative of thinking, creative imagination, and sociopolitical commitments in an academic model of competitive knowledge production.

Insofar as human beings have a fundamental need to be recognized and respected by other human beings, domination psychologically and socially deforms people, and these deformations in turn maintain dehumanizing power relations. The antagonism of oppressed people toward each other is the underside of this fundamental need for recognition.[29] It keeps relations of domination in place by channeling aggression away from the powerful and onto the oppressed. Internalized shame and

---

28. I have coined the expression kyriarchy/kyriocentrism/kyriarchal in order to name the system of domination that goes back to antiquity and is still at work today. Kyriarchy is derived from the Greek *kyrios = emperor, lord, slave master, father, head of household, elite propertied educated male*, and *archein = to rule and dominate.*See my introduction to *Prejudice and Christian Beginnings: Investigating Race, Gender, and Ethnicity in Early Christian Studies*, ed. by Laura Nasrallah and Elisabeth Schüssler Fiorenza (Minneapolis: Fortress Press, 2009) .

29. On the importance of recognition, see Nancy Fraser, "Mapping the Feminist Imagination: From Redistribution to Recognition to Representation," *Constellations* 12, no. 3 (2005): 295–307. For a fuller development of this argument, see my book *The Power of the Word: Scripture and the Rhetoric of Empire* (Minneapolis: Fortress Press, 2007), 7–34.

antagonism of the marginalized against each other is engendered by the discourses of domination. It is a sign that even feminists have internalized the general cultural prejudice that considers wo/men to be "lesser" human beings. This ethos of superiority/inferiority is the psychological mechanism that sustains most relations of domination.

The fundamental need to be recognized as human is constitutive of what it means to be human. This definition of being human needs no specific content other than the satisfaction of this need itself. The need for unconditional recognition and respect as a human being is prior to any other need. Emancipatory theory and theology considers the worth of human beings to be absolute, unchangeable, and not subject to comparison or competition. Such radical equality is not sameness but only the absence of any qualities and pressures to subordinate persons as inferior in order to subject them to the control of the more powerful.

Consequently, it is in the course of personal and political struggles and resistances against domination that the drive for respect and love becomes a drive for autonomy and self-determination. Resistance has two phases or moments that are interdependent: the abolition of relations of domination, and the struggle for autonomy and respect. The possibility of genuine human respect, love, and equality can only be achieved when relations of domination are resisted and transformed into relations of equality. The social character of being human requires that the liberation of one human being from domination is intrinsically dependent on all others attaining it too. This demands a transformation not only of oppressive structures but also of individual consciousness. In consequence, emancipatory biblical interpretation has to focus on such a transformation of consciousness.

TOWARD A RADICAL DEMOCRATIC PEDAGOGY OF BIBLICAL STUDIES

From the nineteenth into the twentieth and now twenty-first centuries, the Bible has been used both as a weapon against emancipatory struggles for equal citizenship in society and church and as a resource for emancipatory struggles for liberation.[30] Biblical interpretation, I

---

30. For theoretical contextualization, see Amy Gutmann, *Democratic Education* (Princeton, NJ: Princeton University Press, 1987); Amy Gutmann and Dennis Thompson, *Democracy and Disagreement* (Cambridge: Belknap Press of Harvard University Press, 1996); Becky W. Thompson and Sangeeta Tyagi, eds., *Beyond a Dream Deferred: Multicultural Education and the Politics of Excellence* (Minneapolis: University of Minnesota Press, 1993); bell hooks,

propose here, is best conceptualized as an integral part of emancipatory struggles for survival, justice, and well-being. If the Bible has been used both against and for wo/men in their diverse struggles, then the goal of biblical interpretation cannot be just *to understand* and *appropriate* biblical texts and traditions. Rather, an emancipatory biblical pedagogy has the task *to change* biblical interpretation and its Western idealist hermeneutical frameworks, individualist practices, and sociopolitical relations of domination. In reclaiming the authority of wo/men as religious-theological subjects who must claim their own spiritual authority for shaping and determining biblical religions, my own feminist work has attempted to reconceptualize the act of biblical interpretation as a moment in the global struggles for radical democracy.

Hence, an emancipatory pedagogy seeks to develop new ways of reading the Bible (and other culturally influential texts) in order to prevent biblical knowledge from continuing to be produced in the interest of domination and injustice. Usually it is assumed that biblical knowledge and reading practices are developed by academic or ecclesiastic leaders and then "translated" into the vernacular language of the "common reader," who in turn is expected to appropriate and apply such knowledge to everyday life. I argue to the contrary, that wo/men struggling for change and recognition as full citizens in society, the academy, and synagogues, mosques, or churches articulate emancipatory knowledge and liberating insights that need to be recognized by scholars and ministers.

Hence, graduate biblical education must enable future biblical scholars, ministers, and religious leaders to attend to such emancipatory biblical knowledge. Future academic and ecclesiastic leaders have to prepare for the task of "translating" such knowledge into academic and religious discourse so that such emancipatory knowledge can become public knowledge and inspire research in the interests of justice for all. In other words, emancipatory biblical interpreters have the task not so much to translate the methods and results of biblical scholarship to a wider audience, but rather to learn from and to cast their lot with wo/men struggling for survival and change in order to be able to translate wo/men's quest for self-esteem and justice into the language and research goals of the academy.

Teaching to Transgress: Education as the Practice of Freedom (New York: Routledge, 1994); Madeleine Arnot and Jo-Anne Dillabough, eds., *Challenging Democracy: International Perspectives on Gender, Education and Citizenship* (New York: Routledge, 2000); bell hooks, *Teaching Community: A Pedagogy of Hope* (New York: Routledge, 2003); Alan M. Olson, David M. Steiner, and Irina S. Tuuli, eds., *Educating for Democracy: Paideia in an Age of Uncertainty* (Lanham, MD: Rowman & Littlefield Publishers, 2004).

Long before postmodern theories, liberation theologies of all colors have not only recognized the perspectival and contextual nature of knowledge and interpretation but also have asserted that biblical interpretation and theology are—knowingly or not—always engaged for or against the oppressed. Intellectual neutrality is not possible in a historical world of exploitation and injustice. However, such a position does not assume the innocence and purity of the oppressed. Neither does it see the oppressed only as victims and not also as agents for change.

Moreover, such a shift from a modern Western malestream to a critical emancipatory frame of reference engenders a fourfold change:

—a change of interpretive assumptions and goals,
—a change of methodology and epistemology,
—a change of individual and collective consciousness, and
—a change of social-religious institutions and cultural-religious formations.

Consequently, a critical emancipatory interpretation does not commence by beginning with the text and placing the Bible at the center of its attention. Rather, interpreters begin with a reflection on their experience and sociopolitical religious location. For such a reflection, interpreters utilize a critical systemic analysis of the kyriarchal[31] oppressive structures that shape our lives and are inscribed in biblical texts and interpretations. In reading biblical texts, a critical emancipatory pedagogy must enable scholars and religious leaders to take their "stand" with wo/men who struggle at the bottom of the kyriarchal pyramid of domination and exploitation because their struggles reveal both the fulcrum of dehumanizing oppression threatening every wo/man and the power of Divine Wisdom at work in our midst.

The challenge today, I argue, is to open the hermeneutical conversation as widely as possible and to enable biblical interpreters to enter this conversation in the interest of struggles for justice. This challenge comes at a time when the paradigm of emancipatory biblical studies is developing its own highly specialized vocabulary and allegiance to the academy or institutionalized religions. Hence, emancipatory biblical

---

31. Rather than advocating a dual systems analysis—imperialism and feminism—as anti-imperial studies and some feminist postcolonial studies seem to do, I have developed a complex analysis of interstructured and multiplicative dominations and have coined the neologism *kyriarchy/kyriocentrism/kyriarchal* (see n. 28). This neologism seeks to express the intersecting structures of dominations and to replace the commonly used term "patriarchy," which is often understood in terms of binary gender dualism. As an analytic category, kyriarchy articulates a more comprehensive systemic analysis of empire, in order to underscore the complex interstructuring of dominations, and to locate sexism and misogyny in the political matrix—or better, "patrix"—of a broader range of dominations.

studies are in danger of becoming "disciplined" and of deriving their theoretical frameworks or taking their measure from the malestream discipline of biblical studies rather than from grassroots movements for ending wo/men's second-class citizenship.

In short, a critical emancipatory pedagogy does not derive its lenses from the modern individualistic understanding of religion and the Bible. Rather, it shifts attention to the politics of biblical studies and its sociopolitical contexts of struggle.[32] Hence, at the center of attention it places wo/men as subjects and agents, as full decision-making citizens. To that end a critical emancipatory pedagogy develops and engages not only a deconstructive but also a (re)constructive approach to interpretation. It struggles to elucidate the ways in which biblical symbols, practices, and texts function in the creation and maintenance of ideas about sex/gender, race, colonialism, class, and religion. It also examines how social constructions of sex/gender, race, colonialism, class, and religion have influenced and shaped theoretical frameworks, theological formulations, and biblical interpretations. A critical emancipatory pedagogy understands the Bible and its own work of interpretation and education as a site of struggle over meaning-making, authorization, and symbolic power.

The pedagogical method to achieve the cultural and religious transformation of relations of domination into relations of radical equality that was developed by the Women's Liberation Movement in the 1970s is consciousness-raising, a process and reflection on experience through which participants grow in feminist awareness. Feminist consciousness insists on wo/men's full citizenship and their freedom for self-definition, self-determination, self-respect, self-esteem, and self-affirmation. Feminist awareness begins with the recognition that wo/men's "lesser" being, inferiority, and oppression are structural and not the result of personal faults. Coming to consciousness is the discovery of structures of socioeconomic domination and the recognition that one belongs to an exploited and oppressed group even if one is individually privileged and well-off. It is the discovery that the personal is political.[33]

However, consciousness-raising must be distinguished from conscientization. Conscientization is a term derived from the Portuguese *conscientização*. It was introduced by Brazilian educator Paulo Freire to

---

32. For an excellent analysis of the "politics of Biblical Studies," see Susannah Heschel, *The Aryan Jesus: Christian Theologians and the Bible in Nazi Germany* (Princeton, NJ: Princeton University Press, 2008).

33. See Jane Kenway and Helen Modra, "Feminist Pedagogy and Emancipatory Possibilities," in *Feminism and Critical Pedagogy*, ed. Carmen Luke and Jennifer Gore (New York: Routledge, 1992), 138–66, esp. 156–57.

designate a learning process in which groups become skilled at recognizing forms and experiences of social, political, cultural, religious, and economic oppression and dehumanization. Such a process of conscientization was developed in literacy training programs for poor Brazilian peasants in order to teach them how to "decode" their situation of poverty and exploitation with the help of systemic sociopolitical analysis.

According to Freire, conscientization means learning to *name* and *change* oneself and one's situation. Freire asserts that humans *"are* because they *are* in a situation, and they will be *more* the more they not only critically reflect upon their existence but critically act upon it."[34] Those who become conscientized see through the sociocultural myth of superiority/inferiority that keeps them in situations of oppression. When people recognize and acknowledge that they are exploited and oppressed, they are empowered to achieve liberation. They do so by becoming committed to their own liberation as well as to that of others and by transforming themselves and their oppressive situations. Conscientization is a critical process, a spiraling dance that is never ending.

In contrast, the scientific ethos of biblical studies insists that readers must silence their interests and abstract from their sociopolitical situation in order to respect the "alien" character of the text and the historical chasm between the contemporary reader and the biblical text. This rhetoric of disinterestedness and presupposition-free exegesis silences reflection on the political interests and functions of biblical scholarship. Its claim to public scientific status suppresses the rhetorical character of biblical texts and readings and obscures the power relations through which they are constituted and kept in place.

Such a suppression of present-day theological socioecclesial locations and religious-theological interests is due largely to the prevailing assumption that the form of exegetical commentary demands scientific objectivity and disinterestedness rather than a self-conscious reading/hearing that is engaged and perspectival. To respect the *rights* of the text, biblical interpreters have to suppress their own questions. Biblical interpretation is here construed in kyriarchal terms insofar as readers have to *submit* themselves to the unequivocal meaning of the text that is established by biblical scholars or religious authorities. Moreover, this scientific model of biblical studies shares in the pathology of modernity, which, according to Jürgen Habermas, splits off expert cul-

---

34. Paulo Freire, *Pedagogy of the Oppressed* (Harmondsworth, Middlesex: Penguin, 1970), 100; see also idem, *Pedagogy of Freedom: Ethics, Democracy and Civic Courage* (Lanham, MD: Rowman & Littlefield Publishers, 1998); idem, *Pedagogy of Hope* (New York: Continuum, 1994).

tures from everyday cultural practices and life. Finally, by understanding the "first" or historical meaning of the biblical text as a deposit of the definitive meaning of the author, historical biblical interpretation runs the risk of "shutting up" the "meaning" of the text in the past and turning it into an artifact of antiquity that is accessible only to the expert of biblical history or philology.

Theologians and ministers in turn are interested in the religious, "spiritualized" meaning of biblical texts for today. Through "application" they seek to liberate the text from its "historical captivity" in order to rescue the message of the Bible for contemporary Christians. One form of this rescue and liberation of the text is accomplished by "updating and actualizing" aspects of it: by "translating" and rendering its mythic images into contemporary frameworks of meaning, by selecting the passages that still speak to us and illumine our own questions, by reducing its world of vision to theological or ethical principles and themes.

Another form of theological "application" of biblical texts is achieved by the method of correlation. This method draws a parallel with the text's discursive situation and present-day religious problem situations. Theological liberals frustrated by the mythological content or outdated injunctions of the Bible look for commentaries that enable them to "squeeze" the living water of revelation and theological truth out of the hard stone of ancient biblical facts; biblical fundamentalists insist on the inerrant literal sense of the text as a "given fact."

Insofar as scientific exegesis tends to foreclose the text's multivalent meanings and does not acknowledge that we always interpret texts from a particular sociopolitical religious location, it is contrary to the practice of conscientization. It overlooks the reality that the practice of interpretation does not simply understand and comprehend texts and symbols (hermeneutics); it also produces new meanings speaking from different sociopolitical locations and from changed rhetorical situations (rhetoric). A rhetorical conceptualization of text and interpretation situates biblical scholarship in such a way that its public character and political responsibility become an integral part of our literary readings and historical reconstructions of the biblical world. Hence, it can function as a practice of conscientization.

This understanding of rhetoric/rhetorical[35] as a communicative practice that involves interests, values, and visions must be carefully distinguished from the popular use of the expression. Popular parlance often

---

35. See my book *Rhetoric and Ethic: The Politics of Biblical Studies* (Minneapolis: Fortress Press, 1999).

labels certain statements as "rhetoric/rhetorical" when it believes them to be "mere talk," stylistic figure, deceptive propaganda—any clever form of speech that is not true and honest and also lacks substance. Rhetoric is often misunderstood as "mere" rhetoric, as stylistic ornament, technical device, or linguistic manipulation, as discourse utilizing irrational, emotional devices that are contrary to critical thinking and reasoning.

When I reclaim the term "rhetoric" for a critical emancipatory pedagogy as a practice of conscientization, I do not use it in this colloquial sense. Indeed, I seek to utilize rhetorical analysis not as one more way of literary or structural analysis, but rather as a means to analyze how biblical texts and interpretations participate in creating or sustaining oppressive or liberating theo-ethical values, sociopolitical practices, and worlds of vision for their respective audiences.

Biblical interpretation understood as a rhetorical or communicative practice lends itself to conscientization insofar as it seeks to display how biblical texts and their contemporary interpretations are political and religious discursive practices. Authorial aims, point of view, narrative strategies, persuasive means, and authorial closure, as well as audience perceptions and constructions—these are rhetorical practices that have determined not only the production of the Bible but also its subsequent interpretations. Moreover, a critical rhetoric of conscientization insists that context is as important as text. What we see depends on where we stand. Our social location or rhetorical context is decisive for how we see the world, construct reality, or interpret biblical texts.

Insofar as emancipatory conscientization seeks to transform academic as well as ecclesial biblical interpretation, it must always have both a theoretical *and* a practical goal. This praxis orientation locates an emancipatory biblical interpretation and pedagogy in the context of radical democratic grassroots movements in society and religion as well as at the intersection of critical emancipatory theories and liberation theologies. Since feminist decolonizing studies, in distinction to functionalist gender studies, are explicitly committed to the struggle for changing kyriarchal structures of oppression in religious, cultural, and societal institutions, they are able to disentangle the ideological (religious-theological) functions of biblical texts for inculcating and legitimating relations of domination.

In short, an emancipatory pedagogy for graduate biblical studies seeks to transform the scientific-positivist ethos of biblical studies into a rhetorical-ethical one. It thereby creates a grassroots democratic space in which feminist and other critical readers/hearers can participate in defining and debating the meaning and significance of biblical texts in contemporary social-political locations and cultural-religious rhetorical situations. Such democratizing deliberations from within particular struggles and political coalitions acknowledge the multiple locations from which emancipatory voices manifest themselves in a diversity of intellectual constructs and competing interest groups.

To the extent that different emancipatory publics articulate their critical analyses, proposals, and strategies differently, it becomes necessary to adjudicate not only between different interpretations of a biblical text but also between competing definitions of the world and alternative constructions of symbolic universes. Such diverse analyses and divergent articulations of emancipatory visions are not simply right or wrong; they are not to be construed as dogmatic positions but are best understood as strategic practices of conscientization and deliberation.

By constantly engendering critique, dispute, and debate with the malestream discipline as well as collaboration with each other, emancipatory biblical practices of radical democratization and conscientization seek more adequate strategies and visions for constructing a different understanding of reality. In so doing, they always must privilege the theories and strategies of those who speak from within the experience of multiplicative kyriarchal oppressions. Clarifying and adjudicating contested concepts and proposals, critical emancipatory biblical studies and pedagogies engender biblical interpretation as a process of grassroots democratization, moral deliberation, and practical solidarity in the midst of diverse and often competing but potentially collaborative emancipatory struggles.

To conclude: The following chapters seek to develop the contours of such an emancipatory pedagogy for graduate biblical studies. This does not mean that they are only of interest to graduate students, professors, and administrators of theological schools and not to readers outside the academy in churches, synagogues, schools, and study groups. Rather, these chapters might be of interest to all who care about the Bible and social justice since they focus on transforming graduate education in the interests of grassroots movements and struggles for justice. They are of significance not only to the academic community but also to all those who desire to realize the kind of contributions graduate biblical education can make to the ethos and vision of a radical democratic society and religious community.

Unlike Dale Martin, I am not so much concerned with the predominance of historical biblical criticism in theological education. Rather,

I am concerned with the use of the Bible in public religious discourses. My central question is this: How are biblical scholars, theologians, preachers, teachers, and communities of faith best educated for participating critically and responsibly in public discourses that use Scripture and biblical rhetoric for unjust undemocratic ends? How do currently existing educational practices teach (or fail to teach) biblical scholars critical self-reflexive and constructive accountability? How, through the resources of the fourth emancipatory paradigm, can future biblical scholars, theologians, and scholars in religion be educated to participate responsibly in public discourses and *to transform* those that deploy the Bible for undemocratic ends?

Even a cursory survey of the discipline of biblical studies and its pedagogical practices indicates that biblical education does not currently equip students for such a task. To check this cursory impression, I joined with Kent Richards, the executive secretary of the Society of Biblical Literature (SBL), to chair a five-year seminar on graduate biblical education at the annual national and international meetings of the society.[36] The contributions of international, senior, and junior scholars not only confirmed the above negative diagnosis; they also indicated increasing interest in changing the standard curriculum of graduate biblical education in order to prepare students, scholars, preachers, theologians, and teachers for radical democratic engagement in both society and organized religion. Hence, this book does not so much focus on how to change curricula, choose methods of interpretation, or analyze texts; rather, it focuses on investigating and transforming the overall frameworks and paradigms of biblical studies on the one hand and the pedagogy and didactics of graduate biblical education on the other.

The first chapter seeks to chart the rhetorical space of graduate biblical studies by articulating the need to transform the discourses of biblical studies and by exploring proposals for such a re-visioning. The second chapter focuses on paradigm criticism and seeks to redescribe the four paradigms that I have developed and refined again and again in my work over the years. I elaborate the fourth emancipatory paradigm in the third chapter, reflect on the discursive struggles within it, suggest a common analytic, and propose a pedagogical model of agency and conscientization. The fourth chapter seeks to articulate further ways in

---

36. See Elisabeth Schüssler Fiorenza and Kent Harold Richards, eds., *Transforming Graduate Biblical Education: Ethos and Discipline* (Atlanta: SBL, forthcoming).

which malestream pedagogical models can be transformed into those that create a radical democratic space and ethos.

Such a pedagogical project, if it is not to remain abstract and under-developed, depends upon benefit from multiple different voices. The metalogue seeks to convey an impression of a radical democratic pedagogy in action. It gathers the voices of eight graduate students (four doctoral and four MDiv/MA level) from Harvard Divinity School, Andover Newton Theological School, and Boston College, who were participants in my seminar on Democratizing/Emancipatory Biblical Studies in the fall of 2008. Both their reflections on the seminar process and their research papers contribute crucial insights to the articulation of an emancipatory pedagogy that the preceding chapters do not fully develop or even address.

Since the pages of a book are limited, it was only possible to include the reflections of the seminar participants here. Their articles appear on the Web site that complements this book. Without the inclusion of the voices of these emerging scholars, ministers, and teachers, talk about a radical democratic ethos would remain just that—talk. The work of the seminar participants opens up the possibility of a different horizon for graduate biblical education. I hope many readers will join in this important work of developing a radical democratic space and a thoroughly egalitarian educational ethos.

1

The Rhetorical Space of Graduate Biblical Studies

I was prompted to start my research on how to change graduate education in the discipline of biblical studies by my experience of the continuing marginalization, trivialization, or total neglect of feminist, postcolonial, or other cultural and ideology critical studies by malestream scholarship. Reports on subfields of the discipline, introductory works, or commentaries still to this day have the tendency to avoid discussing such work as serious scholarship or to relegate it to discreet corners as if it were of interest only to so-called minority scholars. Moreover, such "minority" scholars also have often tended to remain in their little niches of identity politics, to "reinvent the wheel" instead of exploring theoretical commonalities, or to argue against each other rather than against malestream hegemonic scholarship.

Discussing these issues with colleagues, I became more and more convinced that the full citizenship of wo/men required a fundamental change in biblical studies. However, such a change could only be brought about if the ethos and practices of biblical studies, which are inculcated in graduate biblical education in general and doctoral education in particular, were changed. Since my Society of Biblical Literature presidential address more than twenty years ago, many changes have occurred in the field; but the basic structure and rhetoric of doctoral education seems to have remained the same.

CHARTING THE PROBLEM

In my article "Rethinking the Educational Practices of Biblical Doctoral Studies," published in 2003, I argued that the current crisis in critical biblical studies is rooted in a dramatic change not only in disciplinary methods, but more importantly, in social-geopolitical shifts. There are four identifiable problem areas that stand in tension with each other and need to be dynamically integrated.

Diverse Populations

In the last two decades, the population of divinity schools and religion departments—and therefore the character of the*logical education in the United States as a whole—has radically changed. Nondenominational university divinity schools such as Harvard Divinity School have granted full citizenship to populations previously not included, such as Catholics, evangelicals, or Jews. They have also begun to develop interreligious programs in which Buddhist, Confucian, Hindu, or Muslim students are welcomed as equals. Populations from different sociocultural locations and traditions, such as white wo/men, African American, Native American, Asian, Latina/o, gay, lesbian, and transgendered people—those who have traditionally been excluded from theological discourse or from elite religious educational institutions—have been admitted although they and their concerns still are often not highly valued. In addition, second-career students seek the rich intellectual inquiry offered by theological and religious studies.

This change in population requires a change in the kind of knowledge taught and the pedagogy used to communicate it. It requires a complete reconception of an academic disciplinary culture that has been defined not only by false claims to value-neutrality but also by the exclusion of the Other. This change is usually more real in the student body than in the faculty, who understandably show some resistance to such change, since it throws into question professional expertise and traditional academic standards of excellence. It is an extremely serious problem with regard to faculty hiring and promotion.

Furthermore, student-participants from many different Christian denominations and different religious persuasions, cultural contexts, social locations, and international areas seek to be equipped for religious leadership both in religious communities (churches, mosques, synagogues, or temples) and in the academy, society, and culture (communications, law, medicine, or the arts) at large. Hence, it is not only impossible but also inadvisable to devise a set curriculum in terms of traditional ecclesiastical or academic requirements and Eurocentric elite male modes of certification. Rather than spend faculty time on developing fixed curricula, I argue, graduate biblical education needs to focus on evolving educational democratic processes of communication for a multiplicity of religious and cultural communities—processes that are intellectually challenging, while still allowing students the possibility to qualify for academic and professional leadership, irrespective of whether they want or do not want to be ordained or join the clergy.

Additionally, schools have to provide the intellectual resources for those students who want to go on for doctoral work in the study of diverse religious/the*logical disciplines or to earn a degree in religion for leadership in other professions such as, for instance, medicine, business, law, social work, public health, politics, journalism, or education. Finally, the life experiences and the professional know-how of second-career students and lifelong learners must be allowed to enrich their doctoral studies. In light of this overall situation, we need to find educational models that not only insist on difference and diversity as the sine qua non of academic excellence but also stress collaboration rather than competition, allowing for the intellectual integration of such rich diversity.

Globalization of Knowledge

In the past two decades, knowledge—the intellectual capital of religious and academic institutions—has become globalized, or as I would prefer, internationalized and democratized. This has two implications for biblical graduate education and religious leadership: on the one hand, knowledge is no longer the property of male clergy but has become accessible through the communication revolution to anyone who seeks it. As a result, international interreligious dialogue and collaboration has become not only a possibility but also a necessity.

On the other hand, the flood of available knowledge on the internet requires that students learn how to develop intellectual skills of investigation, to articulate ethical criteria of evaluation, and to analyze hermeneutical frameworks of interpretation. What is called for is not knowledge accumulation, but the critical evaluation of knowledge.[1] Hence, thelogical disciplines and religious studies can no longer prove their excellence simply by understanding themselves as depositories of knowledge and scholarship. Today, the computer is such a site of knowledge storage. It can provide knowledge of historical sources, literary parallels, philological data, or foreign-language translations in seconds—knowledge that our predecessors in biblical studies have spent years or a lifetime to find, record, and learn.

It has therefore become increasingly important that students be taught to discriminate between different kinds of knowledge, work collaboratively, recognize intellectual problems, and learn how to debate them with others who have different experiences, standpoints, and belief systems. They need to study how to interpret and critically evaluate not only the rhetoric of biblical texts, but also that of biblical interpreters. A collaborative model of education is called for, a model that is greatly facilitated by the Internet. Students learn from each other in teamwork, write critical evaluation and integration papers, explore different hermeneutical perspectives, lead discussions, explore different ways of communication. Finally, they become skilled at understanding the field and its subfields, as rhetorical constructions that are dependent on the scholar's social location and systematic framework, rather than as an area of scientific data and the*logical givens. The intellectual acuity and excellence of inquiry required today is much harder to achieve, to teach, and to certify than the traditional curriculum of packaged knowledge, competitive standards of evaluation, and skills acquisition that relies on memorization, repetition, and imitation of the great masters.

As a result, academic excellence cannot be judged in light of past models of scholarship but must come under critical scrutiny. This scrutiny highlights the fact that the traditional stress on skills acquisition, training, and practical know-how rather than on theory buys into the mentality of what Stanley Aronowitz calls the "knowledge factory," which turns teachers and professors into technicians of social control.[2]

---

1. In his new book *Save the World on Your Own Time* (New York: Oxford University Press, 2008), Stanley Fish insists that it is not the task of the academician to educate responsible citizens or to foster good moral character. Rather, in his view, the only legitimate goal appropriate to college and university teachers is the transmission and advancement of knowledge and the equipment of students with analytical skills and mastery in methods of knowledge production. They have to investigate problems but not to solve them (12–13). However, this pedagogical view overlooks that knowledge cannot be had "pure" but that it is always conditioned by its contexts, interests, and ideological frameworks. Hence, it needs to be critically evaluated, and students have to be taught how to do so. Such ability of critical evaluation and assessment is also the task of citizens.

2. Stanley Aronowitz, *The Knowledge Factory: Dismantling the Corporate University and Creating True Higher Learning* (Boston: Beacon Press, 2000), 81.

Because of the university's increasingly close ties to business, what was once the hidden curriculum—the subordination of higher education to the needs of capital—has become an open, frank policy of public and private institutions. At the turn of the twentieth century, critics offered strenuous arguments that American universities were far from engaging in disinterested "higher learning," and were actually constituted to serve corporations and other vested interests; today's leaders of higher education seem to wear the badge of corporate servants proudly.[3]

The articulation of excellence in terms of technical skills—data accumulation, quantitative publishing, market-research type evaluations as producing consumer satisfaction—rather than critical pedagogy feeds into this market mentality. Furthermore, the stress on products rather than critical thinking still determines curricular offerings and examinations. For instance, departments have to offer bread-and-butter courses such as Introduction, Paul, Synoptics, and so forth, which are taught in terms of the banking model[4] rather than in terms of critical knowledge and hermeneutical ability. Moreover, ordination boards still tend to test their candidates not on whether they can critically interpret and hermeneutically work with a text or a complex of problems but rather on whether they are able to reproduce packaged scientific theories.

The Dichotomy between Religious and The*logical Studies

The academy also has not yet been successful in overcoming the artificial disciplinary dichotomy between religious and the*logical studies, a dichotomy that has been institutionalized both in departments of allegedly value-neutral studies of religion on the one hand, and religiously committed denominational the*logical schools on the other hand. This split goes very deep, as the American Academy of Religion's Hart Report indicates.[5]

---

3. For the discussion of academic culture and social-political challenges, see, e.g., Thomas Bender and Karl E. Schorske, eds., *American Academic Culture in Transformation* (Princeton, NJ: Princeton University Press, 1997); Philip G. Altbach, Robert O. Berdahl, and Patricia J. Gumport, eds., *American Higher Education in the Twenty-First Century: Social, Political, and Economic Challenges* (Baltimore: Johns Hopkins University Press, 1999); Stacey Lane Tice, Nicholas Jackson, Leo M. Lambert, and Peter Englot, eds., *University Teaching: A Reference Guide for Graduate Students and Faculty* (Syracuse, NY: Syracuse University Press, 2005); Frank Donoghue, *The Last Professors: The Twilight of the Humanities in the Corporate University* (New York: Fordham University Press, 2008).

4. For further elaboration, see chap. 4 (below).

5. Ray L. Hart, "Religious and Theological Studies in American Higher Education: A Pilot Study," *Journal of the American Academy of Religion* 59, no. 4 (1991): 715–82.

This disciplinary split, however, obfuscates the fact that both religious and the*logical studies are not value-detached disciplines; instead, they speak from a particular socioreligious location and position. To avoid this split, I suggest, one has to reconceptualize both religious academic studies and ministerial the*logical studies as situated forms of knowledge. In the past, Christian divinity schools and denominational seminaries functioned to educate future ministers and priests. Such seminaries were denominational (for instance Protestant, Catholic, or Jewish) and followed a required curriculum that led to ordination. Because of the restriction of the*logical studies to clergy education, religious studies has developed as a discipline that supposedly investigates biblical and other religions from a value-neutral, phenomenological, academic standpoint. However, hermeneutics, the sociology of knowledge, ideology critique, feminist critique, critical theory, and especially postcolonial studies have questioned this reifying conceptualization of religious studies.

Moreover, in the last decade or so the Western (Christian) study of other "alien" religions is slowly being transformed. The hegemony of the traditionally Protestant Christian curriculum has been broken, and religious or the*logical studies have more and more felt the need for interreligious and interdisciplinary inquiry. Moreover, scholars of other religions (Jews, Muslims, Buddhists, or Hindus) articulate knowledge about their own religions and Scriptures that is different from the knowledge produced by reifying Western religious studies. Hence, their scholarship often shows similarities with a the*logical studies approach, although they usually do not call their work the*logy because the*logy is a Christian typed term.

Diana Eck has argued that the dialogue between religions has a sociopolitical location.[6] Interreligious dialogue takes place not only in the academy but also on the local communal level and more and more also in public. Hence, future ministers and religious leaders need to be schooled in both ecumenical and interreligious Scripture study and communication. Future biblical scholars or professionals need to acquire the ability to reason the*logically, religiously, and ethically, as well as to critically analyze power relations in the interest of justice for all. The question remains, then, how biblical graduate studies can be so designed that they foster such intellectual capabilities. How can gradu-

---

6. Diana L. Eck, *A New Religious America: How a "Christian Country" Has Now Become the World's Most Religiously Diverse Nation* (San Francisco: Harper San Francisco, 2000).

ate study be shifted from an objectivist study of religions and scriptural or traditional texts to a study of the power of religion and the Bible to foster either violence or justice and well-being?

Political-Religious Fundamentalisms

In the past twenty years, forms of fundamentalism and religious extremism that are explicitly political have emerged in all major religions and in all societies around the globe. Studies of such fundamentalisms have shown that the term can be applied cross-culturally and cross-religiously. These studies have argued that the common denominator of such fundamentalisms is the opposition to modernism and secularism, the distrust of Enlightenment values and institutions, and the contempt for all outsiders or Others, whether within or outside their community.

For instance, Bruce Lawrence has pointed to several characteristics that fundamentalist movements have in common:

1. Such movements are comprised of secondary level male elites.
2. They utilize a technical vocabulary or discourse.
3. They profess totalistic and unquestioning allegiance to sacred Scriptures or religious authority.
4. They privilege the authority of their own leaders and subordinate democratic values and processes to this authority.[7]

Since traditional institutions of higher education often subscribe to a similar positivist understanding of facts and truth—albeit in more academic rather than religious terms—they are not able to articulate discourses and practices that would foster a different radical democratic imaginary that could engender a different form of religious imaginary. Research into the pedagogical procedures that reproduce such fundamentalist thinking in biblical studies is still lacking.

Graduate education in biblical studies compels students who come from a biblicist background to become, in a certain sense, schizophrenic; for example, they may be writing a critical exegesis for a qualifying paper in the academy while preaching biblicist literalism in their church. They generally are not encouraged in a critical learning process to critically

7. Bruce B. Lawrence, *Defenders of God: The Fundamentalist Revolt against the Modern Age* (Columbia: University of South Carolina Press, 1995).

articulate their own faith-based questions, religious experiences, and fundamental convictions. They therefore do not have the opportunity to work through them critically in dialogue with each other and with the major discourses of the field. Rather than receiving encouragement to articulate and to work through their prejudices in the interpretive process, they are often told that they need to adopt the value-neutral, detached stance of the field and remove their own preconceptions or prejudices from inquiry. Yet such a positivist disciplinary conceptualization of hegemonic biblical studies and their educational processes neglects the critical hermeneutical and epistemological insights of the past thirty years. Postmodern biblical studies in turn cultivates a great variety of theoretical methods, subfields, and perspectives, but also does not sufficiently reflect on its own pedagogy. Such a critical pedagogy, I argue, needs to communicate that the*logical and religious studies can be scientifically responsible today only if they become hermeneutically reflective, transdisciplinary, and interreligious.

THE NEED TO TRANSFORM THE DISCOURSES OF BIBLICAL STUDIES

In light of these four developments, it is necessary to re-envision the academic discipline of biblical studies and its pedagogies so that it can attend to a professional identity formation that is not exclusive and antidemocratic. Radical democratic rather than positivist or fundamentalist teaching-learning experiences, however, are generally not part and parcel of graduate education in general and doctoral education in particular. Though much creative teaching is done on the undergraduate level and some on the master's level, doctoral education is still very Eurocentric[8] insofar as it is mostly focused on the classical German or British scientific research university and the master-disciple model[9] of the graduate seminar. Moreover, the dominant ethos of graduate schools often does not appreciate the change in knowledge production and populations, but operates from an outdated model of top-down kyriarchal pedagogy.

---

8. For more on the imbrication of Eurocentric American biblical scholarship with racism, see Shawn Kelley's book, *Racializing Jesus: Race, Ideology, and the Formation of Modern Biblical Scholarship* (New York: Routledge, 2002); as well as the forthcoming collection of essays on *Prejudice and Christan Beginnings: Investigting Race, Gender, and Ethnicity in Early Christian Studies*, ed. Laura Nasrallah and Elisabeth Schüssler Fiorenza (Minneapolis: Fortress Press, forthcoming 2009).

9. For the discussion of this pedagogical model, see chap. 4 (below).

Historical and Institutional Structures

The development of a progressive pedagogy in biblical studies must not overlook its institutional location. Postmodern feminist theory has made us conscious that the way we frame our questions and choose our rhetorical strategies involves issues of power and institutionalization, which need to be made explicit.[10] Hence, decolonizing discourses that seek to decenter the top-down pedagogy of the field must make apparent the historical and institutional structures within which they speak.[11]

The place from which critical feminist pedagogy begins its intervention, the place from which we speak, is the critique of the malestream interpretive community of academic and religious institutions[12] that claims either to be scientific, value-neutral and objective, or to insist on the authority of the Bible. Although the number of wo/men and other underrepresented persons entering the field of biblical studies and enrolling in graduate programs has increased steadily over the past twenty years, no equivalent change in institutional practices has taken place.[13]

Although consistently relegated to the margins, feminist, postcolonial, and other cultural and ideology critical studies continue to deepen and nuance the theoretical and practical tools available for critical engagement with dominant ideological discourses. Kyriarchal discourses have not so much silenced or ignored these challenging and emancipatory discourses, as they have manipulated their marginalization and dialogue in such a way as to maintain their own normative dominance. Consequently, those entering biblical and religious studies still have to adopt the language and discourse of the clerical and academic communities[14] that have silenced us, have excluded us as the Other of the Divine understood as Father and Lord, marginalized us

---

10. Cf. Gayatri Chakravorty Spivak, in *The Post-Colonial Critic: Interviews, Strategies, Dialogues*, ed. Sarah Harasym (New York: Routledge, 1990), 42–43; see also idem, *In Other Worlds: Essays in Cultural Politics* (New York: Methuen, 1987).

11. See my book *The Power of the Word: Scripture and the Rhetoric of Empire* (Minneapolis: Fortress Press, 2007), 11–29, for the discussion of a critical feminist decolonizing approach.

12. In her study of more than 200 women academics, Janice Hocker Rushing points to the damage done to bright young women being mentored by older male scholars who attempt to mold them into their own masculine ideals. See Janice Hocker Rushing, *Erotic Mentoring: Women's Transformations in the University* (Walnut Creek, CA: Left Coast Press, 2006).

13. For pre–1980 statistics, see the Cornwall Collective, *Your Daughters Shall Prophesy: Feminist Alternatives in Theological Education* (New York: Pilgrim Press, 1980), 49–53. In the last decade the number of white wo/men in liberal theological schools surpassed the 50 percent mark, but wo/men of color are still a tiny minority. Moreover, no corresponding curricular changes have been made.

14. For academic frameworks, see especially Elizabeth Kamarck Minnich, *Transforming Knowledge* (Philadelphia: Temple University Press, 1990), 51–175.

as the Other of the scientific Man of Reason,[15] and relegated us to the status of social, religious, and intellectual nonpersons.

It is a well-known fact that until quite recently wo/men were explicitly barred from graduate biblical studies and from seminary education. For instance, Harvard Divinity School just recently celebrated the fiftieth anniversary of wo/men's admission; Roman Catholic wo/men could not receive a the*logical doctorate in the United States until the 1960s. In many countries of the world wo/men still have great difficulty in engaging in doctoral studies. If one recognizes the structural exclusiveness of academic and religious studies, one realizes that wo/men cannot simply be incorporated into this paradigm of the*logical education by an add-and-stir approach. Rather, it becomes imperative to change not only kyriarchal institutional structures but also the pedagogical practices of graduate education.

As long as these public-political locations and interests of biblical scholarship and education are not recognized, wo/men and other academically muted persons will continue to encounter great resistance and remain excluded from the subject position of biblical discourses in the academy. For wo/men and other disenfranchised persons to enter into the dominant discourses of biblical studies as equals, both the systemic interrelation of biblical knowledge and global exclusions must become evident, and the gendered/raced/classed character of biblical studies must be rendered explicit.

The dominant paradigms of graduate biblical education must therefore be scrutinized critically for their pedagogical aims and for their impact on the formation of critical consciousness. According to Stanley Fish, readers are always constrained by the frame of reference provided by the interpretive community to which they belong.[16] If the dominant interpretive community acts somewhat like a police force, defending against unacceptable interpretations, then it becomes important to reflect on the social institutional location of a critical feminist interpretation for liberation in departments of religion and schools of the*logy. For whenever liberation discourses are displaced from their social loca-

---

15. See Genevieve Lloyd, *The Man of Reason: "Male" and "Female" in Western Philosophy* (Minneapolis: University of Minnesota Press, 1984), 108: "Philosophers have at different periods been church men, men of letters, university professors. But there is one thing they have had in common throughout the history of the activity. They have been predominantly male; and the absence of women from the philosophical tradition has meant that the conceptualization of reason has been done exclusively by men."

16. Stanley Fish, *Is There a Text in This Class? The Authority of Interpretive Communities* (Cambridge, MA: Harvard University Press, 1980).

tion in emancipatory movements and become integrated into the practices of kyriarchal institutions, they become subject to the disciplinary pressures and requirements of such institutions.

Like white male students, wo/men and other outsiders who enter the*logical schools have to undertake a double agenda of professionalization: they are to be socialized both into "scientific" thinking and into professional training at once. Like male students, wo/men students must undergo a transformation from a "lay" persona in the religious and educational sense to a the*logical professional one. Such a transformation requires not only that students become familiar with the methods, literature, and technical procedures of academic disciplines, but also that they transform their intellectual religious frameworks. For the most part, students enter graduate biblical studies either because they highly value the Bible as Scripture or see it as a cultural-historical classic; they want to study how the Bible is used in public discourse; they are concerned about the ongoing influence of the Bible in politics and culture; or as future ministers they anticipate preaching regularly on biblical texts. In any case, incoming graduate students' intellectual frame of reference often accords the Bible intrinsic canonical authority, political power, or significant cultural value.

Academic biblical scholarship, in contrast, is rooted in a rationalist approach to the Bible and dedicated to the critical questioning of biblical authority. To undertake an academic or ministerial agenda of professionalization in biblical studies thus entails a change of discursive frameworks either from a discourse of the Bible's acceptance as a cultural icon, or from a discourse of obedience to it as the Word of G*d, toward a critical academic discourse that assumes the authority of inquiry and scholarship in challenging the cultural and doctrinal authority of the Bible.[17]

Academic Professionalization

Professionalization for students means, first of all, that they become socialized into the ethos of biblical studies as a scientific academic discipline. For almost 250 years college education in the United States was

---

17. See the excellent collection of essays by William P. Brown, ed., *Engaging Biblical Authority: Perspectives on the Bible as Scripture* (Louisville, KY: Westminster John Knox Press, 2007).

understood as a "discipline" for training of elite white men in "religious and moral piety."[18] After the Civil War, the new model for the production of knowledge and higher education became that of German scientific research. This transformation of the curriculum replaced religion with science as a rational philosophy claiming to account for the entire universe. This resulted in a galaxy of separate disciplines and departments that accredit persons for a particular kind of professional work. The unifying ethos of objective method, scientific value-neutrality, and disinterested research in the emerging scientific academy unseated the centrality of the Bible and of religion.

This sidelining of the Bible and religion in college and graduate education has gone hand in hand with the professionalization of academic life and the rise of the technocratic university. The impact of this scientific positivist ethos was felt not only in religion but also in all disciplines within the university. The study of literature was compartmentalized under the headings "philology," "the scientific study of modern languages," and "the historical approach to literature." History as a discipline ostensibly sought to establish facts and data objectively, free from philosophical considerations or political interests. It was determined to hold strictly to evidence, not to sermonize or to moralize but to tell the simple truth—in short, to narrate things as they "really happened." However, despite such claims to professional objectivity, virtually every academic discipline operates on the unexamined assumption of academic discourse that equates white male and Western reality with human reality. Intellectual histories and other "canonized" cultural and academic texts have generally assumed that "natural" differences exist between wo/men and men, between slave and free, and have in turn defined wo/men and other colonized peoples as rationally inferior, marginal, subsidiary, or derivative. Wo/men and other colonized intellectuals who have shown leadership and claimed independence have been judged as unnatural, aggressive, and disruptive figures. As Adrienne Rich has put it, "There is no discipline that does not obscure and devalue the history and experience of women as a group."[19] A similar statement could be made about working-class wo/men, wo/men of color, or colonized peoples. The recourse to biological determinism and gender differences is still frequent today in

18. Florence Howe, *Myth of Coeducation: Selected Essays 1964–1983* (Bloomington: Indiana University Press, 1984), 221–30.

19. Adrienne Rich, "Toward a Woman Centered University," in *On Lies, Secrets, and Silence: Selected Prose, 1966–1978* (New York: W. W. Norton, 1979), 134.

scientific debates that seek to defend the kyriocentric framework of academic disciplines as "objective and scholarly."[20]

This positivist ethos of value-free science has also provided the institutional context for the development of academic biblical studies as "hard" science. Just as the developing academic disciplines of literature and history in the last quarter of the nineteenth century sought to model themselves on the natural sciences, so also did biblical studies. Since the rhetoric of biblical studies as "science" in the United States was developed in the political context of several heresy trials at the turn of the twentieth century,[21] the rhetoric of disinterested objectivity continues to reject all overt religious, sociopolitical, or the*logical engagement as unscientific. The aspiration of biblical studies in particular and religious studies in general to "scientific" status within the academy, as well as their claim to universal, unbiased modes of inquiry, denies their hermeneutic-theoretical character and kyriocentric optic. It also masks their sociohistorical location, as well as their sociopolitical or ecclesiastical interests.

Ministerial Professionalization

Students who belong to biblical communities of faith are taken up into a second agenda of biblical professionalization, which reproduces the conflict between the academic-scientific and the doctrinal-religious paradigm of biblical studies. This professionalization entails taking up conflicting subject-positions, especially for students who want to become ministers, priests, teachers, or leaders in religious communities.

Since historical-critical biblical studies came into being in conflict with the ecclesiastical doctrinal model of biblical interpretation, and since they still continue to struggle against ecclesiastical or neoconservative biblicist interferences, academic biblical studies tenaciously hold on to the ethos of scientific objectivity, value-free research, and freedom from all interest in contemporary questions of relevance. While systematic the*logians and scholars of religion vigorously discuss hermeneutics

20. See the critical reflections on the Arizona project for curriculum integration by Susan Hardy Aiken et al., eds., *Changing Our Minds: Feminist Transformations of Knowledge* (Albany: State University of New York Press, 1988), 134–63.

21. See Doug Hill, "Charles Augustus Briggs, Modernism, and the Rise of Biblical Scholarship in Nineteenth Century America," in *The Bible and the American Myth*, ed. Vincent L. Wimbush (Macon, GA: Mercer University Press, 1999), 71–104; Martin Marty, *Modern American Religion*, vol. 1, *The Irony of It All, 1893–1919* (Chicago: University of Chicago Press, 1986). For Roman Catholicism, see Gerald Fogarty, SJ, "The Quest for a Catholic Vernacular Bible in America," in *The Bible in America*, ed. Nathan O. Hatch and Marc A. Noll (New York: Oxford University Press, 1982), 163–80.

and questions raised by epistemological discussions, critical biblical studies often equate "theological" with "apologetic" in order to insist on a value-free, disinterested inquiry into the Bible.

This contradiction between the scientific, value-neutral ethos of academic biblical studies and the opposing ethos of biblical studies as the*logical/canonical studies comes especially to the fore in the tension between the the*logical needs of ministerial students and the academic ethos of value-neutral scientific scholarship. It surfaces as the practical question of how to "apply" the scientific results of historical-critical studies to contemporary pastoral practice and preaching. The numerous commentaries on the lectionary, as well as the countless popularizations of biblical scholarship, testify to this discursive contradiction in biblical studies.

At the root of this contradiction is the presumed opposition between objective scientific inquiry and the*logical commitment to communities of faith. This contradiction has engendered the division of labor between biblical scholars on the one hand, and ministers/preachers on the other hand. Disciplined scientific scholarship is said to restrict itself to the task of philological, archaeological, historical, cultural, and literary analysis. Ministers and church authorities in turn have the task of applying the normative teaching of the text to the contemporary situation, but their the*logical needs are not to interfere in questions of scientific scholarship.

Most North American graduate departments that train future teachers for colleges and the*logical schools operate within this ethos of historical-descriptive, value-neutral biblical studies. They train students to analyze biblical texts as historical sources, as information about ancient history, as literary artifacts, or as cultural classics. Consequently, future teachers and scholars do not learn to theoretically reflect on their own sociohistorical location and the*logical interpretive frames. They are not schooled to articulate and reflect critically on their own questions, interests, prejudices, and commitments. Since they have not learned in a methodological fashion to scrutinize the implicit frameworks and interests of scholarly, popular, or ecclesiastical interpretations of the Bible, they often approach teaching and the*logical education without engaging in disciplined ideological and pedagogical reflection.

Insofar as professors in biblical studies have been trained in graduate departments that subscribe to the notion of positivist, disinterested, value-neutral scholarship, they tend to uncritically import either the antiquarian rhetoric of the discipline or their own doctrinal convictions and sociothe*logical assumptions into their teaching. They are prone to declare that what they teach is "objective scholarship" with universal validity. Consequently, their students are left to bridge the gap between biblical exegesis and their own religious self-understanding or political commitments, between the exegetical-historical, the cultural-postmodern and the public-religious task of biblical interpretation.

The ethos of the discipline does not compel students to ask how biblical interpretation as a discipline is constructed or how scholarship is conditioned by personal experience and social location. Nor does graduate biblical education challenge them to articulate the political functions and ethical implications of dominant scholarship. In short, the pedagogy of biblical studies as a disciplinary field with scientific methods and objective modes of inquiry does not compel students to problematize how and to what end biblical studies as a scholarly or ministerial inquiry is constructed in certain circumstances and how it serves particular interests.

Consequently, students are exposed, for instance, to the deconstructive power of postmodern historical, literary, or cultural-critical methods, but are not taught explicitly how to engage in critical sociothe*logical deconstruction and reconstruction. I remember, for example, entering the*logical education with a biblicist understanding that identified biblical texts with G*d's word and took the Gospels to be accurate accounts of what Jesus really taught and did. I recall that it took me several years to move from this biblicist understanding to one that valued the the*logical freedom to read biblical texts as human witnesses to G*d and to the ministry of Jesus.

Since graduate students have internalized a methodological procedure that consists of value-neutral, descriptive, historical or philological exegesis as a first step and contemporary application as a second step, a step that is not mediated methodologically, they are prone to relinquish the critical-historical or the*logical/ethical inquiry either for the sake of ready-made piety or for scholarship that has no contemporary relevance. Wo/men and others who have traditionally been excluded from graduate biblical education and the articulation of the*logy are often instinctively critical of such dichotomizing dualism in biblical education and reject it as malestream scholarship. However, in so doing, they are also in danger of depriving themselves of critical analytic skills, biblical resources, and historical imagination, which are essential to liberation ministry or teaching that could have public significance.

PROPOSALS FOR RE-VISIONING BIBLICAL STUDIES

Exactly how to address this situation and predicament of graduate biblical studies and education is a difficult matter and needs to be widely debated.[22] In my opinion, it is crucial that we articulate pedagogical theories and strategies for re-visioning biblical studies from a critical decolonizing feminist perspective. Such a re-envisioning of biblical studies would enable us to speak to many different people and situations. In the following, I discuss two recent important proposals that seek to address this problem.

The End of Biblical Studies as We Know It?

It is curious that at this point in time, when religion has again become a much researched and discussed topic, many conservative as well as many liberal and postmodern biblical scholars do not find such a re-envisioning of biblical studies and graduate biblical education in terms of public discourse to be either necessary or desirable. It seems that, even in postmodern academic approaches, the institutional dichotomy between academy and church, rather than a re-visioning of the ethos of biblical studies still takes center stage.

For instance, in *The End of Biblical Studies*, Hector Avalos argues forcefully that biblical studies as we know it must end. He maintains that modern biblical scholarship has shown the irrelevance of the Bible for modern times.[23] But he contends that despite this proven irrelevance, a variety of scholarly disciplines sustain the illusion of the relevance of the Bible. Avalos goes so far as to state that "Bibliolatry is still what binds most biblical scholars together, whether they see themselves as religious or secular, champions of Western culture or multiculturalists, evangelical Christians or Marxist hermeneuticians."[24] Moreover, modern scholarship has proven that the violence of the Bible is a product of

22. See the forthcoming collection of essays initiated by Elisabeth Schüssler Fiorenza and Kent Harold Richards, eds., *Transforming Graduate Biblical Education: Ethos and Discipline* (Atlanta: SBL, forthcoming) which has its origins in a five-year seminar on Graduate Biblical Education held at national and international SBL meetings. The essays explore the current ethos and discipline of graduate biblical education from different social locations and academic contexts. They do so in terms of variegated experiences in graduate biblical studies and provide a critical analysis of these experiences. The majority of the articles are written either by well-known North American scholars, by scholars who are newcomers in the field, or by biblical scholars from different Asian countries. All the contributions offer ideas on how to transform graduate biblical education in such a way that it becomes a socializing power that transforms the present academic ethos of biblical studies.
23. Hector Avalos, *The End of Biblical Studies* (Amherst, NY: Prometheus Books, 2007).
24. Ibid., 340.

ancient cultures whose worldviews, beliefs, and injunctions are no longer compatible with our modern and postmodern ethics and morality.

To make his point that the Bible and therefore biblical scholarship is irrelevant today, Avalos shows how the main subdivisions of biblical studies (translation studies, textual criticism, archaeology, historical Jesus studies, literary criticism, and biblical theology) and their infrastructure (various universities' graduate schools, the Society of Biblical Literature, and the media-publishing complex) render the Bible irrelevant. He concludes:

> So our purpose is to excise from modern life what little of the Bible is being used and also eliminate the potential use of any sacred scripture as an authority in the modern world. Sacred texts are the problem that most scholars are not willing to confront. What I seek is liberation from the very idea that *any* sacred text should be an authority for modern human existence. . . . That is why the only mission of Biblical Studies should be to end Biblical Studies as we know it.[25]

As this quote shows, Avalos seems to be torn between two conflicting reasons as to why biblical scholarship as we know it must be ended. On the one hand, he stresses that biblical studies has to end because it has proven the irrelevance of the Bible. Yet, insofar as biblical studies persists in upholding some of the Bible's relevance and significance, the Bible must continue to be studied by a few agnostic scholars like him as one of the documents of antiquity, many of which have never been translated and studied and hence should receive priority over the Bible.

On the other hand, Avalos argues that biblical scholars must confront the fact that the Bible is upheld as a sacred text that has authority. It is at this second point that the pathos of his argument comes to the fore. He tells us that he comes from a Pentecostal Protestant immigrant home, wanted to become a biblical scholar "to fight atheism," and in the process has come to understand that "atheism was the most honest choice" he could make.[26] As a young scholar he came more and more to the conclusion that

> the pursuit of knowledge for its own sake is simply another way of describing an elite leisure pursuit. I became distressed at how few

25. Ibid., 342.
26. Ibid., 26.

papers actually centered in the idea that knowledge is meant to help people to live in a better world.[27]

Yet, rather than to explore how biblical studies can be transformed so that they can "help people to live in a better world" and to encourage people's ability to challenge the sacred authority of the Bible, he advises that, after weaning humanity from the authority of the Bible, scholars should tend to the thousands of other ancient texts that have not yet been translated. Although he asserts the irrelevance of the Bible, he still recognizes that even though it preaches violence, the Bible still has sacred authority for innumerable people.

To document his claim of the irrelevance of the Bible, he points to a Baylor University 2006 study which showed that 21.9 percent of Protestants and 33.1 percent of Catholics "never" read Scripture.[28] Yet he conveniently overlooks that, according to these statistics, there are still 78.1 percent of Protestants and 66.9 percent of Catholics who *do* read Scripture. Can one merely attribute this fact to the work of biblical scholars who maintain "the illusion of relevance"? Or might there be something in the Bible that still attracts people who are look-ing for a better and more just world? Simply to teach people to reject a sacred book does not enable them to free themselves from its violent and oppressive contents and influences.

While I agree that it is important to identify the violence inscribed in Scriptures, I also think it is necessary to teach how to work con-structively with such scriptural violence. We need to develop a critical pedagogy that teaches people, who love Scripture and accord it great authority for their lives, to read the Bible in a way that enables them to critically assess its ethos and vision.[29] In other words, if one defines the task of the biblical scholar only in negative terms, one is not able to answer the question of how scholarly research and teaching can serve to enhance people's lives and their desires for justice and well-being.

Taking the Bible out of the hands of people and putting it in its place alongside the ancient books that have not yet been translated does not solve the problem because such a displacement of the Bible does nothing to ensure that these other texts do not equally inscribe violence. Looking at this problem from a critical feminist perspective,

27. Ibid., 27.
28. Ibid., 30 n. 14.
29. See also Joseph A. Marchal, "To What End(s)? Biblical Studies and Critical Rhetorical Engagement(s) for a 'Safer' World," *SBL Forum* (n.p.: cited June 2006), http://www.sbl-site.org/publications/article.aspx?articleId=550 (accessed April 8, 2009).

such a rejection of the Bible or the Koran or any other Scripture would also mean that wo/men could claim no language, tradition, and culture since all writings, traditions, and cultures have been elite male-determined and have promoted violence against wo/men. Rather than end biblical studies, I suggest that it is necessary to inquire into the *ends* of biblical studies.

Two Independent Domains of Biblical Studies

Philip Davies recognizes that there is a large gap between what the public thinks biblical scholars do and what they are actually doing. Yet Davies is not so much concerned to re-envision biblical studies in terms of fostering radical democratic discourses as he is concerned with what those discourses can contribute to the life of the academy. He diagnoses the ineffectiveness of biblical studies within the academy and in the wider public, and to remedy this weakness he prescribes the greater academization of biblical studies as an etic, objective discipline that can take its place within the academic discourses of the humanities.[30]

In his book *Whose Bible Is It Anyway?*[31] Davies, like Avalos, attempts to define and establish a "genuine secular academic discipline of biblical studies." He sees secularism not as the opposite of religion, but rather as a cultural discourse in which religious discourses are not in any way privileged. Hence, he constructs a sharp dichotomy between biblical studies and confessional the*logical studies. Also like Avalos, he understands the*logical studies in a dogmatic confessional sense and positions them as the opposite of academic, nonconfessional studies. But unlike Avalos, he postulates two independent domains—that of academy and church—which, in his view, must not interfere with each other, but should be allowed to live alongside each other as long as they do not trespass on each other's domain.

Davies thus draws a sharp distinction between academic biblical studies as humanistic or humanities studies, and confessional biblical studies as committed to Christian faith and life. In order to mark this division, he reserves the term "biblical studies" for the academic study of the Bible, whereas he argues that "Bible study," or the study of Scripture, belongs to the domain of the church. This allows him to concede

---

30. See Philip Davies, "Do We Need Biblical Scholars?" http://www.Bibleinterp.com/articles/Davies_Biblical_Scholars.shtml (accessed April 8, 2009).

31. Philip Davies, *Whose Bible Is It Anyway?* 2nd ed. (New York: T&T Clark International, 2004).

that in synagogues, churches, and mosques but not in the academy, "religious discourse can reign unchallenged."[32]

After establishing these two different domains of biblical studies, Davies argues that they engender two different strategies of critical reading:

> One of them operates "inside the canon" as it were, and evaluates its subject matter in a way that is predetermined ultimately to be positive; in this reading, where Biblical literature equals "scripture," the critic's job is not to evaluate from a disinterested perspective (or set of presuppositions) the values of the text, but ultimately to affirm them.[33]

In other words, the goal of "Bible study" is to understand more fully the rhetorical, historical, or ideological character of the biblical text in order to affirm but not to criticize it. Such "Bible study" can be determined to be an "emic" reading, which adopts the "native" point of view, in distinction to an "etic" reading, which refers to the external description of the objective observer.

In contrast, biblical studies as an academic discipline engenders an "etic" reading, which operates "outside" the canon. It is based on the presupposition that biblical writings and their reception through the centuries "are to be evaluated on the same terms as other known human acts of writing and reception. . . . The values that are adopted . . . are those adopted by the critical observer and applied to other literature. The critic is free to like or dislike, to pass judgment."[34]

Consequently, Davies can uphold the right of a confessional reading, while at the same time championing a disinterested academic reading. He claims that the interest of the church and the academy are easily distinguished, since there is no confusion of what is done in the synagogue, church, or mosque and what in the academic classroom. Although Davies concedes that all discourses are in one way or the other interested, he nevertheless insists that only the etic, nonconfessional discourse of the academy has a range of evaluations and perspectives "that allow Biblical literature to interact with different value systems and to have its own varied value system compared and judged in what is analogous to a 'free market.'"[35]

32. Ibid., Preface.
33. Ibid., 11.
34. Ibid., 12.
35. Ibid., 49.

In short, Davies invokes the rhetoric of unbiased, value-free, dis-interested religious studies as an academic discipline in distinction to the*logical studies, which he terms confessional insofar as they are meant to affirm biblical texts because they are Scripture, not to critically investigate them. He conveniently overlooks that not only the nomen-clature "Scripture" but also the classification "Bible/biblical" is already determined in and through the domain of the church, since it was the church that gathered diverse writings or scriptures into the canon of the Bible. Hence, it is curious that Davies relegates "Scripture" to the church but reclaims "Bible" for the academy. This is surprising, for one, because religious studies has sought to reclaim "Scripture"[36] as cul-tural artifact that must be studied as a religious-cultural document.[37]

Such a dichotomous approach is necessary, Davies argues, because as things stand, the church cannot count on well-trained ministers, nor can the public learn about what biblical scholars do, because in and outside the academy, biblical scholarship is seen as a the*logical confes-sional pursuit. Hence, biblical scholars need to persuade both the acad-emy and the public that they engage in a bona fide academic discipline that contributes to the intellectual life of the humanities. To do so, they have to subscribe to etic, disinterested scholarship. Like Avalos, Davies insists on the academic character of biblical studies, which serves the academy and the wider public but does not interfere with confessional studies and the*logical education.

Hence, in Davies's view, we must "secularize" the Bible and biblical studies "for a secularized world." He spells out what this would mean in the conclusion to his article "Do We Need Biblical Scholars?"

> In short, I would like to see Biblical scholars reclaiming the Bible as their own, seeing in its authors an intellectual elite, aware of and engaged in the major cultural issues of their day, and presenting its ideas in a way that will capture the imagination of anyone interested in the eternal (and unanswered) questions of humanity.[38]

In this reading, the Bible is a product of the elite and the object of study by the academic elite. To be recognized as a part of this academic elite, biblical scholars have to study the Scriptures as a cultural document rather

---

36. Cf. Miriam Levering, ed., *Rethinking Scripture: Essays from a Comparative Perspective* (Albany: State University of New York Press, 1989).
37. Vincent L. Wimbush, ed., *Theorizing Scriptures: New Critical Orientations to a Cultural Phenomenon* (New Brunswick, NJ: Rutgers University Press, 2008).
38. Davies, "Do We Need Biblical Scholars?"

than as a religious one. Yet such a dichotomy between academic and confessional biblical studies not only turns the Bible into a book of the elite, but also reduces the*logical studies to confessional studies. It focuses on developing a pedagogy that enables students to talk to the elites but is not able to empower them to speak to the millions of "fundamentalist" Bible readers who read the Bible in a literalist way because their ministers, pastors, and preachers taught them so. Thus both proposals—that of Avalos as well as that of Davies—deepen the dichotomy that has plagued biblical studies since the modern arrival of biblical criticism.

PROBLEMATIZING THE DUALISTIC-DOMAIN CONSTRUCTION OF THE FIELD OF BIBLICAL STUDIES

The strict territorial segregation of the domains of biblical studies into the domains of the academy and the religious community restricts biblical studies to the territory of either academic disciplines or confessional the*logical studies. Such a dualistic construction of the disciplinary ethos aggravates, rather than alleviates, the problems that biblical studies face. Moreover, it rules out any political or emancipative approaches in biblical studies that are interested in changing societal, religious, or individual mind-sets. It is not able to orient biblical studies to the needs of society and the public, since it is focused either on the academy or on organized religion, but not on a radical democratic imaginary.

Moreover, it must not be overlooked that this division of the discipline as either academic or the*logical is an asymmetric construct that values the academic study of religion more highly, because it is allegedly committed to value-neutrality in the study of the Bible "for knowledge's sake." The study of religion and the Bible, so it is argued, does not succumb to the biased interests of the*logy, which speaks from within a particular religion and is committed to a particular religious community. In this view, the*logy cannot be truly scientific because it is not free from value commitments and disinterestedness. The*logical scholars allegedly act like "missionaries," who want to bring their audiences to commit themselves to a religious faith community.

The academic study of religion is said to be free from ideological commitments because it adopts a neutral scientific framework of research, within which a rational kind of inquiry can take place for the sake of knowledge production. As a scientific discipline, the academic study of religion scrutinizes religious phenomena like empirical facts and studies religion objectively. As a science, it limits itself to understanding the Bible "as it is" and seeks to represent it as "accurately" as possible. Those who object that such an articulation reveals the scientific ethos as another form of ideology have not understood it. Scholarly moral responsibility, according to Max Weber, is to limit itself simply to teaching, research, and writing, to the virtue of plain intellectual activity.

> The only rational action to which scholars, as scholars, are committed, the only moral action to which they are commanded and the only "social responsibility" to which their *professional* position compels them, is to use their energies in order to explain in its full diversity as much as they can of the nature of the world in which they live.[39]

If scholars bring political interests to their scientific discourses—as feminist and other subaltern scholars are wont to do—they are seen as corrupting the "purity" of science. Their research allegedly is no longer ruled just by the demands of logic, since their discourses purportedly no longer belong to the cognitive scientific domain alone but rather promote cultural, political, or religious ends. Just as the*logians who want to persuade students to subscribe to a particular religion compromise the scientific character of their work, so also socially and politically engaged scholars corrupt the "purity" of science by wanting to be socially responsible citizens whose research is no longer sustaining the oppressive aspects of their culture.

Such a rhetoric of disinterestedness is not able to recognize academic biblical and religious studies as public discourses that analyze and promote culturally specific values and thereby are said to function as ideology. Yet such a rhetoric of value-neutrality is in itself ideological because it disregards the feminist and postcolonial critique of science as ideology. As Lorraine Code has pointed out:

> Epistemic responsibility, and the accountability it demands, move to the top of the agenda once one acknowledges the centrality of the question "Whose knowledge are we talking about?" to late twentieth-century feminism. These issues become still more urgent once one admits the extent to which such an acknowledgment politicizes epistemic inquiry.[40]

---

39. Maurice Cowling, *The Nature and Limits of Political Science* (Cambridge: Cambridge University Press, 1963), 210.

40. Lorraine Code, *Rhetorical Spaces: Essays on Gendered Locations* (New York: Routledge, 1995), 17.

Consequently, the central question for biblical studies, whether they are understood as religious or the*logical studies, is not only what methods to use but also who formulates, uses, and deploys them, and to what persuasive ends this is done. In the dispute between those who advocate the scientific study of the Bible and those who champion a the*logical approach, the issue at stake is not so much one of method, but one of values and ideologies.

The scientist notion of the study of religion has widely been criticized. Three dominant perspectives of religious studies—religion as a reality sui generis, as a primarily text-based view of religion, and as a positivistic self-understanding of the study of religion as the science of religion—account for scholarship that renders religion decontextualized and ungendered.[41] Such scholarship moreover represents the "biblical hero" as a collective subject, which is undifferentiated by race, gender, class, ethnicity, or age. It emphasizes religious texts and privileges scholarly elites. Wo/men and other disenfranchised persons who have been excluded from the articulation, teaching, and interpretation of classics such as the Bible are thereby barred from the higher levels of religious authority.

In this scientistic approach, the uniquely religious is understood as the distinctively apolitical, insofar as the need for excluding or marginalizing social and political contents and aspects constitutes it. The distinctly religious allegedly is understandable "only on its own terms." Hence, biblical studies that engage in social-political and intercultural rhetorical analysis are, like the*logical studies, disqualified in this dualistic model of biblical scholarship.

However, such a dualistic conceptualization of biblical and religious studies over and against the*logical studies remains caught up in a modernist argument that does not do justice to our geopolitical situation. In a very perceptive article in the *Chronicle of Higher Education*, Stanley Fish has pointed to the breakdown of the dividing lines drawn by liberalism between academy and religion, reason and faith, truth and belief, or inquiry and revelation. Globalization and our geopolitical situation, he argues, have brought to public consciousness the fact that

> hundreds of millions of people in the world do not observe the distinction between the private and the public or between belief and knowledge and that it is no longer possible for us to regard such per-

---

41. Rosalind Shaw, "Feminist Anthropology and the Gendering of Religious Studies," in *Religion and Gender*, ed. Ursula King, 65–76 (Cambridge, MA: Blackwell Publishers, 1995).

sons as quaintly pre-modern or as needy recipients of our saving (an ironic word) wisdom. Some of these are our sworn enemies. Some of them are our colleagues, many of them are our students,[42]

who are not only seeking knowledge but also inspiration. He relates that when a reporter asked, after Jacques Derrida's death, what would replace high theory and "the triumvirate of race, gender, class" in the future, he spontaneously answered "religion." Hence, there is a growing awareness that it is no longer possible for the academy to keep "the old boundaries in place" and to quarantine "the religious impulse in the safe houses of the church, the synagogue, and the mosque."[43] It is no longer satisfactory to make religion the object of study. Rather, what is necessary is that academicians pay attention to the search of students for inspiration and meaning. If Fish's diagnosis of the academic situation after 9/11 is correct, it would be ironic and tragic if biblical scholars continue to eschew emic biblical meaning-making and restrict themselves to etic teaching *about* the Bible and religion in order to gain academic respectability.

Instead of splitting the field into two irreconcilable domains, one needs to articulate the accountability of biblical studies in an ascending order: the accountability to the academy and its commitment to excellence, the accountability to religious communities and their commitment to truth and justice, the accountability to the search of individuals for meaning and well-being, the accountability to the wider society and its public interests as well as to the ideals of democracy, human rights, and radical equality around the globe.[44]

For biblical studies to practice these responsibilities, its self-understanding needs to shift from a scientific, objectivist, scientist ethos to a rhetoric of inquiry that seeks wisdom. Such a rhetoric of inquiry pays special attention to the argumentative discourses of scholarship and their theoretical presuppositions, social locations, investigative methods, and sociopolitical functions. Since the space of rhetorical discourse is the public and political realm, a rhetoric of inquiry does not need to suppress but instead investigates the sociopolitical frameworks, cultural perspectives, modes of argumentation, and symbolic universes of religious texts and biblical interpretations.[45] It is keenly interested in exploring the

42. Stanley Fish, "One University under God?" in *Chronicle of Higher Education*, January 7, 2005, Chronicle Careers section: 1–11, here 10.

43. Ibid., 8.

44. See Charles Tilly, *Democracy* (New York: Cambridge University Press, 2007); and Thomas Banchoff, ed., *Democracy and the New Religious Pluralism* (New York: Oxford University Press, 2007).

45. For an exploration of rhetoric as argumentation, see Anders Eriksson, Thomas H. Olbricht, and Walter Übelacker, eds., *Rhetorical Argumentation in Biblical Texts* (Harrisburg, PA: Trinity Press International, 2002).

notion of ethos and ethic not only in epistemological-rhetorical but also in pedagogical-didactic terms.

While Christian biblical interpretation is for the most part individualistic and solitary, traditional Jewish interpretation as developed and practiced by feminists points to a radical democratic model. According to traditional rabbinic understanding, study and interpretation of Scripture lead to the redemption of the world because they bring G*d's presence into it. Scripture is the Living Word even in its imperfection and complexities. Hence, investigating and debating Scripture is a sacred activity.

Traditional Jewish Torah study, called Havruta, requires a social context. The Talmud commands: "Make yourself into groups to study the Torah, since the knowledge of the Torah can be acquired only in association with others" (*b. Berakhot* 63b). Echoing this tradition, the Matthean Jesus promises: "Where two or three are gathered in my name, I am there among them" (Matt. 18:20). Biblical meaning must be again and again reconsidered, questioned, debated, adjudicated, and reformulated rather than unquestioningly accepted and obeyed or rejected out of hand. It requires group work and an ethos of communal reading. Consequently, it is important to articulate a collaborative, the*logical, academic, and practical pedagogy for biblical studies in general and biblical/the*logical graduate education in particular.

The exploration of a pedagogy of participation and critical argument in graduate biblical studies, as well as the development of a collaborative model of graduate biblical education, is necessary in order to displace the competitive dualistic model of the academy on the one hand and the individualistic-privatized model of spiritual biblical reading on the other. An emancipative model of teaching and learning is able to conceive of the task of the biblical interpreter in rhetorical-emancipative terms.[46] Rhetoric is aware that texts seek to persuade and to argue; they are address and debate, rather than objective statement and value-free description.

In this model the biblical scholar does not have the task of "popularizing" and "applying" the results of research so that they can be appropriated by the general reader. Rather, a critical feminist rhetorical understanding of biblical studies shifts attention away from biblical interpretation construed as an ever-better explanation of the meaning

---

46. See my book *Rhetoric and Ethic: The Politics of Biblical Studies* (Minneapolis: Fortress Press, 1999) for the development of biblical studies as rhetorical studies.

of the text. It sees biblical interpretation and education as a forum of debate and conversation, a space for becoming conscious of structures of domination and for articulating visions of radical democracy and well-being (salvation) that are inscribed in our own experience as well as in that of biblical texts. Hence, it is necessary to take biblical interpretation both out of the hands of positivist scholarship *and* out of the privatized spiritual realm of the individual solitary reader.

In order to democratize biblical studies, we need to constitute graduate biblical education as a *forum*, a "republic of many voices,"[47] and a space of possibility where the *ekklēsia*, the radical democratic assembly of biblical scholars, students, and general readers, can debate and adjudicate the public and personal meanings of the Scriptures. Hence, the next chapter will explore the paradigms of biblical studies that constitute the pedagogical space of the discipline of biblical studies.

---

47. I have borrowed this title from William Ayers, *Teaching Toward Freedom: Moral Commitment and Ethical Action in the Classroom* (Boston: Beacon Press, 2004), 67.

2

A Republic of Many Voices

Paradigms of Biblical Studies

In chapter 1 we saw that a strict territorial division of the field of biblical studies—into the academy and the religious community—is advocated today with renewed force, restricting biblical studies to the territory of academic disciplines. A conceptualization of biblical studies in terms of territorial dualism—as either the domain of the university or that of institutionalized religion—views the discipline in either/or terms: either as the academic study of religions, or as confessional the*logical studies. Such a dualistic construction of the disciplinary ethos does not have space for a political or emancipatory approach to biblical studies, which is interested in changing societal, religious, or individual mind-sets. It does not conceptualize biblical studies as able to address the needs of society and the public, since biblical studies are located either in the academy or in organized religion and are not envisioned in radical democratic terms.

As a result, the rhetorical space of graduate biblical studies as we have seen is still determined by the dualistic alternative: either biblical studies is beholden to the academy, or it is beholden to the church; it is either academic or the*logical. Such a dualistic conceptualization of the domain of biblical studies is not able to assess the impact of biblical discourses on the democratic ethos and self-understanding of responsible citizens in society and religion. Here I argue that if biblical studies were reconceptualized in terms of a radical democratic republic,[1] then the dualistic-domain construction of "either academy or church/ institutionalized religion" could be overcome, because the exercise of full citizenship takes place in both academy and institutionalized religions as well as in society at large.

It must not be overlooked, however, that this dualistic-domain conceptualization of the discipline as either academic or the*logical is not simply dualistic; it is also an asymmetric dualistic construct that places greater value on the academic study of religion because of its alleged commitment to objectivity, value-neutrality, and the study of the Bible "for knowledge's sake." The study of religion and the Bible supposedly do not succumb to the biased interests of the*logy, which speaks from within a particular religion and is committed to a particular religious community. In this view, the*logy cannot be truly scientific because it is not free from value commitments and interests. The*logical scholars are often reduced to "missionaries," who want to bring their audiences to commit themselves to a religious faith community.

The academic study of religion, in contrast, is said to be free from ideological commitments because it adopts a neutral scientific framework of research, within which a rational kind of inquiry can take place for the sake of pure knowledge production. As a scientific discipline, the academic study of religion scrutinizes religious phenomena like empirical facts and studies religion in a way that is objective and detached. As a science, it limits itself to understanding the Bible "as it is" and seeks to represent it as "accurately" as possible.

In this chapter, I will seek to show that this oppositional dualistic-domain construction of the field can be further illuminated and critically destabilized in and through paradigm criticism.

PARADIGM CRITICISM

While it is tempting to import the dual-domain construction and once again divide paradigm research into the paradigms that are beholden to institutionalized religion and those that are practiced in the academy, such a dualistic-domain construction only obscures the function of the Bible in global societies and individual formation. Hence, it is impor-

---

1. According to the *Encarta Dictionary*, a "republic" is "a group with collective interests: a group of people who are considered to be equals and who have a collective interest, objective, or vocation (*formal*)"; *Microsoft Encarta Dictionary*, s.v. "Republic."

tant to reorient paradigm construction in biblical studies toward a radical democratic vision that fosters intellectual knowledge for change and transformation in global societies, religions, and the intellectual endeavors of individual citizens and scholars.

Paradigm Construction

Thomas Kuhn's categories of "scientific paradigm" and "heuristic model" have provided a theoretical framework[2] for comprehending theoretical and practical shifts in the self-understanding of biblical studies. A paradigm expresses "the shared commitment by the members of a scientific community to a particular form of scientific practice"[3] and is characterized by conceptual coherence and common intellectual interests. It articulates a common ethos and constitutes a community of scholars formed by its institutions and systems of knowledge. At the same time, a paradigm restricts the work of scholars by "blinding scholars to potentially important problems that are literally invisible to their normal science."[4] A paradigm thus can be envisioned as an intellectual and social space and scholarly home.

As a historian of science, Kuhn was interested in explaining change in science. Consequently, he stresses paradigm shifts that are not to be understood in cumulative or progressive terms but rather in competing terms. In a period of crisis, a competing paradigm emerges and subsequently receives acknowledgment and status because "it is recognized as being better at solving acute problems than its competitors. The resultant paradigm shift inaugurates a scientific revolution."[5]

A change of paradigm requires that the new theoretical framework gain a significant number of adherents and that it encompass a substantive alteration of the key issues that are judged to be important in a discipline. Moreover, a shift in scientific paradigm can only take place if and when the institutional conditions of knowledge production are changed. Although Kuhn wanted to restrict the theory of paradigm shifts to the natural sciences, his conceptualization has been used in the humanities in a broad array of disciplines because the key issues are determined by the community of scholars themselves.

2. Thomas S. Kuhn, *The Structure of Scientific Revolutions* (Chicago: University of Chicago Press, 1962).
3. Michael Payne, ed., *Cultural and Critical Theory* (Malden, MA: Blackwell Publishing, 1997), 394.
4. David Macey, *The Penguin Dictionary of Critical Theory* (New York: Penguin Books, 2001), 290.
5. Ibid.

This widespread use of Kuhn's theory of paradigm shift indicates the conditioned nature of all scientific investigation, and demonstrates that no neutral-observation language or value-free standpoint is possible. All scientific investigation demands commitment to a particular research approach and is carried out by a community of scholars dedicated to such a theoretical perspective. Moreover, Kuhn's theory helps us to understand that hermeneutical approaches, like scientific theories, are not falsified but replaced. They are not replaced because we find new "data," but because we find new ways of looking at old problems. Yet it must not be overlooked that Kuhn conceptualizes paradigm construction and paradigm shifts in terms of superiority, exclusivity, and competition. "A paradigm is thus a general theory which has succeeded in its struggle against other competing theories, but which has nevertheless not exhausted all the possible facts with which it has to deal."[6]

In response to the question "What kind of social-political-religious vision and self-understanding do the theoretical and pedagogical practices of paradigm construction support?" one has to point out that paradigm criticism in Kuhn's terms engenders competition and exclusiveness. Such a competitive model for paradigm construction, however, is not the only possible one. Paradigms as exemplary instances of theoretical frameworks and methods are not necessarily exclusive of each other. Rather, they can also be conceptualized as either existing alongside each other, or they can be seen as overlapping or as working in corrective interaction with each other. If paradigms are the cultural discursive practices of scholars, then they can be constructed and related to each other not only in terms of difference but also in terms of commonality. Paradigm shifts as scientific revolutions are, in Kuhn's terms, characterized by "over-and-againstness," incommensurability, and exclusiveness; on the other hand, I suggest that paradigms could also be conceived in terms of difference and shared common ground.

In difference to Kuhn, I argue that it is possible to construct research paradigms in such a way that they are not necessarily exclusive of each other, but rather can be understood as existing alongside and in corrective interaction with each other. Disciplinary paradigms are not hermetically closed off from each other but interact with each other on the level of method and in terms of a common area of inquiry. For this reason, paradigms must not necessarily be construed as standing in

6. Andrew Edgar, "Paradigm," in *Cultural Theory: The Key Concepts*, ed. Andrew Edgar and Peter Sedgwick (New York: Routledge, 2002), 268.

exclusive competition with each other but can also be seen, I suggest, as overlapping in some ways and in other ways as excluding each other. For this reason, paradigms can also be constructed in democratic terms as promoting collaboration, interaction, and dialogue/debate. However, if their stakeholders should do so, paradigms may no longer be conceptualized in terms of competition and over-and-againstness but should be understood in terms of both difference and shared common ground.

Paradigm research best constructs a typology of shifting, overlapping practices that shape and determine the discipline of biblical studies and biblical interpretation on the whole. Hence, one needs to critically analyze the construction of existing paradigms as to how open they are for the possibility of exchange and collaboration. Paradigms or exemplary instances of theoretical frameworks and methods can continue to be construed as existing over and against each other or as interacting with each other; they can be seen as overlapping or exclusive of each other, depending on their overall reconstructive ethos. They can utilize each other's methodological approaches and can work in corrective interaction with each other's theoretical perspectives.

The existing paradigms of biblical interpretation that have historically developed are therefore best imagined as overlapping circles, each constituting its own platform and space from which to speak. Each paradigm articulates a common ethos and constitutes a community of readers formed by common institutions and systems of knowledge. The discussion of existing paradigms therefore needs to pay special attention to exclusionary tendencies on the one hand, and overlapping interests of paradigms on the other.

A corrective conceptualization of biblical studies paradigms that understands them as consisting of diverse platforms or interpretive spaces allows one to shift the dual-domain rhetoric of "either academy or religious community" to that of different interpretive spaces that overlap and interact with each other. Rather than focusing on the paradigms of biblical studies as entities that are exclusive of each other, it is important to emphasize the aspects and methods that are compatible with and corrective of each other. Their overlap constitutes the ever-shifting heart or common ground of biblical studies on the whole, whereby the incompatible elements of each paradigm—those which would be at the center in a competitive construction—become progressively decentered.

The rhetoric of over-and-againstness and competitiveness is the factor that, according to Kuhn, engenders the emergence of a new paradigm. Consequently, in order to transform a paradigm into one of intellectual collaboration and dialogue, one needs to pay special attention to the elements that are articulated in radical critique of the preceding paradigm—not in order to preserve them, but to change them. It is true that paradigms are permeable, but the aspects of their theoretical framework, epistemological presuppositions, and institutional discourses that have been articulated over and against the preceding paradigm are exclusive of each other.

While one can and must, for instance, deploy literary, archaeological, historical, cultural, sociological, anthropological, philological, and other methods in the process of a particular interpretation, one can do so only after carefully investigating the epistemological presuppositions of these methods, their theoretical epistemological frameworks, and the institutional discursive practices operative in them. Consequently, one cannot promiscuously mix up theoretical frameworks and different discursive locations—such as religious dogmatism, historical positivism, cultural relativism, or emancipatory ideology critique—without losing one's theoretical and practical footing.

As cultural discursive practices, paradigms are both theoretical and institutional formations that develop not only distinct methodological approaches, but also distinct disciplinary languages, cultures, and loyalties. Practitioners are judged by professional criteria of excellence maintained by the dominant current hegemonic paradigm, and students are socialized into its disciplinary practices. For instance, the question of whether a book is "scholarly" or not is usually judged in terms of the hegemonic paradigm and not usually in terms of an emerging paradigm that would ask for competence in demystifying structures of domination inscribed by the practices of the dominant paradigm. Therefore, it is necessary to make explicit the different methodological approaches and theoretical frameworks articulated in the construction of competitive paradigms in order to deconstruct them.

For instance, students in biblical studies who are coming from a biblicist, religious background to divinity schools and departments of religious or the*logical studies are generally required to skillfully engage philological, historical, or literary academic methods. They are less encouraged, however, to explore the theoretical, often areligious, self-alienating, and marginalizing underpinnings of these methods. Within a fundamentalist religious paradigm, for instance, students learn to understand biblical authority in terms of kyriarchal obedience, often without knowing that this paradigm also has understood biblical authority in terms of empowering possibility.

Or within a positivist-scientific paradigm, students are socialized into accepting historical facticity, value-neutrality, and disinterestedness as authoritative, but they are not challenged to reflect on the kyriarchal tendencies of the scientific ethos, which marginalizes and objectifies the Others as distinct from elite, white, Western men. Yet to be able to create a radical democratic space of inquiry, students need to learn how to analyze the theoretical-epistemological frameworks, institutional locations, and ethical visions embedded in and promoted by the different paradigms of biblical studies. Paradigm criticism, I submit, could also enable them to locate themselves, their previous education, and professional goals epistemologically and practically. Hence, it is important to look critically at two leading proposals for paradigm construction in biblical studies.

Paradigm Construction in Biblical Studies

Intercultural Postcolonial Paradigm Criticism

Fernando Segovia has advocated a critical reflection on the discourses of biblical studies in light of paradigm criticism.[7] He charts four paradigms in biblical studies in terms of *modern and postmodern* academic biblical criticism rather than in terms of the overall history of biblical interpretation. Segovia is concerned with debunking historicist criticism, which has been dominating biblical studies and education for some time. While he focuses on the understanding of texts in the academy, he also situates biblical criticism within Christian studies and is concerned with the function of Scripture in the ongoing life of "actual flesh-and-blood religious communities."

Segovia charts the following four paradigms:

1. *Historical Criticism*, which uses the text as *means*, was according to him the dominant paradigm through the 1970s.
2. *Literary Criticism*, which dislodged historical criticism in the 1980s, analyzes the text as *medium*.
3. *Cultural Criticism*, an umbrella term that encompasses lines of inquiry such as socioeconomic and ideological analysis, neo-Marxist,

7. See also Fernando F. Segovia, "Pedagogical Discourse and Practices in Cultural Studies," in *Teaching the Bible: The Discourses and Politics of Biblical Pedagogy*, ed. Fernando F. Segovia and Mary Ann Tolbert (Maryknoll, NY: Orbis Books, 1998), 137–67.

and various forms of sociological analysis, understands the text as *medium and means.*

4. *Intercultural, Diasporic, or Postcolonial Criticism,* finally, takes account of the influx of marginal voices and locates the meaning of the text in the encounter between the text and the flesh-and-blood reader.

While Segovia is quite constant in his delineation of the first three paradigms, he seeks again and again to name and clarify the fourth paradigm, where he locates his new work. Though at first he called this paradigm "cultural studies" in order to distinguish it from cultural criticism,[8] he later qualified it as "intercultural" or "diasporic" studies, which are a part of postcolonial studies.[9]

Because Segovia is concerned with establishing his own postcolonial approach as the fourth paradigm, he stresses the proliferation of differences within this paradigm that are generated by a postcolonial approach. Yet he does not construct the fourth paradigm as an umbrella paradigm capable of gathering together the diverse ideology-critical emancipative approaches in biblical studies by forging common ground. In *Interpreting beyond Borders,* Segovia first discusses the difference between his diasporic Christian approach and the Jewish diasporic understanding of Daniel Boyarin. Then he proceeds to distinguish his reading approach by comparing it with other Christian intercultural approaches such as the *reading-with* style of Gerald West, the *androcritical reading* of Daniel Patte, and finally, the *dialogical reading* of Kwok Pui-lan, which he sees as "the plural face of postmodernism via postcolonialism, grounded in Asia."[10] Segovia concludes that all three proposals "break with the competitive strain of scientific reading" and alternatively emphasize a dialogical reading. He points out that the differences between these three approaches result from their different discursive matrices: oppositional modernism, postmodernism by way of textually based poststructuralism, and postmodernism

---

8. Fernando F. Segovia, "Introduction: 'And They Began to Speak in Other Tongues'; Competing Modes of Discourse in Contemporary Biblical Criticism," in *Reading from This Place: Social Location and Biblical Interpretation in the United States,* ed. Fernando F. Segovia and Mary Ann Tolbert (Minneapolis: Fortress Press, 1995), 1–32; Fernando F. Segovia, *Decolonizing Biblical Studies: A View from the Margins* (New York: Orbis Books, 2000), 3–52.

9. Fernando F. Segovia, "Biblical Criticism and Postcolonial Studies: Toward a Postcolonial Optic," in *The Postcolonial Bible,* ed. R. S. Sugirtharajah (Sheffield: Sheffield Academic Press, 1998); idem, "Notes Towards Refining the Postcolonial Optic," *Journal of the Study of the New Testament* 75 (1999): 103–14; idem, *Decolonizing Biblical Studies,* 119–142; idem, "Interpreting beyond Borders: Postcolonial Studies and Diasporic Studies in Biblical Criticism," and "Reading-Across: Intercultural Criticism and Textual Posture," in *Interpreting Beyond Borders,* ed. Fernando Segovia (Sheffield: Academic Press, 2000), 11–35, 59–83.

10. Segovia, "Reading-Across: Intercultural Criticism and Textual Posture," 78.

by way of reader-based postcolonialism. Intercultural reading and the dialogical imagination approach of Kwok share in common the post-modern-postcolonial matrix, but neither reflects countermodernism or poststructuralist postmodernism. Yet Segovia also stresses that while postmodern intercultural criticism questions texts, readings, and readers on all levels, it especially does so on the political level of agenda and location. It engages in a process of evaluation and critique throughout. However, he neither considers the feminist critique of "ludic postmodernism" nor compares his intercultural-postmodern-dialogical paradigm with a critical feminist-emancipatory construction of paradigms, which I have developed.

Although Segovia knows of my prior construction of disciplinary paradigms, he does not critically discuss and develop his paradigm construction in dialogue with mine. Rather, he opts for a different construction and suggests a different nomenclature since he is compelled to distinguish the fourth paradigm from both the second paradigm of literary criticism and the third paradigm of cultural criticism, which share his emphasis on the reader. He does so on the grounds of a different analysis that distinguishes the four disciplinary paradigms in terms of textual hermeneutics and reading approaches.

In short, Segovia identifies the three paradigms of historical, literary, and cultural criticism as hegemonic paradigms in the academic discipline of biblical criticism on the basis of his method and interdisciplinary approach, adding an emerging fourth paradigm of cultural studies or intercultural/diasporic/postcolonial criticism that does not emphasize texts but focuses on readers in their different historical, cultural, political locations. Such a fourth paradigm has become possible because of the development of interpretive and interdisciplinary postmodern, intercultural, diasporic postcolonial approaches in the academy.

Because Segovia correctly debunks the scientific-positivist paradigm as Western colonialist, he argues that the scientific paradigm of biblical studies in its historical and literary forms must be decentered because it has legitimized Western imperialism. Since Segovia is invested in debunking the scientific-positivist-hegemonic paradigm, he is not interested in highlighting its critical accomplishments. Moreover, he is compelled to omit the premodern the*logical-religious paradigm, which is considered to be beholden to the church. Such an omission of the religious-the*logical paradigm does not imply a rejection of this paradigm, however, because Segovia knows that actual flesh-and-blood readers are mostly located within church and religion rather than the academy. He thereby attempts to avoid importing a dual-domain ethos into the fourth paradigm but ultimately does so by failing to explicitly acknowledge a place in the academy for the*logical-religious frameworks and methods.

This delineation of the genealogy of the field as limited to the modern and postmodern paradigm practically restricts biblical studies to the academy and to "scientific" methods because it does not take into account the the*logical-religious paradigm, which is the oldest paradigm in biblical studies and is accountable to both the academy and organized religious communities. Such neglect results in the eclipse of the biblical readings that are engendered by religious communities and have as their goal spiritual nourishment, critique of oppressive structures, cultivation of vision, and religious-ethical motivation of flesh-and-blood readers. Therefore, Segovia's omission of this paradigm is puzzling since its adherents are of great concern to him. It is even more puzzling that Segovia has, to my knowledge, never explored this omission, although it took center stage in the discussion of feminist interpretation in the 1980s and 1990s.[11]

However, the eclipse of the religious-the*logical paradigm is questionable not just in terms of feminist but also in terms of postcolonial emancipatory concerns, since both feminist and postcolonial studies derive their strength not primarily from the academy but especially from social-political movements for justice. Because most postcolonial and feminist biblical readers are not located in the university but in communities of faith, the religiously based paradigm of biblical studies must not be eclipsed. If it is, one restricts scholarly work to the academy and cuts off its influence on and utility for communities of faith, communities that constitute a significant part of the democratic public.

Critical Feminist Decolonizing Paradigm Criticism

At this point it might be helpful to look at my own somewhat different construction of paradigms. In my book *Bread Not Stone: The Challenge of Feminist Biblical Interpretation*,[12] I proposed three paradigms: (1) the *doctrinal paradigm*, which understands the Bible as the word of G*d; (2) the *historical paradigm*, which sees it as a book of the past; and (3) the

---

11. See Letty Russell, ed., *Feminist Interpretation of the Bible* (Philadelphia: Westminster Press, 1985).

12. Elisabeth Schüssler Fiorenza, *Bread Not Stone: The Challenge of Feminist Biblical Interpretation* (Boston: Beacon Press, 1984), 25–33. This chapter was a revised form of my article "For the Sake of Our Salvation: Biblical Interpretation and the Community of Faith," in *Sin, Salvation, and the Spirit*, ed. D. Durken (Collegeville, MN: Liturgical Press, 1979), 21–39.

practical-the*logical paradigm, which understands the Bible as a root model rather than as an archetype. With this paradigm construction, I simultaneously sought both to counter the antiquarian ethos of biblical studies and to relocate academic biblical interpretation within engaged and dialogical communities of faith. Ecclesiastical as well as academic biblical interpretation should once again serve the people of G*d.

The new practical-the*logical paradigm, which I proposed then, was prepared, I argued, by two developments in biblical studies: form and redaction criticism as well as by the hermeneutical discussion. Whereas form and redaction criticism have shown that the Bible is not an exegetical or doctrinal tradition but a living tradition of the communities of faith, the hermeneutical discussion has made obsolete a value-free, objectivist, and positivist study of biblical texts. Hence, it is necessary to have a critical evaluation and assessment of biblical texts and their function in contemporary sociopolitical and religious communities.

Obviously, this form of paradigm construction is firmly located within a the*logical discussion and seeks to gain distance from both the doctrinal paradigm and the historical-positivist paradigm. In line with Latin American liberation the*logy, I argued that the proposed model was dialogical, practical, and emancipatory—oriented toward living communities of faith rather than just to the past, in the way that elite academic scholarship tended to be. In difference to Latin American liberation theologies, I contended that the emerging practical model of interpretation must first be critical, approaching the text with a hermeneutics of suspicion. This frame allowed me subsequently to develop the emerging fourth feminist interpretive paradigm as that of emancipatory praxis. Consequently, I developed this fourth paradigm not primarily in conversation with the three hegemonic paradigms of biblical studies, but rather in conversation with feminist and liberation the*logical-theoretical frameworks and approaches.

Like the third pastoral paradigm, a fourth paradigm was emerging that placed the Bible into the hands of people. Now, however, it is made explicit that these interpreters are gendered. Since the first two paradigms excluded wo/men throughout the centuries from the authoritative interpretation of the Bible, the third and fourth paradigms of biblical studies call for a critical feminist reader able to evaluate biblical texts and interpretation "for the sake of wo/men's salvation, that is, well-being." Segovia's assumption that it was only the third cultural paradigm that shifted attention from the text to the reader must be corrected. It is the feminist the*logical paradigm that has first sought to shift the scholarly focus on texts to the community of interpretation. It could do so because it connected with the religious-hermeneutical tradition and sharpened it by adding ideology-criticism, which called for an ethos of interpretation.

In my book *Rhetoric and Ethic*, almost fifteen years later, I sought to rename the four paradigms of interpretation that I had sketched out in *Bread Not Stone* as follows: (1) the doctrinal-fundamentalist, (2) the scientific-historical, (3) the hermeneutic-(post)modern, and (4) the rhetorical-emancipatory paradigms.[13] This reformulation was undertaken in light of the discussions that had been engendered by postmodern and various emancipatory approaches in biblical studies. Since these discussions did not acknowledge or even take into account a critical feminist paradigm of liberation, I thought it was necessary to do so.

If one compares the nomenclature used in *Bread Not Stone* with that used in *Rhetoric and Ethic*, one can see the critical points of difference. In the context of resurgent global fundamentalisms, I renamed the first paradigm "doctrinal-fundamentalist" and qualified the second as the scientific-positivist paradigm. Learning from Segovia's paradigm criticism, I renamed the third paradigm "(post-)modern cultural paradigm" and broadened the fourth paradigm by naming it "rhetorical-emancipatory"—as opposed to just "feminist-emancipatory"—in order to create an intellectual space for all the different approaches that utilize an analysis of the rhetoric of power.

The basic paradigms that I have articulated in *Bread Not Stone* and refined and renamed again and again take the premodern paradigm of interpretation into account. Such a paradigm construction, I submit, is not only able to comprehend the struggle between the first and subsequent paradigms, but also to underscore the affinities of the first and the succeeding paradigms. Hence, my genealogy of biblical studies reads somewhat differently from that of Segovia. Moreover, it parts way with Kuhn's competitive exclusivist-paradigm construction.

A comparison with Segovia's paradigm construction shows that we differ formally only with respect to the first paradigm, since my four basic paradigms take the premodern paradigm of interpretation into account, whereas Segovia's paradigm construction is restricted to the academy. Although we use a different nomenclature for the fourth paradigm, I believe that we are envisioning a similar restructuring of biblical studies.

---

13. Elisabeth Schüssler Fiorenza, *Rhetoric and Ethic: The Politics of Biblical Studies* (Minneapolis: Fortress Press, 1999), 31–56.

In light of the dual-domain discussion, I want to broaden my understanding of the first paradigm further by stressing that biblical studies as academic studies are not only scientific, cultural, and emancipatory studies, but also religious and the*logical studies. In addition, scientific and cultural-emancipatory studies, like religious-the*logical studies, may not be restricted to the questions and interests of the academy. They, too, must become radical democratic studies responsible to all the people.[14]

In formulating such studies, one needs to be careful not to import the dualistic-domain construction of the field. Whereas in Segovia's model such importing of the dualistic-domain construction is done by omitting the religious-the*logical paradigm, I have also done so in previous attempts by labeling the first paradigm of interpretation as "doctrinal" rather than as religious-the*logical.[15] However, such a labeling does not do justice to the wide-ranging reach and sophistication of this paradigm. It unwittingly promotes the dualistic-domain conception that eliminates religious discourses from academic biblical studies on the one hand and critical-historical/hermeneutical-emancipatory discourses from the biblical interpretation of communities of faith on the other.

REDESCRIBING AND RENAMING THE FOUR PARADIGMS OF BIBLICAL STUDIES

In light of the preceding discussions, I again want to insist on the acknowledgment of the first paradigm, but rename it as (1) the *religious-the*logical-scriptural paradigm*. Partially following Segovia, I will redescribe the second paradigm as (2) the *critical-scientific-modern paradigm*. I also want to qualify the third paradigm as (3) the *cultural-hermeneutic-postmodern paradigm*, and broaden the fourth paradigm by renaming it (4) the *emancipatory-radical democratic paradigm*.

The Religious-The*logical-Scriptural Paradigm

The first paradigm, which I renamed as the *religious-the*logical-scriptural paradigm*, was for centuries the dominant paradigm of Christian and Jewish biblical interpretation. It understands the biblical record as

---

14. Lori Anne Ferrell, *The Bible and the People* (New Haven, CT: Yale University Press, 2008), discusses the Bible's profound impact on readers over the centuries.
15. See my book *Rhetoric and Ethic*, chap. 2.

sacred Scripture and hermeneutically explores what it means to say that, as Scripture, the Bible is the revealed, authoritative Word of G*d. Under the*logical interpretation, Douglas Knight lists the following approaches focused on the authority of the Bible: canonical criticism, apocalypticism, evangelical biblical interpretation, Hebrew Bible and New Testament inner-biblical interpretation, inspiration of the Bible, orthodox biblical interpretation, biblical the*logy, Hebrew Bible and New Testament the*logy.[16]

This paradigm of biblical interpretation is at home not simply in biblical communities of faith but also in both institutional religions and the academy. Like the second academic paradigm, which has been practiced by a class of elite educated gentlemen, it was the domain of learned clergymen. Until the beginning of the twentieth century, wo/men and other marginal people had been explicitly excluded, by both law and custom, from this as well as from the subsequent scientific-modern paradigm. The Bible as the holy book of Jews, Christians, and Muslims—albeit in very different forms and ways— has become authoritative for communities of faith in and through the codifications and interpretations of educated clergymen.

The ancient and medieval Christian method of interpretation sought to establish a fourfold sense of Scripture: the literal (historical), the tropological (moral), the allegorical, and the anagogical (future-oriented) meanings of a text. Jewish hermeneutics developed a similar but distinctive method of interpretation that was called *PaRDeS* (Paradise): *Peshat* seeks for the plain sense of the text, *Remez* means the implied or allegorical sense, *Derush* involves legal and narrative exegesis—comparing terms from different places, and *Sod* is the mystical sense of a text.

Beginning with humanism and the time of the Protestant Reformation, this open-ended, dynamic, but doctrinally controlled mode of medieval interpretation changed. The Reformation taught on the one hand that Scripture can be understood by everyone, and on the other hand that "Scripture alone" (*sola scriptura*) is self-interpreting and that it alone is the foundation of faith. This teaching brought about the following two changes: it democratized Scripture reading, and it doctrinalized its hermeneutics.

The first change—the democratization of Scripture reading—led to a multiplicity of contradictory readings of Scripture, which could be used as legitimizations for diverse groups and struggles, resulting in the

---

16. Douglas A. Knight, ed., *Methods of Biblical Interpretation* (Nashville: Abingdon Press, 2004), 209–74.

European Wars of Religion. These wars, which for thirty years devastated Europe, led to the second change: a demand for either a rational criticism or a dogmatic understanding of Scripture. Baruch (Benedict) Spinoza (1632–77), one of the fathers of the modern critical-historical interpretation of Scripture, argued the following in his *Theological-Political Treatise*:

> We see nearly all men (sic) parade their own ideas as the Word of God, their chief aim being to compel others to think as they do, while using religion as a pretext. We see, I say, that the chief concern of theologians on the whole has been to extort from Holy Scripture their own arbitrarily invented ideas, for which they claim divine authority.[17]

Hence, a reasoned study of Scripture is called for, one that studies the language, content, and historical circumstances of biblical writings. The truth of Scripture transcends its context and speaks to reason. The divine revelation of Scripture preaches "true virtue"; that is, it teaches "to obey God with all one's heart by practicing justice and charity."[18] This summary of divine revelation echoes the great commandment of Jesus in Matthew 22:37–40 and

> calls to mind the schema (Deut. 6:4ff.) and the injunction to serve the neighbor (Lev. 19:18), the latter passage being the most common summary of the Torah made by the rabbis. Hence, the truth of Scripture is common to Christian and Jew.[19]

In a similar hermeneutical move, Martin Luther (1483–1546) had articulated the gospel as a "canon" by which to evaluate biblical texts as to whether they belonged to sacred Scripture. To that end, he formulated the dogmatic principle "what brings forth Christ" as the measuring rod. The orthodox successors of the Reformers, however, did not follow Luther but introduced the traditional dogmatic principle of "verbal inspiration" and the principle of biblical infallibility.[20] They insisted that the Bible was identical with the Word of G*d. Thus they

17. Baruch Spinoza, *Tractatus theologico-politicus*, trans. Samuel Shirley, intro. Brad S. Gregory (Leiden: E. J. Brill, 1989), 140; for his political thought and stress on democracy, see Joseph Dunner, *Baruch Spinoza and Western Democracy* (New York: Philosophical Library, 1955); Etienne Balibar, *Spinoza and Politics* (New York: Verso, 1988).

18. Spinoza, *Tractatus*, 55.

19. Roy A. Harrisville and Walter Sundberg, *The Bible in Modern Culture: Theology and Historical Critical Method from Spinoza to Käsemann* (Grand Rapids: Wm. B. Eerdmans Publishing Co., 1995), 42.

20. Robert M. Grant with David Tracy, *A Short History of the Interpretation of the Bible* (Philadelphia: Fortress Press, 1984), 97.

could use the Bible as the infallible foundation and proof text for a set of dogmatic convictions. Interpretation became a set of rules that allowed us to read the text in such a way as to confirm our dogmatic preunderstanding.

The so-called pietistic movement, in turn, deplored such a doctrinal reading and stressed the personal spiritual experience of interpreters. Literalist fundamentalism, in contrast, insists that the biblical message proclaims universal moral values and truth. Like modern orthodoxy and modern science, it claims that this truth can be positively established and proven. Thus it stresses verbal inspiration and calls for Christians to accept without question the Bible as the direct, inerrant Word of G*d. This emphasis on verbal inerrancy asserts that the Bible and its interpretation transcend ideology and particularity. It obscures the power relations and interests at work in biblical texts and interpretations. Such a fundamentalist approach eschews a critical the*logical hermeneutics that takes the linguisticality and historicity of biblical texts into account.

In contrast to the fundamentalist model of reading the Bible—which, as James Barr has shown, is strongly influenced by the epistemology of positivist modern scholarship[21]—the*logical studies typically understand the Bible in one of the following ways: either "in terms of the model of the classic" with its disclosure of existential truth (David Tracy), or in terms of the "literary model with its emphasis on intratextuality" (Hans Frei), or in terms of "the cultural linguistic model of thick description" (George Lindbeck). Alternatively, they might understand it in terms of the model of a "broad reflective equilibrium" (Francis Schüssler Fiorenza) between the reconstructive interpretation of a tradition, the examination of relevant background theories, the consideration of warrants, the attentive engagement with diverse communities of discourse, and a normative rhetorical practice.[22]

Such religious the*logical scholarship is, however, rarely seen as a part of biblical studies; instead, it is restricted to the discourses of systematic the*logy and hence has little influence on students in biblical studies. The dual-domain split of biblical studies is, as a result, sustained by such a dualistic disciplinary location. Hence, critical the*logical reflec-

21. James Barr, *Fundamentalism* (London: SCM Press, 1981); idem, *Beyond Fundamentalism: Biblical Foundations for Evangelical Christianity* (Philadelphia: Westminster Press, 1984).

22. See the excellent review of Francis Schüssler Fiorenza, "From Interpretation to Rhetoric: The Feminist Challenge to Systematic The*logy," in *Walk in the Ways of Wisdom: Essays in Honor of Elisabeth Schüssler Fiorenza*, ed. Shelly Matthews, Cynthia Briggs Kittredge, and Melanie Johnson-DeBaufre (Harrisburg: Trinity Press International, 2003), 17–45.

tion cannot become fruitful and effective in the discipline of biblical studies. This is also the case for the innovative practice of Scriptural Reasoning, which is inspired by Jewish traditions of interpretation and seeks to bring Christians, Jews, and Muslims together in a collegial context to study the Bible. Scriptural Reasoning has been summarized as follows by David Ford:

> Its combination of recognition of the plain sense with discernment of an applied sense is at the heart of what I call a wisdom inter- pretation of scripture. This is the central way in which scriptural reasoning copes with the abundance of meaning: by trying to take as much of it as possible into account, by always giving priority (as Judaism, Christianity and Islam traditionally do) to the plain sense, and by risking a contemporary midrashic sense that has emerged out of wisdom-seeking conversation across traditions and disci- plines. This contemporary sense is a performance of interpretation for now. It does not seek to be normative knowledge or the only valid interpretation.[23]

This religious-the*logical performative model of interpretation stresses dialogue, mutual respect, and getting to know one another's traditions; it understands Scriptural Reasoning as an art and perfor- mance that risks border crossings and cultivates an ethos of engage- ment. It works with "a triadic semiotic that assumes that meaning arises out of the relationship between the sign, referent and community of interpreters that reads the text," whereas "much contemporary biblical scholarship utilizes a dyadic sign/referent model for assigning meaning to scripture."[24]

The Critical-Scientific-Modern Paradigm

The *critical-scientific-modern paradigm* has been practiced in biblical studies as a Euro-American historical-factual and formalist literary par- adigm because it uses a dyadic sign/referent model, according to which each sign refers to one object or concept of interpretation. Hence, it has claimed that it is able to establish the one true meaning of a text

23. David F. Ford, "An Interfaith Wisdom: Scriptural Reasoning between Jews, Christians and Muslims," in *The Promise of Scriptural Reasoning*, ed. David F. Ford and C. C. Pecknold (Malden, MA: Blackwell Publishing, 2006), 1–22, here 15.
24. Steven Kepnes, "A Handbook of Scriptural Reasoning," in Ford and Pecknold, *The Promise of Scriptural Reasoning*, 23–39, here 30.

by using the appropriate philological, historical, and literary methods of analysis. The distinction is usually made between historical criticism on the one hand, which includes archaeology, textual criticism and translation, lexicography and philology, history of religions, form criticism and tradition criticism, orality criticism, social-world criticism and sociological interpretation; and literary criticism on the other, which includes source and redaction or composition criticism as well as genre, rhetorical, narrative, reader-response, canonical criticism, structuralism, and the New Criticism.[25]

This paradigm was developed in the context of the European Reformation, Renaissance, and Enlightenment over and against the control and authority of the churches. Its social institutional location is the positivist understanding of science in the modern university. The scientific principle of the Enlightenment was institutionalized in the modern university as the positivist paradigm of knowledge that gives primary import to evidence, data, and empirical inquiry—that is, to the "logic of facts."

Since this positivistic ethos of scientific biblical criticism is not only a part of the academy but has also become popularized by literalist fundamentalism, it is important to critically explore the degree to which religious and academic communities have internalized the presuppositions of the modern scientific-positivistic paradigm of historical and literary criticism. Although the scientific-positivist paradigm demands objectivity, disinterestedness, and value-neutrality in order to control what constitutes the legitimate, scientifically established, true meaning of a text, it is patently *kyriocentric* and *Eurocentric*.

In the nineteenth and early twentieth centuries, the scientific ethos of value-free scholarship, which was presumed to be untainted by social relations and political interests, was institutionalized in professions that assure the continuation of the dominant disciplinary ethos. Nancy Leys Stepan and Sander Gilman, among others, have pointed out that the professional institutionalization of scholarship as value-neutral, apolitical, universal, empirical, and methodologically objective science—as an "unbiased arena of knowledge"—was not a "natural" outcome of unbiased study but rather

> a social outcome of a process whereby science was historically and materially constituted to have certain meanings, functions and inter-

25. Cf. William Baird, "New Testament Criticism," in *Anchor Bible Dictionary*, ed. D. N. Freedman, vol. 1 (New York: Doubleday, 1992), 730–36.

ests. In a complex series of innovations, science's epistemological claims were given definition and institutional representation in the form of new scientific societies and organizations sharply delimited from other institutions. These innovations were tied not only to industrialization, but also to the politics of class and the closing of ranks of bourgeois society. . . . Race and gender were also crucial in the construction of modern science, insofar as science was defined as "masculine" in its abstraction, detachment and objectivity.[26]

This professionalization of the academic disciplines engendered theoretical dichotomies such as "pure and impure," or theoretical and applied science. Dualistic opposites such as rational and irrational, objective and subjective, hard and soft, male and female, European and colonial, and secular and religious—all were given material form not only in professional disciplines but also in their discursive practices. For instance, the methodologically dense, scientific, depersonalized, empirical-factual text of the research paper emerged as a new, standardized academic genre. This genre replaced the more metaphorically porous, literary varied, and readable forms of writing that were accessible to both academics and the nonscientific, "popular" reader.

The development of biblical studies as a scientific discipline adopted a similar scientific, professional, elite male ethos.[27] The Society of Biblical Literature (SBL) was founded in 1880,[28] around the same time that the American Philological Association (1869), the American Social Science Association (1869), the Archaeological Institute of America (1879), the Modern Language Association (1883), and the American Historical Association (1884) were initiated. The formation of these organizations was largely driven by the desire to establish each field as "legitimate," as value-free, objective, and "scientifically rigorous."

The feminist historian Bonnie G. Smith, for example, has argued that the ethos of the American Historical Association cultivated a value-detached, "gender-neutral" community of scholars and developed an

26. Nancy Leys Stepan and Sander L. Gilman, "Appropriating the Idioms of Science: The Rejection of Scientific Racism," in The "Racial" Economy of Science: Toward a Democratic Future, ed. Sandra Harding (Bloomington: Indiana University Press, 1993), 170–93, here 173; see also Londa Schiebinger, The Mind Has No Sex? Wo/men in the Origins of Modern Science (Cambridge, MA: Harvard University Press, 1989).

27. For the medical profession, see Anne Witz, Professions and Patriarchy (New York: Routledge, 1992); for the notion of professional authority, see the sociological study by Terrence J. Johnson, Professions and Power (London: Macmillan, 1972).

28. For the history of biblical studies in North America, see the various published contributions of Thomas Olbricht, such as "Alexander Campbell in the Context of American Biblical Studies," Restoration Quarterly 33 (1991): 13–28; idem, "Biblical Interpretation in North America in the 20th Century," in Historical Handbook of Major Biblical Interpreters, ed. Donald K. McKim (Downers Grove, IL: InterVarsity Press, 1998), 541–57; and idem, "Histories of North American Biblical Scholarship," Current Research in Biblical Studies 7 (1999): 237–56.

"objective" narrative in the course of professionalization as "a modern scientific profession." Its practices were not only unconcerned with considerations of gender, class, politics, culture, or society at large; they also openly required "a commitment to objectivity" over and above such categories as class and gender. They demanded "the strict use of evidence, the taming of historical narrative to a less rhetorical style, the development of archives and professional libraries, the organization of university training in seminars and tutorials, and in the case of the United States, a commitment to democratic access to the profession based on ability." In addition, professionalizing historians attempted to eliminate all personal or subjective meaning from their work. Thus historians created a space inhabited by an invisible "I," one without politics, without an ego or persona, and certainly ungendered.[29]

Like its brother profession, the American Historical Association, the SBL was founded by Protestant "gentlemen"[30] who were, for the most part, "European trained in such universities as Berlin, Heidelberg, Halle, and Tübingen."[31] Even though the overall theoretical position of the SBL was apparently "impartial," seeking to make available "a forum for the expression and critique of diverse positions on the study of the scriptures," the position of the so-called higher criticism won increasing influence.[32] This professional scientific stance was complicated in biblical studies by the struggle of the discipline to prove its scientific "value-neutral" character within the Enlightenment university, which had only quite recently more or less successfully thrown off the shackles of religion. It also was marked by the struggle to free itself from the dogmatic fetters of the Protestant and Roman Catholic[33] churches. This conflict emerged between the advocates of scientific "higher criticism" and those interested in safeguarding the the*logical "purity" of the Bible in the "heresy trials" at the turn of the twentieth century.

As we have seen in the first chapter, the same rhetorical tension still remains inscribed in the self-understanding of biblical studies as a pro-

29. Bonnie G. Smith, "Gender, Objectivity, and the Rise of Scientific History," in *Objectivity and Its Other*, ed. Wolfgang Natter, Theodore Schatzki, and John Paul Jones III (New York: Guilford Press, 1995), 52.

30. *Journal of Biblical Literature* 9 (1890): vi.

31. See Jerry Wayne Brown, *The Rise of Biblical Criticism in America, 1858–1870: The New England Scholars* (Middleton, CT: Wesleyan University Press, 1988); the above references to Thomas Olbricht's work; and Ernest W. Saunders, *Searching the Scriptures: A History of the Society of Biblical Literature, 1880–1980* (Chico, CA: Scholars Press, 1982), 6.

32. Saunders, *Searching the Scriptures*, 11.

33. For the history of Roman Catholic scholarship, see Gerald Fogarty, SJ, *American Catholic Biblical Scholarship: A History from the Early Republic to Vatican II* (San Francisco: Harper & Row, 1989); for Jewish scholarship, see S. David Sperling, ed., *Students of the Covenant: A History of Jewish Biblical Scholarship in North America* (Atlanta: Scholars Press, 1992).

fession and in its discursive practices today.[34] Emblazoned in the profession ethos of biblical criticism is the conflict surrounding how the Bible should be studied. Should it be viewed as a collection of ancient texts, or as a normative document of biblical religions? Is the critical study of the the*logical meaning and normativity of traditions and scriptures part of the research program of biblical studies, or must it be left to confessional theology? Is it part of the professional program of "higher criticism" to study the communities of discourse that have produced and sustained scriptural texts and readings in the past and still do so in the present? Finally, does competence in biblical criticism entail the ability to engage in a critical, theoretical, interdisciplinary metareflection on the the*logical work of biblical studies? Would this require that students of the Bible be trained not only in textual-historical analysis but also in the ideological analysis of social and political discursive positions and social-religious-political relations of the discipline and its practitioners?

In short, biblical studies' aspiration to "scientific" status in the academy and its claim to universal, unbiased modes of inquiry both deny its hermeneutical-rhetorical character and mask its sociohistorical location as well as its sociopolitical or ecclesiastical interests. The phenomenological, literary, comparative, and history of religions approaches can be situated either in this or the following paradigm, depending on whether they stress objectivism and value neutrality or hermeneutic empathy.

The Cultural-Hermeneutic-Postmodern Paradigm

The third, *cultural-hermeneutic-postmodern paradigm*, in contrast to the modern positivist paradigm, underscores the rhetorical character of biblical knowledge and acknowledges the symbolic, multidimensional power of biblical texts and artifacts. This third, *cultural-hermeneutic-postmodern paradigm* is not so much concerned to prove authoritative truth, or to establish historical "facts" and literary structures, as it is to *understand* and, if need be, *deconstruct* sacred texts and their function in the life of peoples. It is best understood as a cultural paradigm in its hermeneutic and postmodern forms. The Postmodern Bible Collective identifies various approaches gathered under this paradigm: reader-response criticism; structuralist and narratological criticism—

---

34. See Harrisville and Sundberg, *The Bible in Modern Culture*; for more recent work, see John Barton, *The Nature of Biblical Criticism* (Louisville, KY: Westminster John Knox Press, 2007).

both of which I would attribute to the second, preceding paradigm, the critical-scientific-modern paradigm; poststructuralist criticism; rhetorical criticism; psychoanalytic criticism; ideological criticism; feminist and womanist criticism; but it does *not* include Latino/a, Asian, African, indigenous/Native American, or postcolonial criticism.[35]

The term postmodernism encompasses a great variety of cultural practices and celebrates pluralism, playfulness, indeterminism, and relativism. However, I understand postmodernism not as antimodernism, but rather in terms of Lyotard's redefinition: "as a 'rewriting' of modernity."[36] In a similar fashion, Zygmunt Bauman states: "Postmodernity is modernity coming to terms with its own impossibility; a self-monitoring modernity, one that consciously discards what it was once unconsciously doing."[37] An important aspect of poststructuralism[38] and postmodernism is its adoption of rhetoric as a key category and its understanding of the rhetoricity of language. Some thinkers seek to overcome the traditional prejudice that sees rhetoric as ornamental, flowery language or as "mere" talk by stressing the carnevalesqueness and playfulness of language. Others stress that the ideas, values, and worldviews we express are socially and politically constructed in language. Still others argue that a postmodern appropriation of rhetoric is able to articulate critical political analyses and discourses.

Hermeneutics[39] also recognizes the rhetorical character of language, but focuses on understanding and meaning. It conceives of Scripture as cultural icon and construes it as a dialogue partner or divining agent. Or to use another metaphor, it sees the sacred text as a multicolored tapestry and texture of meaning and likens the reading of the Bible to the reading of the great books, or classics, of Western culture, whose greatness does not consist in their accuracy as records of facts, but depends chiefly on their symbolic power to transfigure human experience and symbolic systems of meaning. Postmodern criticism stresses the indeterminacy, ambiguity, fragmentation, and multidimensionality of text and mean-

---

35. Elizabeth A. Castelli et al., eds., *The Postmodern Bible* (New Haven, CT: Yale University Press, 1995).

36. Peter Sedgwick, "Postmodernism," in *Cultural Theory: Key Concepts*, ed. Andrew Edgar and Peter Sedgwick (New York: Routledge, 2002), 296.

37. Zygmunt Bauman, *Modernity and Ambivalence* (Ithaca, NY: Cornell University Press, 1991), 272.

38. See Stephen Moore, *Poststructuralism and the New Testament: Derrida and Foucault at the Foot of the Cross* (Minneapolis: Fortress Press, 1994); Moore concludes (117), "In the context of Biblical Studies, poststructuralism would be historical criticism's id, the seat of its strongest antiauthoritarian instincts—historical criticism unfettered at last from the ecclesiastical superego that has always compelled it to genuflect before the icons it had come to destroy."

39. See Francis Schüssler Fiorenza, "History and Hermeneutics," in *Modern Christian Thought*, ed. James Livingston and Francis Schüssler Fiorenza, vol. 2 (Upper Saddle River, NJ: Prentice Hall, 1999), chap. 11; and the collection of essays edited by Kurt Mueller-Vollmer, *The Hermeneutics Reader* (New York: Continuum, 1988).

ing; proclaims the collapse of grand narratives; questions the possibility of articulating the truth; and "disdains all pretensions to objectivity."[40] Yet hermeneutics still has one foot in the modern scientific paradigm.

The word *hermeneutics* derives from the Greek word *hermēneuein* and means to interpret, exegete, explain, or translate. It owes its name to Hermes, the messenger of the gods, whose task is to mediate the announcements, declarations, and messages of the gods to mere mortals. His proclamation, however, is not just a communication and mediation but always also an explication of divine commands in such a way that he translates them into human language so that they can be comprehended and obeyed.

Hermeneutics can be understood with Derrida as a matter of the free play of signs[41] and with Rorty[42] as merely keeping the lines of communication open; yet hermeneutics, according to Gadamer,[43] has the task of translating meaning from one "world" into another.[44] It is a matter of practical understanding that involves the Aristotelian virtue of *phronēsis*: practical judgment and adjudication that is not secured by an a priori method, but rather by the process of understanding.

As a discipline, philosophical hermeneutics has its roots in biblical interpretation. It is best understood as a theory and practice of interpretation that explores the conditions and possibilities of understanding— not just of texts, but of other practices[45] as well. As such, hermeneutics is not so much a disciplined scientific method and technique, but more of an epistemological perspective and approach.[46]

Since Schleiermacher, Dilthey, and Gadamer,[47] hermeneutics has stood over and against scientific positivism, maintaining that understanding takes place as a process of engagement in the hermeneutical circle or spiral, which is characterized by the part/whole relation. It stresses that understanding is not possible without preunderstandings

---

40. Sedgwick, "Postmodernism," 297.

41. Jacques Derrida, "The Ends of Man," in *Philosophy and Phenomenological Research* 30 (1969): 31–57.

42. Richard Rorty, *Philosophy and the Mirror of Nature* (Princeton, NJ: Princeton University Press, 1979), 315.

43. See Hans Georg Gadamer, *Truth and Method*, trans. and ed. Garrett Barden and John Cumming (New York: Seabury Press, 1975); and idem, *Philosophical Hermeneutics*, ed. and trans. by David E. Linge (Berkeley: University of California Press, 1976).

44. See Richard Bernstein, "What Is the Difference That Makes a Difference? Gadamer, Habermas, and Rorty," in *Hermeneutics and Modern Philosophy*, ed. Brice R. Wachterhauser (Albany: State University of New York Press, 1986), 343–76.

45. Paul Ricoeur's theory of interpretation has argued that action may be regarded as a text. If an action, like a text, is a meaningful entity, then the "paradigm of reading" can also be applied to socioreligious practices. See Paul Ricoeur, *Hermeneutics and the Human Sciences*, ed. and trans. John B. Thompson (Cambridge: Cambridge University Press, 1981), 197–221.

46. See Wachterhauser, *Hermeneutics and Modern Philosophy*, 5.

47. See Ricoeur, *Hermeneutics and the Human Sciences*, 43–62.

or prejudices, and therefore that understanding is always contextually dependent. Hermeneutics does not ground intelligibility in the "pregiven, essentially changeless human subject, but in the public sphere of evolving, linguistically mediated practice."[48] Thus hermeneutics seeks to remain open for change and difference.

Hermeneutics insists, furthermore, on the linguisticality of all knowledge, on its contextuality and its immersion in tradition. It stresses that human understanding can never take place without words and outside of time. Hermeneutics comprises seven key theoretical emphases: *empathy, historicity, linguisticality, tradition, preunderstanding, fusion of horizons,* and *the classic,* with its notion of *effective history.* All of these are problematic from a critical feminist perspective because they do not sufficiently take into account relations of domination and power. In what follows, I will focus on four of these central concepts of hermeneutics because they are also emphasized in postmodern discourses. These are historicity, linguisticality, tradition, and the fusion of horizons.

First, *historicity (Geschichtlichkeit) and contextuality* are central to hermeneutic method. Historicity signifies both our participation in, and the fact that we belong to, history and renders us historical beings through and through. It colors our rational capacity to know and make sense of the world. By shaping our preunderstandings and prior assumptions, historicity makes it impossible for us scholars of religion to free ourselves from the impact of our own historical context in order to represent other religions or times "as they actually are." As scholars, we can produce more or less true accounts, but we can never free ourselves from the influences of our own historical context and location.

Moreover, historicity means that human texts such as the Bible can never be reduced to an essential ahistorical core or to one universal meaning that is the same in all historical circumstances. Rather, texts—like people—must be understood in the contexts of their historical circumstances, languages, and the communities in which they were articulated. According to the hermeneutical perspective, we human beings are neither given an immutable essence by God or nature, nor do we make ourselves (at least not as isolated individuals). We are defined rather by the particular mode of historical existence in which we find ourselves, a mode that shapes us just as we also actively shape it in cooperation with others.[49]

---

48. Wachterhauser, *Hermeneutics and Modern Philosophy*, 8.
49. Ibid., 7.

Second is *linguisticality*. Hermeneutics further insists that all knowledge and understanding is determined by and mediated through language. Language transports meaning from one context to another. The
notion of linguisticality underscores the view that all understanding is
historically and culturally mediated. By learning a language or the discourse of specialized fields of study, we come to understand our world
and ourselves. Feminist analyses have emphasized that grammatically
masculine, so-called generic language is a major cultural force in maintaining women's second-class status in culture and religion. If, as Wittgenstein says, the limits of our language are the limits of our world,[50]
then grammatically masculine language that operates to construct the
universe of women and men in androcentric or—better—kyriocentric
(that is, slave-master, lord, father, elite-male-centered) terms engenders
a world in which wo/men are marginal or not present at all.

Hence, it does not suffice to simply analyze the kyriocentric
religious-cultural language, tradition, or cultural classic. What is necessary is to change them by understanding language as an instrument of
power and ideology rather than simply as descriptive and communicative. Language is always rhetorical. Hence, a poststructuralist approach
would insist that hermeneutical theory must be braided with rhetorical
theory, for rhetoric not only inscribes but also makes explicit the relation of language and power in a particular moment.[51]

> If all language is rhetorical, if even objectivity is the product of a
> certain strategy, then discourses are no longer to be measured in
> terms of their adequacy to an objective standard (which Nietzsche's
> perspectivism exposes as a myth) but rather to be analyzed in terms
> of their strategic placement within a clash of competing forces them-
> selves constituted in and through the very rhetorical dissimulations
> they employ.[52]

Third, *tradition* is a foundational term in hermeneutics and biblical
studies. Gadamer stresses that we always stand within a tradition, and
he likens this to our standing within a river of life. Hermeneutics is
the attempt to understand the stream of tradition of which texts, like
interpreters, are a part. However, Gadamer understands tradition in

50. On religious language and hermeneutics, see Dan R. Stiver, *The Philosophy of Religious Language: Sign, Symbol and Story* (Cambridge: Blackwell Publishers, 1996), 37–111.
51. See Cheryl Glenn, *Rhetoric Retold: Regendering the Tradition from Antiquity through the Renaissance* (Carbondale: Southern Illinois University Press, 1997); Lorraine Code, *Rhetorical Spaces: Essays on Gendered Locations* (New York: Routledge, 1995).
52. John Bender and David Wellbery, *The Ends of Rhetoric* (Stanford, CA: Stanford University Press, 1990), 27.

affirmative ways as "belonging," rather than in critical terms as a place of distortion and domination. To belong to a tradition, he observes, means to have a shared language and/or understanding. Still, hermeneutics does not sufficiently problematize the fact that traditions are rhetoricized, valorized, and shaped by the interests of those in power. The emphasis of hermeneutics on tradition and its authority clearly stands in tension with poststructuralist understandings and goals, which for ethical and political reasons reject all essences, be it the essence of truth or language or being. For instance, John Caputo points to the antiessentialism of Derrida regarding tradition:

> For Derrida the tradition is through and through something "constituted," an effect, radically contingent, reformable, reconstructible, not possessed of some deep identity, some essential truth or core that cuts off in advance the coming of the other. . . . That is why Derrida would not embrace the rhetoric of a fusion of horizons, for it is only in the breach of the horizon that the other manages to gain a hearing.[53]

Fourth is *fusion of horizons*. Gadamer understands the hermeneutical event as a fusion of horizons (*Horizontverschmelzung*). All interpretation involves a fusion of horizons between the horizon of the text and that of the reader, between past and present, between the classic and its contemporary interpreters. Such a fusion of horizons presupposes a conception of the actual course of history,

> linking the past with the present situation and its horizon of the future [that] form the comprehensive horizon within which the interpreter's limited horizon of the present and the historical horizon of the text fuse together.[54]

In the process of interpretation we have to inquire into the unspoken horizon of meaning of the text to be understood as well as into our own limited horizons. The well-known "hermeneutical circle"[55] means that understanding can take place only if we situate a phenomenon in a larger context: the parts of some larger reality can only be grasped in

---

53. John D. Caputo, *More Radical Hermeneutics: On Not Knowing Who We Are* (Bloomington: Indiana University Press, 2000), 58.

54. Wolfhart Pannenberg, "Hermeneutics and Universal History," in Wachterhauser, *Hermeneutics and Modern Philosophy*, 135.

55. The concept of the "hermeneutical circle" was first developed by Heidegger; see Martin Heidegger, *Being and Time*, trans. John MacQuarrie and Edward Robinson (London: SCM Press, 1962); see also Hans Georg Gadamer, "Hermeneutics and Social Science," *Cultural Hermeneutics* 2 (1975): 307–16.

terms of the whole. What we can do in this to-and-fro action of the hermeneutical circle or spiral is fuse or broaden our horizon with the horizon of the text and vice versa.

The image of the fusion of horizons seeks to articulate effective hermeneutic communication. The appropriation of a tradition through understanding can be likened to translation. The horizon of the present is not formed without the past. Such an interlacing of horizons belongs to the very conditions of hermeneutic work. No horizon is closed because we are able to place ourselves in another point of view and to comprehend another culture. However, it has been pointed out that Gadamer does not mean to say that past and present are separate horizons, although the image suggests two distinct horizons melting or flowing into each other. When we understand the past, with its many differences, we are expanding our horizon, not stepping out of our horizon into the other horizon.[56]

Yet if we understand the fusion of horizons either as expanding our horizon with that of the text's horizon or as submission of one's own horizon to that of the text, that means to construe understanding in kyriarchal terms either as appropriation or as submission.[57] Rather than conceiving understanding as a fusion of horizons, it is necessary, as Susan Shapiro has argued,[58] to articulate hermeneutics as rhetoric. If horizon means "the field to which the perceptual object belongs," or is the "inactual, nonthematic halo that surrounds and decisively affects the structure of the thematic object,"[59] then hermeneutics must become a critical inquiry into the rhetoricity of the structures of domination and goals of emancipation inscribed in biblical texts.

To summarize, the *cultural-hermeneutic-postmodern paradigm* is not so much concerned to prove authoritative truth, or to establish historical "facts" and literary structures, as it is to *understand* and, if need be, *deconstruct* sacred texts and their function in the life of peoples. It does not assume that the text represents a given divine revelation, a window to historical reality, or a textual world enclosed in itself. It also does not understand historical artifacts and literary sources as data and evidence. Rather, it sees them as perspectival discourses that construct a range of

---

56. David Couzens Hoy, "Is Hermeneutic Ethnocentric?" in *The Interpretive Turn: Philosophy, Science, Culture*, ed. David R. Hiley, James F. Bowman, and Richard Shusterman (Ithaca, NY: Cornell University Press, 1991), 165.

57. Derrida's breach of horizon to make room for and welcome the Other with hospitality is likewise not able to critically evaluate and reject violent texts that are seen as personifications of the Other.

58. Susan Shapiro, "Rhetoric as Ideology Critique: The Gadamer-Habermas Debate Reinvented," *Journal of the American Academy of Religion* 62, no. 1 (1994): 123–50.

59. Caputo, *More Radical Hermeneutics*, 424.

symbolic universes. Since alternative symbolic universes engender competing definitions of the world, texts cannot be reduced to one single, definitive meaning. Competing interpretations are therefore not simply either right or wrong. Rather, they constitute different ways of reading and of constructing historical and religious meaning.

Like the modern scientific paradigm of biblical criticism, the cultural-hermeneutic-postmodern approach to biblical interpretation is also located in the university, divinity schools, and other cultural institutions. Three decades ago the historical-positivist and literary-formalist paradigms of scientific biblical interpretation reigned in the Anglo-American academy; today hermeneutical and postmodern epistemological discussions abound—discussions that are critical of both the dogmatic-the*logical and the positivist-scientific ethos of biblical studies. Feminist, postcolonial, and liberation the*logical interpretations have moreover played a great part in the postmodern hermeneutical transformation of academic biblical scholarship, which is often not acknowledged in malestream biblical scholarship.[60] These approaches have insisted on critical evaluation and transformation by the marginalized subjects of interpretation and refused to relinquish the liberationist claims to truth, the possibility of transformation, and the vision of a more just world. Hence, a new emerging paradigm is called for.

The Emancipatory-Radical Democratic Paradigm

Postmodern hermeneutic-cultural and emancipatory-postcolonial analyses meet in their critique of modernity, insofar as modernity's achievements have been bought at the price of misogyny, colonialism, and slavery. Postmodernism rejects the notion of emancipation and truth; but liberationist, postcolonial, and feminist criticisms argue that modernity failed to accomplish the emancipation it promised. The liberation movements of the last centuries insisted that their calls for emancipation must be realized.

In contrast to nihilist postmodern criticism, the voices from the margins of biblical studies argue that the subjugated others cannot afford to abandon either the notion of being historical subjects and agents or the possibility of knowing the world and the divine differently. Rather,

---

60. See, however, Burke O. Long, "Scholarship," in *Handbook of Postmodern Biblical Interpretation*, ed. A. K. M. Adam (St. Louis: Chalice Press, 2000), 227–32.

the critical voices from the margins of religious communities and the academy maintain that we who are the "subordinated and silenced others" must engage in a political and theoretical process of constituting ourselves as subjects of knowledge, history, and interpretation.

With Jürgen Habermas, a representative of the Frankfurt School's critical theory, a critical feminist hermeneutics of liberation, over and against the hermeneutical program and postmodern nihilism, insists on emancipation and the question of power as integral to understanding, linguisticality, tradition, and the classic. Habermas distinguishes

> three basic forms of our scientific interest in knowing about the world: the empirical-analytical, the hermeneutical-historical, and the critical-emancipatory. We seek to know in order to control social and natural realities (the empirical-analytic interest), to qualitatively understand and interpret such realities (the hermeneutical-historical interest), and to transform our individual and collective consciousness of reality in order to maximize the human potential for freedom and equality (the critical-emancipatory interest).[61]

Whereas hermeneutics is concerned with the surplus of meaning, critical theory focuses on the lack and distortion of meaning through contextualization and relations of domination. Like feminist criticism, critical theory also stresses the distortion of language and tradition. The endurance of the classic, for instance, is not so much due to its outstanding representation of meaning as to the persistence of kyriarchal power constellations that legitimate it and in turn are legitimated by it. Cultural and religious linguistic practices and traditions have been constituted within unequal power relationships. A feminist critical theory thus insists on and makes possible the concrete analysis of structures of power and domination. It engages in interpretation for the sake of ideology critique.

A fundamental assumption of critical theory holds that every form of social order entails some forms of domination, and that critical emancipatory interests fuel the struggles to change these relations of domination and subordination. Such power relations engender forms of distorted communication that result in self-deception on the parts of agents with respect to their interests, needs, and perceptions of social and religious reality. The*logically speaking, they are structural sin. As a corrective to unquestioned relations of domination,

61. Raymond A. Morrow with David D. Baron, *Critical Theory and Methodology* (Thousand Oaks, CA: Sage Publications, 1994), 146.

the notion of ideology must be situated with a theory of language that emphasizes the ways in which meaning is infused with forms of power. . . . To study ideology is not to analyze a particular type of discourse but rather to explore . . . the modes whereby meaningful expressions serve to sustain relation of domination.[62]

John B. Thompson has pointed to three major modes or strategies that are involved in the way ideology operates: legitimization, dissimulation, and reification (literally, to make into a thing).[63] All three modes can be identified in the discourses of wo/men's silencing and censure. *Legitimization* is an appeal for legitimacy on traditional grounds, whereas dissimulation conceals relations of domination in ways that are themselves often structurally excluded from thought. Or as Jürgen Habermas puts it, ideology serves to "impede making the foundations of society [and, I would add, of religion] the object of thought and reflection."[64]

Reification, or *naturalization*, represents a transitory as well as a culturally, historically, and socially engendered state of affairs as if social structures were permanent, natural, outside of time, or directly revealed by G*d. This ideological strategy comes to the fore in, for instance, the questionable the*logical arguments for wo/men's special nature. Ideology moreover contributes to the distorted self-understanding of oppressed people who have internalized belief in the legitimacy of their own subordination and innate status as inferior. Religious texts and traditions that represent and mystify kyriocentric texts and kyriarchal structures of domination as revealed truth call for ideology critique.

Hence, in the past three decades, a new *fourth paradigm of interpretation*—which I have dubbed *the emancipatory-radical democratic paradigm*—has been evolving, one that inaugurates not just a hermeneutic-scientific but also an ethical-political-emancipatory turn. This paradigm has engendered contextual approaches such as African, Asian, indigenous, Euro-American, Latino/a, mujerista, womanist, cross-cultural biblical studies, as well as ideology-critical approaches, such as cultural studies, ideological criticism, and feminist, postcolonial, gender, and queer studies.[65] This paradigm of biblical interpretation is not new; it has a long history in political-religious struggles for emancipation and radical democracy.

62. Ibid., 130–49.
63. John B. Thompson, *Studies in the Theory of Ideology* (Cambridge: Polity Press, 1984), 254.
64. Jürgen Habermas, "Ideology," in *Modern Interpretations of Marx*, ed. Tom Bottomore (Oxford: Blackwell, 1981), 166.
65. Cf. Douglas A. Knight, ed., *Methods of Biblical Interpretation* (Nashville: Abingdon Press, 2004), 297–384.

This *fourth* paradigm is not so much interested in dogmatic proof, spiritual edification, scientific facts, or cultural sublimation. Rather, it investigates the ways in which scriptural texts and icons exercise influence and power in cultural, social, and religious life. Its commitment to change structures of domination and practices of dehumanization compels it to explore how biblical texts function in specific social locations and religious contexts. Working within this paradigm, one investigates how Scripture is used to inculcate mind-sets and attitudes of submission and dependency as "obedience" to the will of G*d, and examines the interpretive practices that condition people to accept and internalize violence and prejudice. One furthermore searches for visions of equality, freedom, and well-being for all of creation, which are historically unrealized possibilities inscribed in Scriptures.

Whatever its proper name will turn out to be, this fourth paradigm seeks to redefine the self-understanding of biblical interpretation in ethical, rhetorical, political, and radical democratic terms. It understands the biblical reader to be a "public," "transformative" subject who is able to communicate with a variegated public and seeks to achieve personal, social, and religious transformation for justice and well-being.

CONCLUSION

Studying the genealogy of biblical studies from the perspective of emancipatory movements and the public square helps one to realize that scriptural meaning-making has been practiced, for the most part, not only by elite Western-educated clergymen but also for the benefit of Western cultural and capitalist interests. A Western doctrinal or scientific approach declares its own culturally particular readings as universal divine revelation or scientific data that may not be questioned.

Scripture is understood either as an absolute and true oracle of the will of G*d that cannot be challenged but must be obeyed, or as a storehouse of antiquity, a cultural classic. Scripture may reveal timeless truth and universal principles and give definite answers to modern-day problems and questions, it may teach scientific data and historical facts, or it may elaborate hegemonic cultures. The form of biblical interpretation most closely associated with colonialism is manifested not only in otherworldly evangelicalism and literalist fundamentalism, which are oriented toward the salvation of the soul, but also in scientific malestream biblical scholarship.

Whenever we read/hear/interpret Scripture or any other text, we read/hear/interpret it by engaging one or more of these paradigms of interpretation. But whereas the three hegemonic malestream paradigms of interpretation do not enable a critical process of reading that indicts the dehumanizing power of scriptural texts, the critical-emancipatory-political paradigm seeks to do so by making explicit the critical hermeneutical lenses and goals with which it approaches the Scriptures. While the other three paradigms obfuscate the fact that they also have sociopolitical and cultural-religious interests and goals, the rhetorical-emancipatory paradigm openly confesses that it engages in biblical interpretation for the sake of conscientization and well-being.

This fourth paradigm stresses experience, social location, relations of power, and interested perspectives of interpreters, as well as the rhetoricality of text and interpretation and the institutional locations that determine all four paradigms of biblical studies. It seeks to research and lift into consciousness the legitimizing, dissimulating, and reifying or normalizing functions of ideology at work in biblical interpretation. It does not stand accountable to either the academy or the church, but seeks to analyze the power structures of both in relation to the wider public and political-societal structures.

Two of the four paradigms—the scientific positivist and the hermeneutical—are clearly located in the modern university and academic community. In contrast, the first *religious-the*logical-scriptural paradigm*, which is omitted by Segovia, has as its social location religious institutions and communities such as the Christian church or the Jewish synagogue, as well as the academy. The fourth, *intercultural/interreligious-emancipatory-radical democratic paradigm*, in turn, is at home in social movements for change or subaltern communities that are critical of and seek to transform relations of domination in society and in religions, including those that are inscribed in and sustained by Holy Scriptures.

Yet, when placed into the context of the two-domain discussion, the fourth paradigm is in danger of being either restricted to the academy or relegated to the religious community. In both cases, it loses its power to transform the kyriarchal discourses of society, religion, and academy. Conversely, when the first paradigm is restricted to the domain of religion and mistakenly labeled as doctrinal rather than as religious-the*logical paradigm, its academic-intellectual as well as its societal impact is overlooked. Finally, restricting the second and third paradigms to the academy robs them of their religious and societal power for change.

Rather than conceptualizing the four paradigms of biblical studies as competitive, I suggest that we envision them as "a republic of many voices." By republic, I mean "a group of people who are considered to be equals and who have a collective interest."[66] To liken biblical studies to a republic would mean to acknowledge the different voices in the four different paradigms of biblical studies as equals, whose collective interest is biblical criticism. Rather than construing them as canceling each other out in competition with each other, I suggest that we envision them as actively communicating with each other as equals, albeit each with a different accent. They can also be imagined as overlapping moving circles that deepen and correct each other. This requires that they abandon their positivist and exclusivist tendencies and claim a radical democratic common space of interpretation.

I do not, however, understand biblical criticism in the negative sense as simply disapproving of and criticizing the Bible for what is wrong or bad about it. Rather, I understand it in the sense of the Greek verb *krinein*, which means to assess, distinguish, evaluate, or judge the Bible, its language, origins, transmission, history, interpretations, worldviews, and theologies. To conceptualize biblical studies as a "republic of many equal voices" is to see it as a space for people to dialogue, debate, argue, and collaborate with each other, to seek not only to understand the diverse voices of biblical texts but also to explore, assess, and evaluate them in terms of their impact on contemporary publics and religious communities. This would mean, however, that practitioners must be able to critically reflect on the ideological elements and aspects of their preferred paradigm that prevents such collaboration.

In consequence, graduate education would need to provide opportunities for students both to become literate in all four paradigms of interpretation *and* to develop their capacities for critical-theoretical analysis and intersubjective communication. This would require a re-vision of the curriculum to encompass not only linguistic and methodological specializations but also the exploration of critical theories and the ethics of interpretation. It would entail not only to learn the different theoretical "dialects" of the field but also how to engage in fruitful communication and constructive argument.

However, the voices of the emerging fourth paradigm are still struggling to be acknowledged as equals, as those whose voices are no longer marginalized or passed over with silence. Consequently, it is vital

66. *Microsoft Encarta Dictionary*, s.v. "Republic."

to develop a pedagogy of communication and teaching that is able to harness the critical possibility, the power for change, and the transformation that are inscribed in all four paradigms of biblical studies. It is even more important that such a pedagogy enable practitioners of the fourth paradigm to collaborate with each other in staking out a shifting ever-expanding common ground of inquiry and dialogical approach.[67] Hence, in the next chapter we need to explore the theoretical frameworks and pedagogical structures that must be developed for the fourth paradigm to take its place as an equal in the "republic of many voices" in biblical studies.[68]

---

67. For such an attempt see now *They Were All Together in One Place? Toward Minority Biblical Criticism,* ed. by Randall C. Bailey, Tat-siong Benny Liew, Fernando F. Segovia (Atlanta: Society of Biblical Literature, 2009).

68. Although I am arguing here for the full citizenship of the fourth paradigm in the "republic of many voices," there was a general concern noted by the seminar that the fourth paradigm could be established as the paradigm that sets the rules for the republic. This anxiety seems to have been due to the fact that I, as the seminar instructor, had clearly identified myself as working from within the framework of the fourth paradigm, and hence this paradigm took center stage in our discussions. In consequence, the marginality of the fourth paradigm could not be experienced in the seminar.

3

Fashioning a Radical Democratic Discourse

In this chapter I want to focus on the fourth emancipatory-radical democratic paradigm after having discussed in the last chapter all four paradigms of biblical studies. In the preceding chapter I have argued that biblical studies has to be conceptualized in such a way that all four paradigms of biblical studies can be envisioned as overlapping spheres rather than constructed as in competition with and as displacing each other. Disciplinary equality, however, does not mean that all four paradigms should become the same. Rather, the discourses of the discipline need to interface with each other in order to intellectually and practically fructify each other. This understanding of paradigms as disciplinary sites accountable to different publics entails the need to create a radical democratic discursive space for graduate biblical education, where future scholars and ministers can learn the methodological "languages" and intellectual grammar of each paradigm while at the same time specializing in one of them.

To envision and create such a radical democratic space of biblical studies, it is necessary that each paradigm is recognized in its own right as well as that all of the paradigms seek to study the Bible in the interest of a radical democratic society of justice and well-being. Only in such a radical democratic discursive space can the marginal voices—previously excluded from the*logical, historical, and cultural academic biblical studies—achieve "full citizenship." Moreover, only in such a radical democratic discursive space can the work of the first three paradigms become ethically sophisticated and politically adequate to the public undertaking of biblical studies.

This chapter focuses on the fourth emerging emancipatory-radical democratic paradigm, which is still not recognized as an equal partner in many graduate studies programs. In order to construct biblical studies as a radical democratic space or "republic of many voices," the fourth paradigm, and its path-breaking work, needs to be recognized as a disciplinary equal. Here I am not making a liberal claim for the inclusion of the fourth paradigm on terms of the academy or the religious community. I am rather asserting the necessity for the fourth paradigm to be recognized as a significant area of the discipline that is essential to a biblical studies curriculum.

Creating an intellectual radical democratic space requires that biblical studies be refashioned in such a way that it constitutes a critical and reflexive public discourse. In the horizon of the fourth rhetorical-emancipatory paradigm, exegetical, historical, and hermeneutical inquiry of the other three paradigms needs to engage in critical readings and evaluations of biblical discourses in terms of a critical analytics of power and a public, radical democratic ethos. Questions such as "How has this text been used in the past, and how is it used today to defy or corroborate hegemonic political systems, laws, science, medicine, or public policy?" must become central to all four paradigms. How has biblical interpretation been used, and how is the Bible still used either to protect powerful interests or to engender sociocultural, political, and religious change? How is the Bible used to define public discourse and groups of people? What is the vision of society that is articulated in and through biblical texts? Is Scripture used to marginalize certain people and to legitimate racism and other languages of hate? If so, how is it so used? Is Scripture used to intervene in discourses of injustice? If so, how is it so used? Such questions must become as central to the discipline as exegetical-historical and literary-anthropological questions.

Committing biblical research to asking such questions, I suggest, would engender a transformation in the self-understanding of biblical studies. It would effectively change biblical studies into a rhetorical-ethical public discourse. Yet to be successful, one needs to carefully analyze what stands in the way of such a transformation. As I have pointed out repeatedly in my work, the scientist-positivist ethos, which is still virulent in religious and biblical studies, is the main obstacle to such a discursive shift from a scientistic-hermeneutical to a rhetorical-political model of biblical studies, or from a kyriarchal-Eurocentric to a radical-egalitarian-cosmopolitan model.

If one conceptualizes the overall task of paradigms in terms of the fourth paradigm in political rather than just in disciplinary terms, one can understand a paradigm as "a public intellectual sphere" where "citizen interpreters" come together to debate and discuss the Bible in terms of their own theoretical frameworks, approaches, and interests. Such public spheres—the academy, the church/synagogue, the school, and individual space—are overlapping and not exclusive of each other. To communicate with each other, the citizen interpreters need to be clear not only about their different theoretical languages but also about the different emphases and goals of the four paradigms of biblical studies. I contend that by articulating the four paradigms of biblical studies as different and overlapping practices in the public sphere, the dichotomizing tendencies that still haunt the discipline can be overcome.

In such a political imaginary, the fourth paradigm can be seen as creating a "radical democratic ideology critical, public space," from where to interact with and challenge the the*logical/religious, the historical, and the cultural academic paradigms. The emphasis of the fourth paradigm on ideology-critique and on the analysis of power enable it to facilitate border exchanges between the interfacing paradigms of biblical studies. To do so, however, it needs to create the conditions for equal citizenship in its own public sphere by articulating a theoretical platform capable of fostering critical and constructive exchanges and learnings between the different approaches that inhabit this diverse and ever-shifting paradigm. It needs to carefully pay attention to all the theoretical voices in its midst, avoid dualistic over-and-against constructions, and create a common ground for its work of producing emancipatory-radical democratic knowledges. In the following I will attempt to delineate the emerging contours of the fourth emancipatory-radical democratic paradigm from within which I speak and contribute a critical analytic and method of interpretation.

DELINEATING THE FOURTH EMANCIPATORY PARADIGM

Certain specific models and methods of interpretation seem to have emerged as constitutive of the fourth paradigm. As discussed in the

Postmodern Bible,[1] they are poststructuralist criticism, rhetorical criticism, psychoanalytic criticism, feminist and womanist criticism, and ideological criticism. Under ideological criticism are listed feminist, liberationist, Native American, African American, contemporary Jewish, and political hermeneutics as well as Marxist, materialist, and sociopolitical analysis. However, they are generally not recognized as disciplinary equals but only as fringe endeavors by malestream biblical studies. For instance, Manfred Oeming's *Contemporary Biblical Hermeneutics*,[2] a translation from the German, recognizes a plethora of methods at work today in biblical studies, but under "Methods Focused on Readers and Their Worlds" lists only Liberation The*logy and Feminist Exegesis. Oeming's Hermeneutical Square, which categorizes the many methodological approaches in biblical studies into four areas—reality behind the text, authors and their worlds, texts and their worlds, and readers and their worlds—has affinities with the four paradigms I have suggested. Yet I would rename his methodological umbrellas in rhetorical terms: texts and their symbolic-religious worlds, texts and their sociopolitical worlds, and interpreters and their political-religious worlds.[3]

The collection of essays *Methods of Biblical Interpretation*,[4] which appears under the name of Douglas A. Knight and is excerpted from *Dictionary of Biblical Interpretation*,[5] in turn has three rubrics that encompass the fourth paradigm: contextual approaches, liberation or ideological approaches, and gender-based approaches. Under contextual approaches are listed: Afro-centric, Asian, cross-cultural, Euro-American, Hispanic-American, mujerista, and womanist biblical interpretation as well as biblical interpretation and the Holocaust. Under liberation or ideological approaches one finds the following entries: cultural studies, ideological criticism, liberation theologies, and postcolonial biblical interpretations. The section on gender-based approaches has only two entries: gay/lesbian interpretation and feminist interpretation. In this conceptualization the nomenclature divides the constituents of the fourth paradigm into three different areas. Although major approaches are missing despite attempts to be comprehensive, this collection documents two things: on the one hand, it demonstrates that

1. Elizabeth A. Castelli et al., eds., *The Postmodern Bible* (New Haven, CT: Yale University Press, 1995).

2. Manfred Oeming, *Contemporary Biblical Hermeneutics: An Introduction* (Burlington: Ashgate, 2006).

3. I would not want to restrict interpretation to reading but rather to stress the subjects and agents of interpretation. I favor the category "interpreter" over "reader" because everyone is able to interpret but not everyone is able to read, since the majority of illiterate people in the world are wo/men.

4. Douglas A. Knight, *Methods of Biblical Interpretation* (Nashville: Abingdon Press, 2004).

5. John H. Hayes, *Dictionary of Biblical Interpretation* (Nashville: Abingdon Press, 1999).

the methodological approaches of the fourth paradigm are beginning to be recognized among the established methods of the discipline. On the other hand, it indicates the difficulty of becoming competent in a discipline characterized by a steady proliferation of methods and progressive articulations of increasing diversity.

Naming the Fourth Paradigm

Without doubt, the fourth paradigm has gained ground in the past twenty years or so, but insofar as its approaches are often listed under different disciplinary headings and rubrics, it seems not to have yet found its own intellectual profile and institutionalization. Scholars working in the horizon of the fourth paradigm meet under the governorship of traditional academic biblical studies organizations, such as the Society of Biblical Literature (SBL), the Catholic Biblical Association(CBA), or the Society for New Testament Studies (SNTS); and they still seek access to a discipline that has been articulated by their exclusion. The same is true for graduate education. Hence, the voices of the fourth paradigm remain situated in the margins of biblical studies insofar as their work is measured as to how much it adapts to the standards of the hegemonic the*logical, scientific, and cultural paradigms.

Students from different societal and religious kyriarchal locations have still to do "double or triple work." They still are admitted to biblical studies in many schools under the conditions of the scientific-positivist paradigm; they have to internalize the disciplinary languages of the dominant Euro-American malestream paradigms before they are allowed to use the theoretical approaches articulated in the fourth paradigm. Often they are still not able to articulate their own particular interpretive interests in the dissertation even if they have passed the hurdles of initiation into the historical and the*logical paradigms or the cultural-literary paradigms through comprehensive exams.

Since the fourth paradigm has not been able to develop its own organizational structures and common theoretical framework, it usually is not recognized as an equal partner in the conversation, even though it has greatly changed the discourses of the field in the past forty years or so. Moreover, little attention has been paid to how the multifarious different approaches can collaborate with each other rather than cancel each other out, or dominate one another by theoretical exclusion or submission. To show that the critical and constructive work that has been located in the space defined as margin/center can be articulated and continued "otherwise," I have argued that one has to shift focus from the discourse on margin/center to an understanding of biblical studies in terms of overlapping, shifting circles that interface with each other. Graduate biblical education needs to foster facility in the theoretical languages of all four paradigms, as well as the ability to articulate one's own theoretical approach within one of the paradigms. Hence, it is important that the fourth paradigm formulate its own theoretical approach and pedagogy.

However, the fourth paradigm seems to be characterized by innumerable social and religious locations, local struggles, and theoretical languages, each insisting on its difference from the others, as well as countless critical discourses that provide theoretical legitimizations to such a multitude of differences. Each group insists on its own theoretical voice, grievance, and identity; the paradigm is thus in danger of splintering like broken glass into a myriad of pieces. At the same time, there are tendencies of unification that operate either by excluding or by subsuming other voices and approaches. Hence, it is important to articulate a critical framework and vision that is flexible enough to enable communication between the different directions in the fourth paradigm without silencing, excluding, or subsuming any of them in a master-subordinate relationship. It is also important to do so if we do not want graduate biblical education to continue to co-opt the intellectual powers of students coming from very different social and religious locations. In my work, I have therefore attempted to do this by articulating one possible shared framework and analytic that seeks to engender a discussion of paradigm formation.

In *Rhetoric and Ethic*, I have named the fourth paradigm "rhetorical-emancipatory" in order to suggest a common orientation for the methodological and theoretical inquiry of the fourth paradigm. In my view, all the different theoretical approaches of the fourth paradigm share an understanding of language as rhetorical, and moreover they engage the rhetoric of inquiry in order to assess the ideological implications and impact of biblical texts and contemporary interpretations of the Bible. Because of the fourth paradigm's interest in the liberation and well-being of everyone, I have suggested that its rhetoric must be qualified as emancipatory in order to ensure that it does not end up in the endless play of postmodern differentiations. This qualification appreciates the roots of the fourth paradigm in social-religious struggles against domination, and harkens back to liberation the*logical discourses even as it speaks with a critical accent. It also does not need to pass over its critical feminist theoretical roots with silence and forgetfulness.

Both the terms "feminist" and "emancipation" are often critically problematized and rejected as remaining caught up in the discourse of modernity. Moreover, both terms are often used in a derogatory fashion—in Germany, for instance, feminists are often labeled pejoratively as *Emanzen*. However, these objections are determined not by the affiliation of feminism or emancipation with modernity, but rather by its political orientation. As a political term, feminism—like liberation studies—is considered to be ideological because of its advocacy stance and struggle for wo/men's full citizenship in society and religion.

However, it must not be overlooked that emancipatory and emancipation are political terms that recall the process of liberation from slavery, servitude, exploitation, and captivity. Emancipation inaugurates democratic citizenship. Hence, the term seems to be an appropriate term for naming those interpretive discourses of biblical studies that have as their goal the overcoming of the intersecting and multiplicative structures of domination and the achieving of well-being for everyone without exception.

Whatever its proper name will turn out to be, the different articulations of the fourth paradigm understand biblical scholarship as an ethical, rhetorical, political, cultural, and emancipatory discourse. They see the scholar in religion as a "public,"[6] "transformative,"[7] "connected," or "integrated" intellectual who is able to communicate with a variegated public, and who has as her goal personal, social, and religious transformation for justice and well-being.

Conceptualizing the Fourth Paradigm as a Forum of Many Voices

I have continued to argue that scholarship within the frame of the fourth paradigm needs to understand biblical texts as rhetorical discourses that are to be investigated in terms of their persuasive power and argumentative functions in particular historical and cultural situations and constellations of power. Such an argument rejects the

6. For reflections on scholarly engagement with public, political issues, see Cynthia Briggs Kittredge, Ellen Bradshaw Aitken, and Jonathan A. Draper, eds., *The Bible in the Public Square: Reading the Signs of the Times* (Minneapolis: Fortress Press, 2008).

7. For the expression "transformative intellectual," see "Teaching and the Role of the Transformative Intellectual," in *Education Still under Siege*, by Stanley Aronowitz and Henry A. Giroux, 2nd ed. (Westport, CT: Bergin & Garvey, 1993).

Enlightenment typecasting of rhetoric as stylistic ornament, technical skill, linguistic manipulation, or "mere words," and maintains not only "that rhetoric is epistemic but also that epistemology and ontology are themselves rhetorical."[8] At the heart of rhetoric are both the ethical and the political. As political and religious discursive practices, biblical texts and their contemporary interpretations involve authorial aims and strategies, as well as audience perceptions and constructions.

Since the sociohistorical location of rhetoric is the public of the *polis*, the fourth rhetorical-emancipatory paradigm situates biblical scholarship in such a way that its public character and political responsibility become an integral part of its contemporary readings and historical reconstructions. It insists on an ethical, radical democratic imperative that compels biblical scholarship to contribute to the vision of a society and a religion that are free from all forms of kyriarchal inequality and oppression. I suggest that such a theoretical model and epistemological framework enables the different voices within the fourth paradigm to move toward the articulation of a critical ethics and rhetoric of inquiry.

This fourth paradigm of biblical studies is in the process of being articulated today all around the world in different religious, intellectual, and cultural contexts. Insofar as they interact with postmodern critical theory and have problematized the Enlightenment's notion of the universal transcendental subject as the disembodied voice of reason, emancipatory feminist and postcolonial discourses have facilitated the emergence of this fourth paradigm. They have done so in order to insist that the excluded Others of elite propertied men must not only be included, but also acknowledged as equal, diverse partners.[9] These discourses have elaborated that the political-social and intellectual-ideological creation of the devalued "colonialized" Others goes hand in hand with the creation of the Man of Reason as the rational subject positioned outside of time and space.[10] He is the abstract knower and

---

8. Richard Harvey Brown, *Society as Text: Essays on Rhetoric, Reason, and Reality* (Chicago: University of Chicago Press, 1987), 85. See also, e.g., John S. Nelson, Allan Megill, and Donald McCloskey, eds., *The Rhetoric of the Human Sciences: Language and Argument in Scholarship and Public Affairs* (Madison: University of Wisconsin Press, 1987); Hayden White, *Topics of Discourse: Essays in Cultural Criticism* (Baltimore: Johns Hopkins University Press, 1978); John S. Nelson, "Political Theory as Political Rhetoric," in *What Should Political Theory Be Now?* ed. John S. Nelson (Albany: State University of New York Press, 1983), 169–240.

9. Brian K. Blount, *Cultural Interpretation: Reorienting New Testament Criticism* (Minneapolis: Fortress Press, 1995), 3, correctly argues that "if one wants to achieve a non-ideological method of biblical interpretation, the perspectives of the societal marginal must be included." Such an inclusion will result in a multicolored rainbow of biblical interpretation. However, insofar as he positions his new approach as "cultural" interpretation, which has as its explicit goal the production of a nonideological reading, he remains within the third paradigm of biblical interpretation.

10. See my article "The Politics of Otherness: Biblical Interpretation as a Critical Praxis for Liberation," in *The Future of Liberation Theology: In Honor of Gustavo Gutiérrez*, ed. Mark Ellis and Otto Maduro (Maryknoll, NY: Orbis Books, 1989), 311–25.

disembodied universal speaker of Enlightenment science and knowledge who has arrogated to himself a G*d's-eye view of the world.

In contrast to some forms of postmodern criticism, the voices from the margins of biblical studies insist that the colonialized others cannot afford to abandon the notion of the subject and the possibility of knowing the truth and of envisioning the world differently. Rather, they are adamant that the subordinated others must engage in a political and theoretical process of constituting their selves as subjects of knowledge and history.[11] Those previously excluded from the academy have to use what they know about the world and about wo/men's lives for critiquing the dominant culture of the academy and for constructing a heterogeneous public that allows for the recognition of particular voices and fosters appreciation of difference.

The Fourth Paradigm as a Critical Postmodern Discourse

Modern "scientific" studies have, in the name of "pure reason," promoted a mode of inquiry that denies its own rhetorical character and masks its own historicity in order to claim scientific, historical certainty and value-detached objectivity.[12] This modern posture of value-neutral inquiry in the interest of pure reason, as well as its claims to universality, has been thoroughly challenged by diverse postmodern discourses, such as philosophical hermeneutics, the sociology of knowledge, ideology critique, and critical theory.[13] As David Lyon has observed,

> Modernity as a deeply European event is all about the massive changes that took place at many levels from the mid-sixteenth century onwards. . . . Modernity questions all conventional ways of doing things, substituting authorities of its own based in science, economic growth, democracy, or law. And it unsettles the self; if identity is given in traditional society, in modernity it is constructed. Modernity started out to conquer the world in the name of Reason; certainty and social order would be founded on new bases. . . .

11. See, e.g., Elisabeth Schüssler Fiorenza and Shawn Copeland, *Feminist Theologies in Different Contexts* (Maryknoll, NY: Orbis Books, 1996); Elisabeth Schüssler Fiorenza, *The Power of Naming: A Concilium Reader in Feminist Christian Theology* (Maryknoll, NY: Orbis Books, 1996); and Ursula King, ed., *Feminist Theology from the Third World: A Reader* (Maryknoll, NY: Orbis Books, 1994).

12. David Tracy, *Plurality and Ambiguity: Hermeneutics, Religion, and Hope* (New York: Harper & Row, 1987), 31.

13. See also Jürgen Habermas, *Moral Consciousness and Communicative Action* (Cambridge, MA: MIT Press, 1995), 4: "Modernity is characterized by the rejection of substantive rationality typical of the religious and metaphysical world-views and by a belief in a procedural rationality and its ability to give credence to our views in the three areas of objective knowledge, moral-practical insight, and aesthetic judgment."

The achievement of modernity is astonishing. In the space of a few decades a transformation began in Europe that would alter the world in unprecedented and irreversible ways.[14]

The ideal of the European-American Enlightenment was critically accomplished knowledge in the interest of human freedom, equality, and justice, and under the guidance of pure and abstract reason. Its principle of unqualified critical inquiry and assessment did not exempt any given reality, authority, tradition, or institution. Knowledge is not a given, but a culturally and historically embodied language that is therefore always open to probing analysis and relentless criticism.

This scientific principle of the Enlightenment was institutionalized in the modern university as the empiricist paradigm of knowledge, which gives primary importance to evidence, data, and empirical inquiry—to the "logic of facts." This modern logic relies on abstraction for the sake of rigor, evidence, and precision. At the same time, this scientific principle has also engendered three major correctives that underscore the complexity, particularity, and corruption of reality. The *aesthetic* corrective stresses experiential concreteness and intuitive imagination over rationalist abstraction; the *cultural* corrective insists, over and against the universalizing tendencies of the Enlightenment, on cultural autonomy and on tradition as wisdom and heritage of a particular community; and the *political* corrective asserts that there is no pure reason as an instrument of knowledge that could lead to a just society. In the beginning was not pure reason, but power. The institutions of so-called pure reason—the sciences, scholarship, and the university—all hide from themselves their own complicity in societal agendas of power.[15]

These three correctives seek to move scholarly discourses beyond Western modernity without relinquishing its emancipative achievements. Most importantly, by critically demonstrating that the standard for the Enlightenment's claims about selfhood, reason, and universality was elite Western man, feminist postmodern thinkers have shown that the rights and knowledge of the modern elite male subject were underwritten by the negation of such rights to his devalued others, such as wives, children, slaves, aliens, natives, and other disenfranchised wo/men. The accomplishments of the Enlightenment and its transformation of European society were achieved in the interest of the "Man of Reason" (Genevieve

14. David Lyon, *Postmodernity* (Minneapolis: University of Minnesota Press, 1994), 21.
15. For documentation, see my essay "Commitment and Critical Inquiry," *Harvard Theological Review* 82 (1989): 1–11.

Lloyd) and at the cost of his devalued Others. It is at this crossing point that critical feminist, emancipative, and postcolonial discourses meet in their critique of modernity, an era whose achievements have been bought at the price of racism, misogyny, and colonialism.

Although critical feminist scholarship has trail-blazed the rhetorical, ethicopolitical paradigm of biblical and religious studies, the pioneering contributions of feminist theory and the*logy are seldom recognized in the malestream discourses that deliberate the status of the discipline. Hence, my theoretical proposals not only continue to encounter resistance in the hegemonic centers of biblical and religion studies, but also tend to receive only a token acknowledgment or none at all in the malestream discourses of the margins.[16] Its constructive proposals are not seriously discussed because of the identity politics and discursive struggles within the fourth paradigm.

DISCURSIVE STRUGGLES WITHIN THE FOURTH PARADIGM: FROM MARGIN TO POSTCOLONIALISM

Margins, Postcolonialism, and Liberation Hermeneutics

R. S. Sugirtharajah has been very influential in articulating the theoretical frame "center-margins" of the fourth paradigm. In the introduction to the third edition of his landmark work *Voices from the Margins*, Sugirtharajah asserts five substantial changes that have taken place in the fifteen years since the first appearance of this book. He does so with the intent to move from margin-discourse to postcolonial discourse:

1. While in the first and second editions the margins still could be imagined as an ideal forum of dispute and site of protest and change, today the margins have been hijacked and taken over by reactionary forces.

2. Whereas approximately fifteen years ago the Bible could be envisioned as an emancipatory tool for the people, today it has become a lethal weapon in the hands of extreme fundamentalists.

3. In the past two decades we have seen not only an increasing fragmentation of the discipline of biblical studies but also the fragmentation and co-optation of identity-driven hermeneutics.

---

16. I think here, for instance, of the rewriting of the discipline by Blount, Segovia, Wimbush, or Sugirtharajah, whose work I greatly admire in spite of the fact that they give only token recognition to the breakthrough brought about by critical feminist theory applied to biblical studies.

4. Whereas most articles in the first editions were written as counter-discourses in the idiom of liberation the*logy, this new edition recognizes the demise of liberation the*logy and its replacement by postcolonial studies. Postcolonial studies are first of all critical of the Bible rather than seeing it as an instrument of liberation. Such a critical stance is necessary, since in the current conservative political climate "liberation" is equated with terror or the American occupation of Iraq.

5. Finally, Sugirtharajah argues that today the voices of diasporic intellectuals are central, whereas the 1980s were the times of the subaltern voices. The emergence of "diasporic" hermeneutics, however, raises for him the question of whether one can articulate a geographically shaped hermeneutics far removed from its original territorial or national location. It is unclear who the new "authentic voices" are and where the margins are to be located.[17]

In short, it seems that the location "on the margins" has become difficult to sustain, not because the Euro-American center of biblical studies has further marginalized these approaches, but because the margins in themselves can no longer be conceptualized and articulated as a critical space of protest and liberation. Although Sugirtharajah seems not to take note of my paradigm discussion in *Rhetoric and Ethic*, he would probably argue in a similar fashion against the epithet "emancipatory."

According to Sugirtharajah,[18] liberation the*logy had its roots in the Christian church and its social location in the third world. It catered not to the expert reader, but to the "ordinary" reader. However, liberation hermeneutics has been co-opted by the mainstream and, in the end, has become triumphalistic. Its exclusivist Christian tone is jarring in the multireligious and polycultural contexts of today. He reads the majority of the contributions to the first edition of *Voices* as examples of such liberation hermeneutics, which "privileged the Bible as a sound and secure book for the faithful."

Sugirtharajah observes that whereas the "aim of the liberation hermeneutic was to interpret and make the text secure for the faithful," postcolonialism, which he proposes has replaced liberation hermeneutics, "perceives its task as critiquing, problematizing and exposing contradictions and inadequacies in both the text and its interpretations."[19]

17. R. S. Sugirtharajah, ed., *Voices from the Margins: Interpreting the Bible in the Third World*, rev. and expanded, 3rd ed. (Maryknoll, NY: Orbis Books, 2006), 3–6.
18. Ibid., 4–6.
19. Ibid., 5.

Further, while liberation the*logy celebrated a monotheistic G*d who is on the side of the poor and oppressed, postcolonial scholarship, which for the most part is no longer the*logical, scrutinizes the colonizing tendencies of such a G*d in order to understand the many-layered polytheistic context out of which early Christianity also emerged. While a liberation hermeneutic was rooted in popular movements for change and adopted a sociopolitical analytic, postcolonial criticism and "diaspora" studies seem firmly rooted in the academy and located in the first world. Postcolonial studies with their call for a critical, interdisciplinary, expert reader are the product of postmodernity.

At first glance, it seems that with postcolonial studies the "voices from the margin" have arrived in the Euro-American intellectual center, speaking perfectly its postmodern theoretical academic languages, whereas those who stayed "at home" in Africa, India, or Latin America remain at the margins, continuing the sociopolitical-economic analysis of their situation inherited from liberation theologies. Their key issues might be HIV/AIDS, base communities, gay marriage, capitalism, development, environment, free trade, or the World Trade Organization. Hence, the margins can no longer be maintained in and through identity politics since such a politics has become co-opted by those in power and has fragmented the voices of the margin into exclusivist arguments and claims.

As a result, a dualistic framing of the margins emerges in the introduction to the third edition of *Voices from the Margins*. On the one side, we find liberation hermeneutics, church, third-world, and "ordinary readers" lined up, while on the other side stand postcolonialism, the academy, and diasporic expert readers located in the first world. I suggest that such a construction of emancipatory interpretation in terms of binary oppositions could have been avoided if a critical feminist hermeneutics of liberation had not been excluded from the presentation of the "voices from the margin." Instead, Sugirtharajah advocates the replacement of liberation hermeneutic with postcolonial and diasporic discourse.

It is striking that a critical feminist hermeneutic does not appear in its own right either in the introduction or in the content of the new edition of *Voices from the Margins*. The "margin" is conceptualized as singular and unitary, as the third world. Hence, in contrast to postcolonial hermeneutics, critical feminist liberationist readings cannot constitute their own intellectual domain and section in the book, but are subsumed under other section headings such as "subaltern, postcolonial, or popular readings."

Just as in malestream theory, so also in *Voices from the Margin*, feminist interpretation has been subsumed under other reading strategies that have been developed without a critical analysis of gender and its intersections with race, class, and imperialism. I assume that this is the case because the margin is constituted in liberation the*logical terms geographically as third world in opposition to the Euro-American center, which is understood as first world. Since, however, a critical feminist hermeneutics of liberation has been articulated not only in the third but also in the first world, it cannot find its place on the margin if the margin is conceptualized as unitary. In contrast, a postcolonial hermeneutic is awarded its own section on the basis of its roots in the third world, although its representatives in biblical studies have their home, for the most part, in the academy of the first world.

Biblical Interpretation and Intercultural Criticism

Fernando Segovia also has carefully discussed the contributions of liberation the*logy to the emerging fourth paradigm of biblical studies.[20] He recognizes that there are multiple strands of liberation hermeneutics and sees them as part of a new paradigm in biblical studies, which in his earlier work he called cultural or ideological criticism. In his view, ideological criticism centers on the "flesh-and-blood reader," immersed in history and culture. It emerged, according to Segovia, in the 1980s and 1990s in biblical studies.

Segovia's analysis focuses on the strand of liberationist interpretation that concerns itself with questions of social class and has been articulated especially in Latin America. He carefully discusses and evaluates socioeconomic criticism, its theoretical grounding, its principles of analytic practice, and the historical Jesus as its the*logical foundation. Underscoring liberation the*logy's importance for the development of cultural and ideological criticism in biblical studies, Segovia concludes his review:

> No critical movement has been, in my opinion, as uniformly forthcoming regarding its context and perspective as socioeconomic criticism. From the outset it pointed to material poverty as both

---

20. Fernando F. Segovia, "Liberation Hermeneutics: Visiting the Foundation in Latin America," in *Toward a New Heaven and a New Earth: Essays in Honor of Elisabeth Schüssler Fiorenza*, ed. Fernando F. Segovia (Maryknoll, NY: Orbis Books, 2003), 106–32.

its external driving force and its internal reading optic and did so while emphasizing the need of the critic to share in some way the life of the poor. . . . In so doing, not only did it pursue the thematic of poverty in the Bible in a sustained and systematic way, it also proceeded to reread and reinterpret the whole of the Bible in light of this thematic.[21]

Yet Segovia also critically points out that this monolithic optic overlooked the complexity and diversity of the Bible so that Christian Scriptures could emerge as a manifesto of liberation. In addition, this monolithic optic also ignored other oppressions and marginalizations such as those based on gender, race, or culture. Moreover, while quite radical in socioeconomic terms, this optic was quite conservative in the*logical matters. However, Segovia does not discuss a critical feminist hermeneutics of liberation as an important third conversation partner for the trenchant critique of "much of U.S. academic postcolonialism."

Although Segovia stresses "the key role [that] socioeconomic criticism played in the history of the discipline,"[22] he, like Sugirtharajah, seems to think nevertheless that liberation hermeneutics must be replaced by postcolonial studies because the former is not sufficiently critical of the Bible—a statement that could not be made if a critical feminist hermeneutics of liberation and the feminist hermeneutical debates in the 1980s were taken into account. Thus, Segovia also constructs the following dualistic alternative: either the Bible is liberationist, or it is colonialist—a dichotomy that a critical feminist liberation hermeneutic has worked hard to overcome.

This either-or stance does not take the cautionary judgment of Gayatri Spivak regarding "much of U.S. academic postcolonialism" into account when it not only relinquishes socioeconomic criticism as an important hermeneutical area of biblical interpretation, but also overlooks the theoretical work of a critical feminist hermeneutics of liberation and its importance for articulating the fourth paradigm of biblical studies. Such a critical feminist hermeneutics of liberation is not primarily rooted in Latin American liberation the*logy, but rather in the wo/men's liberation movements that emerged in the 1970s not only in the United States, but also around the world. In the context of these variegated movements, first-world feminist liberation hermeneutics emphasized the critical and deconstructive task of interpreting the Bible by stressing

21. Ibid., 127.
22. Ibid., 129.

the ideological role of the Bible in wo/men's subordination, exclusion, and exploitation. The voices from oppressed second- and third-world communities, on the other hand, emphasized the Bible's and religion's sustaining power in the struggles for liberation. Both articulations have insisted on wo/men as subjects of biblical interpretation.

I argue that the emancipatory voices in biblical interpretation must continue to insist that the subjugated and marginalized others cannot afford to abandon either the notion of being historical subjects and agents or the possibility of knowing the world and the divine differently. Rather, the critical voices in religious communities and the academy must continue to maintain that those who are the marginalized, the "subordinated and silenced others," must engage in a political and theoretical process of constituting ourselves as subjects of knowledge, history, and interpretation.

In short, from the vantage point of a critical feminist liberation hermeneutics and rhetoric, the change from an allegedly parochial Christian liberation hermeneutic to a sophisticated academic postcolonial theory can be seen as the reinscription in biblical studies of the modern-postmodern antagonism between church and academy, between the*logical and religious biblical studies, between sociopolitical and literary-conceptual analytics. These dichotomies have relegated biblical interpretation to the positivist sophistry of the ivory tower or the parochial piety of the church, and thereby prepared the way for the deadly fundamentalisms that plague public biblical discourses today. If the optic and self-understanding of postcolonial criticism is shaped by the Western academy, then one must ask both whether and how it is able theoretically to reflect on the role of the Bible in the liberation struggles of wo/men, who are at the bottom of the kyriarchal pyramid of domination in a world of global capitalism.

Postcolonial and Sociopolitical Biblical Criticism

The move to replace a socioeconomic liberation hermeneutics with postcolonial criticism does not critically reflect on the negative impact that the displacement of such a hermeneutics by academic postcolonial studies would have on the present sociopolitical context of biblical studies. In order to take the economic-political contemporary context of neoliberal globalization into account, postcolonial criticism is in need of not only the insights of the socioeconomic liberation hermeneutic, but also the hermeneutics of suspicion put forward by critical feminist biblical studies. I suggest that it is only through this recognition that postcolonial criticism can provide comprehensive analytic approaches capable of both identifying the kind of power inscribed in Scripture, as well as analyzing the Bible's power of persuasion in the context of the global capitalism that conditions all biblical readings today.

Marxist theory possesses tools for such analysis of the Bible in a capitalistic context, but Roland Boer has pointed out that both post-colonial theory and postcolonial biblical criticism seek to steer clear of the Marxist tradition. He argues that "postcolonial theory seems to have forgotten two crucial dimensions of the possibility of its existence: history and Marxism,"[23] and he goes on to write that

> the forgetting of Marx is necessary for the constitution of postcolo-nial criticism: in light of the enabling role of Marxism in postcolo-nial theory, that theory can only exist by excluding that which keeps it functioning. What is outside the system provides the glue that keeps the system running.[24]

In agreement with Boer, David Jobling elaborates that, by eclips-ing the Marxist tradition, postcolonial biblical criticism "narrows the options of people in struggle." In his view postcolonial biblical criti-cism faces several problems:

> Given how much of its base resides in Western universities, it risks not only losing some of its closeness to local struggles, but also becoming another intellectual fad within the Western globalizing machine. An opposite danger is that it makes itself into a kind of counter-globalization, by conceiving the world in terms of only a single struggle between "developed" and "undeveloped" regions.[25]

Rather than abandon liberation the*logy with its stress on the Marxist tradition, postcolonial biblical criticism needs to rediscover its Marxist roots if it wants to account for the ongoing struggles not only of resis-tance but also of liberation.

Because of its alliance with postmodernism and its primary aca-demic location in literature and philosophy departments, the tendency

---

23. Roland Boer, "Marx, Postcolonialism, and the Bible," in *Postcolonial Biblical Criticism: Interdisciplinary Inter-sections*, ed. Stephen D. Moore and Fernando F. Segovia (New York: T&T Clark International, 2005), 166–83, here 166.

24. Ibid., 170.

25. David Jobling, "'Very Limited Ideological Options': Marxism and Biblical Studies in Postcolonial Scenes," in Moore and Segovia, *Postcolonial Biblical Criticism*, 184–201, here 191.

of postcolonial criticism has been to privilege the act of reading over sociopolitical analysis. As a consequence, postcolonial criticism has not sufficiently focused on global structures of exploitation and domination. In response to Ella Shohat's question "When exactly does the postcolonial begin?"[26] Arif Dirlik at first answers facetiously: "When Third World intellectuals have arrived in First World academy." He then concludes more seriously:

> It begins with the emergence of global capitalism, not in the sense of an exact incidence in time but in the sense that the one is a condition of the other. . . . What is remarkable, therefore, is not my conclusion here, but that a consideration of the relationship between postcolonialism and global capitalism should be absent from the writings of postcolonial intellectuals: this is all the more remarkable because this relationship is arguably less abstract and more direct than any relationship between global capitalism and postmodernism, since it pertains not just to cultural/epistemological but to social and political formations.[27]

Economic globalization[28] has been created with the specific goal of giving primacy to corporate profits and values and installing and codifying such market values globally. Globalization has been designed to amalgamate and merge all economic activities around the world within a global monoculture. In many respects, wo/men are suffering not only from the globalization of market capitalism but also from the sexual exploitation instigated by it.

In the time of capitalist neoliberal globalization, the line between the haves and the have-nots increasingly spans the entire globe, with the West (i.e., Europe and the United States) becoming more and more part of this global "equalization of the oppressed." Neoliberal globalization is evoking a future where a handful of the world's most well-to-do families may pocket more than 50 percent of the world's $90 trillion in assets and securities (stocks, bonds, etc). Moreover, relentlessly rising global temperatures are bound to create catastrophic conditions worldwide, and the poor of the world will be the hardest hit. The predict-

---

26. Ella Shohat, "Notes on the Postcolonial," *Social Text* 31/32 (1992): 103.
27. Arif Dirlik, "The Postcolonial Aura: Third World Criticism in the Age of Global Capitalism," in *Dangerous Liaisons: Gender, Nation, and Postcolonial Perspectives*, ed. Anne McClintock, Aamir Mufti, and Ella Shohat (Minneapolis: University of Minnesota Press, 1997), 501–28, here 519–20.
28. See Jan Nederveen Pieterse, ed., *Christianity and Hegemony* (Oxford: Berg Publishers, 1992), 11–31; see also Paul E. Sigmund, "Christian Democracy, Liberation Theology: The Catholic Right and Democracy in Latin America," in *Christianity and Democracy in Global Context*, ed. John Witte Jr. (Boulder, CO: Westview Press, 1993), 187–207.

able results of the neoliberal economic model, which was made in the United States, are socially unjust, politically destabilizing, culturally destructive, and ecologically unsustainable. It is this global interconnectedness of exploitations that challenges postcolonial intellectuals, in Gayatri Chakravorty Spivak's words, to "learn to be responsible as we must study to be political."[29] Hence, she is highly critical of "much of U.S. academic postcolonialism," which is, according to her, "as much a strategy of differentiating oneself from the racial underclass as it is to speak in its name."[30]

However, Boer charges that Chakravorty Spivak herself, together with Edward Said and Homi Bhabha, have contributed to this situation by occluding the Marxist prehistory of postcolonial theory. Chakravorty Spivak did so, he charges, by introducing Derridean deconstruction as a useful tool for reading for the other voices. Said did so by disempowering Gramsci's notion of hegemony, leaving out categories crucial to hegemony such as class, class conflict, and political economics; instead, following Bhabha, "mimicry, hybridity, and border crossing became the key to reinterpreting the texts of colonial encounters."[31] Rather than dismissing these critics, however, Boer refers to the different reading strategy of Ernst Bloch, who reads the Bible not only as "riven with class conflicts," but also looks for "traces of subversion and rebellion in class and economic terms." What is needed is therefore a sophisticated interpretation, "one that reads back and forth between the ideological, social, and economic contradictions"[32] inscribed in the text.

In a very learned and carefully researched article, Fernando Segovia has sought to map "the postcolonial optic" in biblical studies in and through a judicious, critical analysis of the field of postcolonial studies on the whole, and has argued that the postcolonial optic foregrounds the political. He seeks for the confluence of postcolonial and biblical discourses

> similar to those already at work between biblical studies and such other fields as Feminist Studies, Third World Studies, Minority Studies, Gay, and Lesbian Studies. In effect, just as feminist criticism foregrounds the question of gender, liberation criticism that of class, minority criticism that of ethnicity and race, and queer

---

29. Gayatri Chakravorty Spivak, *A Critique of Postcolonial Reason* (Cambridge, MA: Harvard University Press, 1999), 378.

30. Ibid., 358.

31. Boer, "Marx, Postcolonialism, and the Bible," 170.

32. Ibid., 178–89.

criticism that of sexual orientation, so, I would argue, does postcolonial criticism highlight the question of geo-politics—the realm of
the political at the translocal or global level with specific reference to
the phenomenon of imperial-colonial formations.[33]

He immediately realizes that such a characterization does not do
justice to the actual work done by these diverse optics in biblical criticism, because feminist theory is concerned with more than "gender,"
and the same applies mutatis mutandis to liberation, minority, queer,
and postcolonial criticism.[34] Nevertheless, Segovia believes it is useful
for "charting the terrain within ideological discourse and criticism." He
is only concerned, however, with the confluence of postcolonial theory
and postcolonial biblical criticism and hence he does not explore the
confluence of postcolonial biblical criticism with the other political
criticisms at work in biblical studies.

In his conclusion, Segovia emphasizes that the political, postcolonial study of early Christianity should foreground and emphasize the
unequal relation of inequality and the unequal relation of domination
and subordination at work in the imperial-colonial. It "should affect
and should be affected by other studies with a similar focus on unequal
relations—Feminist, Liberation, Minority, Gay and Lesbian Studies.
A tall order, indeed, but of the essence."[35] I could not agree more. But
the question still remains how such a "mutual affection" can be conceptualized. If it is of the essence, it needs to be carefully spelled out
and explored.

The Feminist Postcolonial Challenge

In Laura Donaldson's discussion of the feminist contribution to the
volume on *Postcolonial Biblical Criticism*, she indicates that such interaction is envisioned as a contribution:

> Such haunting surfaces instead consideration of disability, gender
> and indigeneity—all of which serve to disrupt and reconfigure post-
> colonial criticism. That, in turn, emerges as the distinctive contri-
> bution of feminism to postcolonialism: a reading that is at once

---

33. Fernando F. Segovia, "Mapping the Postcolonial Optic in Biblical Criticism: Meaning and Scope," in Moore
and Segovia, *Postcolonial Biblical Criticism*, 23–78, here 23.
34. Ibid., 23 n. 1.
35. Ibid., 75–78.

oppositional and multidimensional, allowing for the rescue of all the silenced voices everywhere and thus in keeping with the vision of planetarity advanced by Spivak.[36]

Here the relation is construed in gendered terms. In line with the cultural "feminine," the work of feminism is seen as a "contribution" to postcolonialism, which is itself construed as the cultural "masculine" represented by Spivak, its feminine figure of legitimization. It is not clear, however, how the postcolonial optic needs to change if it should seriously consider and learn from an intersectional feminist analysis.

A similar problem emerges from Tat-siong Benny Liew's excellent argument that race/ethnicity and postcolonialism "are conceptually connected with, or maybe even embedded in each other," but "that there are also productive differences between the two."[37] So far so good! But then he goes on to discuss the "contributions" that race/ethnicity theories can make to postcolonialism. He mentions that many Christian Testament scholars who are committed to racial/ethnic justice are suspicious of "postmodernism's or postcolonialism's tendency to (over)emphasize textuality, hybridity, and multiplicity," and that they see it as "a fragmentation of [politics], or even a flight from politics."[38] He points out that this anxiety is shared only by certain postcolonial critics, but presumably not by all. Yet, rather than the need to explore these concerns of some scholars, Liew emphasizes the necessity "to converge (not collapse) the interpretive optics of race/ethnicity and postcolonialism." In the next sentence he refers to Sugirtharajah, "who has given a couple of very instructive examples of how the tunnel vision on race/ethnicity ends up (dis)missing certain colonial dynamics in one's reading of the New Testament."[39] It seems that "convergence" of voices means either "contribution to" or "correction by" postcolonialism, but it does not intend a radical challenge to the essentializing postcolonial analytic framework.

Such a challenge to the postcolonial analytic framework needs to focus on the subjects or agents who are articulating the postcolonial optic, their struggles for justice, and their goals for doing so. The subjects of racial/ethnic analysis are scholars committed to racial/ethnic justice; the subjects of critical feminist analysis are scholars committed to justice for wo/men on all levels of the kyriarchal pyramid; the subjects

---

36. Ibid., 14.
37. Tat-siong Benny Liew, "Margins and (Cutting) Edges: On the (Il)Legitimacy and Intersections of Race, Ethnicity, and (Post)Colonialism," in Moore and Segovia, *Postcolonial Biblical Criticism*, 114–65, here 125.
38. Ibid., 129.
39. Ibid., 129 n. 21.

of Marxist analysis are scholars engaged in the struggle for justice of those exploited by global capitalism; the subjects of Queer Studies are scholars dedicated to justice for lesbians, gays, and transgendered people. Yet postcolonial scholars are understood "to *read* the politics and policies as well as the material factors that are always already embedded in our institutions and societies."[40] Is the task of postcolonial biblical scholarship only to "read" the power politics and material conditions embedded in our societies and religions? Or is it also to engage in the struggles for justice for colonized people, and hence for changing societies and religions? If the latter is the case, then postcolonialism needs to be fashioning its voice in such a way that it is able to collaborate with the other critical voices within the fourth paradigm rather than trying to establish its own voice as a hegemonic one.

For genuine collaboration to happen between the different theoretical approaches in the fourth paradigm, critical scholarship has to be reconceptualized as a part of activism, a part of the struggle for justice and the survival of wo/men living on the bottom of the kyriarchal pyramid of global capitalism. For them to come into view, we need to develop a common critical political optic that can factor in all the critical approaches of the fourth paradigm without subsuming or excluding one.

With Jobling, we need to ask, "How do we bring together sites of struggle which are not only invisible to each other but which might not even be recognized by each other as sites of struggle?"[41] For scholars working within the fourth paradigm, it is therefore important to adopt a shared complex analysis in order to be able not only to talk, reason, and argue with each other, but also to analyze texts in terms of their inscribed power structures and functions within such structures of domination.

TOWARD A SHARED ANALYTIC: INTERSECTIONAL ANALYSIS OF KYRIARCHY

In my view, we need such a shared analytic to critically trace the intersectional social and discursive structures of domination and subordination inscribed in biblical texts and still at work today. For that reason, I have proposed the analytic concept of kyriarchy to theorize the intersecting dominations and subordinations engendered by race, class, gender, het-

40. Ibid., 151–53.
41. Ibid., 197.

erosexuality, age, ableism, or imperialism-colonialism—an analytic that has as of yet found little recognition or serious discussion by biblical scholars.[42] In my view, only a complex intersectional analytic would disrupt the positivist ethos of modern scientism and religious fundamentalism as well as the postmodern ethos of multiplicity, hybridity, instability, and endless play of meaning in the interest of subversion, resistance, struggle, change, and transformation. Such a critical analytic of domination was developed especially in the 1990s by black feminist theorists, whose work has been situated at the intersections of race and gender.

If and whenever mainline liberal, radical, or socialist-Marxist scholars have paid attention to the objections of Two-Thirds-World feminists, they have tended to adopt an "adding on" approach of listing oppressions. This add-and-stir procedure ignores the fact that structures of oppression crisscross and feed upon each other in wo/men's lives. Such an adding-on method conceptualizes the oppression of wo/men not as an interlocking, multiplicative, and overarching system of domination, but as parallel discrete structures of domination. To list parallel oppressions, or to speak of "dual-system oppression" (patriarchy and capitalism, or patriarchy and colonialism), obscures the multiplicative pyramidal interstructuring of the relations of domination that position wo/men of different social status differently.

Indeed, such an adding-up feminist approach disregards the historical interstructuring of race, class, gender, age, and nation as forms of stratification that develop together out of the same set of dominations and that therefore need to be changed simultaneously. Structures of wo/men's oppression are not just multiple but also multiplicative: racism is multiplied by sexism, multiplied by ageism, multiplied by classism, multiplied by colonial exploitation. Hence, feminist theory and practice needs to be (re)conceptualized as practices of struggle against intersecting oppressions; it must make wo/men's *differing* experiences of multiplicative oppressions central to all feminist discourses.

Intersectional Analysis

The term "intersectionality" was coined by the legal scholar Kimberly Crenshaw and entails the notion that subjectivity is constituted by the

---

42. See David Jobling, "'Very Limited Ideological Options,'" 196 n. 22, who refers only to another feminist, Sharon Ringe, "Places at the Table: Feminist and Postcolonial Interpretation," in *The Postcolonial Bible*, ed. R. S. Sugirtharajah (Sheffield: Academic Press, 1998), 136–51.

mutually multiplicative vectors of race, gender, class, sexuality, and imperialism. It has emerged as a key theoretical tool in critical feminist and race studies' efforts to subvert race/gender and other binaries of domination. It also seeks to respond to criticisms that it elides intra-group differences while at the same time recognizing the necessity of group politics. Jennifer Nash in turn observes that "intersectionality invites scholars to come to terms with the legacy of the exclusions of multiply marginalized subjects from feminist and anti-racist work" and "to draw on the ostensibly unique epistemological position of marginalized subjects to fashion a vision of equality."[43] Bonnie Thornton Dill studied this emerging method of social analysis in 2001 and defined it as "in the process of being created."[44] Dill argues that intersectional scholarship is grounded in the experience of those whose identity is constructed at the intersections of race, gender, and ethnicity. The goal of this work "at the intersections" is to contribute to a more just world.

The theory of intersectionality has been articulated as a threefold theory, as a theory of marginalized subjectivity, as a theory of identity, and as a theory of the matrix of oppressions. In the first version, intersectional theory refers only to multiply marginalized subjects; in the second version, theory seeks to illuminate how identity is constructed at the intersections of race, gender, class, sexuality, and imperialism; the third version stresses intersectional theory as a theory of structures and sites of oppression. Race, sex, gender, class, imperialism are seen as vectors of dominating power that create coconstitutive social processes that engender the differential simultaneity of dominations and subordinations.

Leslie McCall in turn describes three methodological approaches to intersectionality, which she defines primarily "in terms of . . . how they understand and use categories to explore the complexity of intersectionality in social life."[45] She calls the first approach "anti-categorical complexity," which uses a methodology that deconstructs the analytical categories of race, gender, class, sexuality, and imperialism. McCall terms the second approach "intra-categorical complexity" because scholars working in this mode focus on "people whose identity crosses the boundaries of traditionally constructed groups."[46] Finally, the third

---

43. Jennifer C. Nash, "Rethinking Intersectionality," *Feminist Review* 89, no. 1 (2008): 1–15, here 3.

44. Bonnie Thornton Dill, "Work at the Intersections of Race, Gender, Ethnicity, and Other Dimensions of Difference in Higher Education," *Connections: Newsletter of the Consortium on Race, Gender, and Ethnicity of the University of Maryland*, Fall 2002, 5–7, http://www.crge.umd.edu/publications/news.pdf (accessed on April 8, 2008).

45. Leslie McCall, "The Complexity of Intersectionality," *Signs* 30, no. 3 (2005): 1771–1800, here 1773.

46. Thornton Dill, "Work at the Intersections," 5.

approach, termed "intercategorical complexity," requires that scholars adopt "existing analytical categories" to analyze "the relationships of inequality among social groups."[47]

The first approach renders categories of analysis suspect because they have no foundations in reality; this approach deploys postmodernist discourse, which "attempts to move beyond essentialism by pluralizing and dissolving the stability and analytic utility of the categories of race, class, gender, sexuality." The third, in contrast, seeks to use categories of analysis strategically and holds that "the relations of domination and subordination that are named and articulated through the processes of racism and racialization still exist and they still require analytic and political specification and engagement."[48] In short, it is important to pay attention to the material and discursive significance of categories in order to analyze how they are "produced, experienced, reproduced and resisted in everyday life."[49] The interactive complexity of the social and discursive relations of inequality within and across analytical categories is at the heart of intersectional analysis.

In such a social analytic of dominations, a *status* rather than an *identity* model of social organization is appropriate. A status model of social analysis is able to examine the institutionalized structures and value patterns of domination for their effects on the relative status of social actors in a given society (and thus also in a text). If such status inscriptions constitute persons as peers, capable of participating on a par with each other, then we can speak of status equality or grassroots democracy; if they are not peers, then we speak of domination. Wo/men's struggles for radical democratic equality seek to abolish relations of domination and to establish those of subordinated status as full partners and peers.

The social structures in which we are positioned are interpreted in and through cultural, political, and religious discourses. Since we cannot stand outside of interpretive frameworks available in our society and time, we make sense out of life with their help. For instance, one person might be influenced by neoconservatism and believe that her social position results from the fact that she worked harder in life than the wo/man on welfare who lives down the street. Another person influenced by right-wing religious fundamentalism might explain the

47. McCall, "The Complexity of Intersectionality," 1773.
48. M. Jaqui Alexander and Chandra Talpade Mohanti, *Feminist Genealogies, Colonial Legacies, Democratic Futures* (New York: Routledge, 1997), xvii.
49. McCall, "The Complexity of Intersectionality," 1783.

situation by the fact that he is blessed by G*d because of his virtuous life, whereas the unmarried mother on welfare has gravely sinned and therefore needs to be punished. Again, another wo/man might believe that her success as a wife and mother is due to her feminine attractiveness and selfless dedication to her husband and children, and that the fate of the wo/man on welfare is due to her lack thereof.

If we always have to resort to existing interpretive discourses for making sense of our lives or of biblical texts, then the importance of social movements for justice becomes obvious. Since malestream hegemonic discourses provide the frameworks in which we make meaning in oppressive situations, emancipatory discourses must provide analyses that illuminate not only the choreography of oppression but also the possibilities for a radical democratic society and religion. Emancipatory discourses are able to articulate an emancipatory self- and world-understanding only within the context of radical democratic movements that shape theories and thereby help to exploit the contradictions that exist between the diverse sociohegemonic discourses.

Here the distinction between a person's *structural position* and her *subject position* becomes important. Every individual is *structurally* positioned within social, cultural, economic, political, and religious systems by virtue of birth. No one chooses to be born white, black, Asian, European, mixed race, poor, healthy, male, or female. Persons find themselves always already positioned by and within structures of domination, and the chances they get in life are limited by them. For example, people are not poor or homeless because they have low motivation, faulty self-esteem, or poor work habits. Rather, people are poor or homeless because of their *structural position* within relations of domination.

In contrast to a structural position, a *subject position* is variable, open to intervention, and changeable, but also limited by hegemonic structures of domination. According to the theorists Ernest Laclau and Chantal Mouffe,

> A "subject position" refers to the ensemble of beliefs through which an individual interprets and responds to her structural positions within a social formation. In this sense an individual becomes a social agent insofar as she lives her structural positions through an ensemble of subject positions.[50]

50. Anna Marie Smith, *Laclau and Mouffe: The Radical Democratic Imaginary* (New York: Routledge, 1998), 58–59.

The relationship between a *subject position* and a *structural position* is quite complex since our self-understandings are always already determined by our *structural position*, with its rewards and pressures. Thus a person might be theoretically able to live her structural positions through a wide range of subject positions, but practically might be restricted to a rigidly defined and closed set of available interpretive frameworks. Hence comes the importance of emancipatory movements and the different interpretive frameworks they articulate.

An Intersectional Analytic of Kyriarchy

Feminist theory has made a range of such interpretive frameworks and categories available for shaping people's *subject positions*. It has provided various social analytics for diagnosing and changing wo/men's structural positions in and through the articulation of different *subject positions*. Key analytic concepts and categories with which to read in a feminist fashion have been developed either as reverse discourse to the binary intellectual framework of systemic dualisms, or in a critical-liberationist-intersectional frame.

The interpretation of wo/men's oppression solely in terms of gender dualism has been problematized for years by socialist-Marxist feminists, as well as by third-world feminists. They have pointed out, on the one hand, that wo/men are oppressed not only by heterosexism but also by racism, classism, and colonialism. On the other hand, they have rejected the mainstream feminist definition of patriarchy, which holds that men are the oppressors and wo/men the victims, as well as the tenet that culture, history, and religion are man-made.

Instead, these theorists have argued consistently that wo/men of subordinated races, nations, and classes are often more oppressed by elite white wo/men than by the men of their own class, race, culture, or religion. As a result of this contradiction in wo/men's lives, neither the interconnection between the exclusion of wo/men and all other "subordinates" from citizenship nor its ideological justification in terms of reified "natural" sexual/racial/class/cultural differences has been given sufficient attention. In order to map and make visible the complex interstructuring of the conflicting status positions of different groups of wo/men, I have argued that patriarchy must be reconceptualized as *kyriarchy*, a neologism derived from the Greek word *kyrios* (Lord, master, father, husband) and the verb *archein* (to rule, dominate). Kyriarchal analysis can be deployed against the structures of domination in the past and in the present.

Kyriarchy in classical antiquity was the rule of the emperor, lord, slave master, husband, and thus of the elite freeborn, propertied, educated gentleman, to whom disenfranchised men and all wo/men were subordinated. In antiquity, kyriarchy was institutionalized either as imperial or as a democratic political form of ruling. Kyriarchy is best theorized as a complex pyramidal system of intersecting multiplicative social and religious structures of superordination and subordination, of ruling and oppression. Kyriarchal relations of domination are built on elite male property rights as well as on the exploitation, dependency, inferiority, and obedience of wo/men.[51]

Kyriarchy as a sociocultural and religious system of domination is constituted by intersecting multiplicative structures of oppression. The different sets of relations of domination shift historically and produce a different constellation of oppression in different times and cultures. The structural positions of subordination that have been fashioned by kyriarchal relations of domination and subordination stand in tension with those required by democracy. Hence, in the context of Greek democracy, Western political philosophy has engaged in discourses and debates to justify such structures of domination. These political discourses of subordination that shape the subject positions of domination have been mediated by Christian Scriptures and have decisively determined modern forms of democracy.

Rather than identifying kyriarchy with binary male-over-female domination, it is best to understand the political system denoted by the term in the classical sense of antiquity. Modern democracies are still structured as complex pyramidal political systems of superiority and inferiority, of dominance and subordination. As kyriarchal democracies, they are stratified by gender, race, class, religion, sexuality, and age *structural positions*, which are assigned to us more or less by birth. Yet how people live these structural kyriarchal positions and how they respond to them is conditioned not simply by the mere fact of these structural positions themselves but also by the subject positions through which they live their structural kyriarchal positions. An essentialist approach assigns to people an "authentic" identity—of gender, as an example—that is derived from our structural position; on the other

---

51. In order to continue in the process of consciousness-raising and becoming aware of how language functions, readers might want to list, as an intellectual, critical exercise, all people who are meant here by the expression "wo/men."

hand, our subject position becomes coherent and compelling through its political discourse, interpretive framework, and theoretical horizon, which I have termed the ideology of kyriocentrism.

Thus, a critical feminist analytic does not understand kyriarchy as an essentialist ahistorical system. Instead, it articulates kyriarchy as an heuristic (derived from Greek and in this use meaning "exploratory") concept, or as a diagnostic, analytic instrument that allows one to investigate the multiplicative interdependence of gender, race, and class stratifications as well as their discursive inscriptions and ideological reproductions. Moreover, it helps one understand that people inhabit several structural positions of race, gender, class, and ethnicity. If one of them becomes privileged, it constitutes a nodal (entangling) point. In any particular historical moment, class may be the primary modality through which one experiences gender and race; in other circumstances, gender may be the privileged position through which one experiences race and class.

Rather than tracing the different historical formations of kyriarchy in Western societies and biblical religions, I direct attention here to the classic and modern forms of democratic kyriarchy and its legitimating discourses. *Greek kyriarchal democracy* constituted itself by the exclusion of the Others, who did not have a share in the land but whose labor sustained society. Freedom and citizenship not only were measured over and against slavery but also were restricted in terms of gender. Moreover, the socioeconomic realities in the Greek city-state were such that only a few select freeborn, propertied, elite, male heads of households could actually exercise democratic government. According to the theoretical vision—but not the historical realization—of democracy, all those living in the polis, the city-state, should be equal citizens, able to participate in government. In theory, all citizens are equal in rights, speech, and power. As the assembly or congress (Greek *ekklēsia*) of free citizens, people came together in order to deliberate and decide the best course of action for pursuing their own well-being and for securing the welfare of all citizens. In practice, however, most of the inhabitants of the city-state were excluded from democratic government.

This classic Greek form of kyriarchal democracy was both kyriocentric and ethnocentric. It drew its boundaries in terms of dualistic polarities and analogies between gods/humans, Greeks/barbarians, male/ female, human/beast, culture/nature, civilized and uncivilized world. The boundaries of citizenship were constituted through civilization, war, and marriage. The structuring dividing lines ran between the men who owned property and those who were owned, between those who were rulers and those who were ruled, between those who as superiors commanded and those who as subordinates had to obey, between those who were free from manual labor and had leisure for philosophical and political activity and those who were economically dependent and whose labor was exploited. This mapping of kyriarchy as an overarching system of domination, however, must not be misconstrued as a universal ahistorical master paradigm. Rather, it is best understood as a particular concrete reflection of the sociopolitical situation and the common good of the Athenian city-state.

This Roman kyriarchal model of imperial power was legitimated by Neo-Aristotelian philosophy, which has found its way into the Christian Scriptures in the form of the kyriarchal injunctions to submission. The First Epistle of Peter, for instance, admonishes Christians who are servants to be submissive even to brutal masters (2:18–25) and instructs freeborn wives to subordinate themselves to their husbands, even to those who are not Christians (3:1–6). Simultaneously it entreats Christians to be subject and give honor to the emperor as supreme, as well as to his governors (2:13–17). The post-Constantinian ancient church most closely resembles this Roman imperial pyramid in Christian terms.

At first, the *modern Western form* of democratic kyriarchy, or kyriarchal democracy, excluded propertied and all other freeborn wo/men, as well as immigrant, poor, and slave wo/men from the democratic right to elect those who govern them. "Property" and elite male status by birth and education, not simply biological-cultural masculinity, entitled men to participate in the government of the few over the many. Hence, modern political philosophy continues to assume that propertied, educated, elite Western Man is defined by reason, self-determination, and full citizenship, whereas freeborn wo/men and other subordinated peoples are characterized by emotion, service, and dependence. Wo/men are seen not as rational and responsible adult subjects but as emotional, helpless, and childlike, subject to exploitation.

Modern political thought elaborates two aspects of kyriarchal power: one seeking to secure species reproduction, the other sexual gratification. The first one sustains the kyriarchal order by wielding control over wives, children, servants, and wealth. The second one articulates kyriarchal power as masculine-phallic power, which wields control over those it desires. In modern capitalist societies, "father-right" operates primarily on an institutional structural level; on the other hand, "masculine" or phallic power operates primarily but not exclusively on a linguistic-ideological level. Kyriarchal power operates not only along the axis of gender but also along the axes of race, class, culture, and religion. Its "politics of dominations" fashions ideological subject positions that are like "the foundation[s] . . . around which notions of domination are constructed."[52]

Since there are not many cross-cultural studies of non-Western kyriarchy, I am especially grateful to Hisako Kinukawa for pointing to the "emperor system" of Japan as an example of such a form of kyriarchal relations of domination. The Japanese emperor system consisted of the emperor standing at the apex of the imperial pyramid; his various agents came from the nobility and ruled the country socially, culturally, and politically. The emperor system was supported by state Shintoism and consisted of a pyramid of domination, with the emperor on top and the people divided into four descending classes of samurai, farmers, craftsmen, and merchants as well as the poor and despised outcast class. Although the nationalist Japanese emperor system was replaced by democracy in 1945, its shame culture, values, and politics are still perpetuated today, especially in and through the patriarchal family, which is a small-scale model of the emperor system.[53]

In conclusion, I want to stress the following structural aspects of kyriarchy:

1. Kyriarchy is a complex pyramidal system of dominations that works through the violence of economic exploitation and lived subordination. However, this kyriarchal pyramid of gradated dominations must not be seen as static but as an always changing net of relations of domination.

2. Kyriarchy is realized differently in different historical contexts. Democratic kyriarchy or kyriarchal democracy was articulated differently in antiquity and modernity; it is different in Greece, Hellenism, Rome, Asia Minor, Europe, America, Japan, or India; it is different in Judaism, Islam, or Catholicism.

3. Not only the gender system but also the stratification systems of race, class, colonialism, and heterosexism structure and determine this kyriarchal system. These structures of domination, racism, heterosexism, classism, and colonialism intersect with each other in a pyramidal fashion; they are not parallel but multiplicative. The full power of

52. See bell hooks, *Talking Back: Thinking Feminist, Thinking Black* (Boston: South End Press, 1989), 175.
53. Hisako Kinukawa, *Wo/men and Jesus in Mark: A Japanese Feminist Perspective* (New York: Orbis Books, 1994), 15–22.

kyriarchal oppression comes to the fore in the lives of wo/men living on the bottom of the kyriarchal pyramid.

4. In order to function, kyriarchal societies and cultures need a servant class, a servant race, a servant gender, a servant religion. The existence of such a servant class is maintained through the ideologies of kyriocentrism, which are internalized through education, socialization, and brute violence and rationalized by malestream scholarship. It is sustained by the belief that members of a servant class of people are by nature or by divine decree inferior to those whom they are destined to serve.

5. Both in Western modernity and in Greco-Roman antiquity, kyriarchy has been in tension with a democratic ethos and system of equality and freedom. In a radical democratic system, power is not exercised through "power over" or through violence and subordination, but through the human capacities for respect, responsibility, self-determination, and self-esteem. This radical democratic ethos has again and again engendered emancipatory movements that have insisted on the equal freedom, dignity, and justice for all.

6. Feminist political theorists have shown that the classical Greek philosophers Aristotle and Plato variously articulated a theory of kyriarchal democracy to justify the exclusion of certain groups of people, such as freeborn wo/men or slave wo/men and men from participation in democratic government. These groups of people were not fit to rule or to govern, the philosophers argued, because of their deficient natural powers of reasoning. Such an explicit ideological justification and kyriocentric theory need to be developed at a point in history when it becomes increasingly obvious that those who are excluded from the political life of the polis (the city-state)—such as freeborn wo/men, educated slaves, wealthy metics (alien residents), and traveling mercenaries—are actually indispensable to it. Philosophical rationalizations of the exclusion of diverse people from citizenship and government are engendered by the contradiction between the democratic vision of the city-state and its actual kyriarchal socioeconomic and political practices.

7. The contradiction between the logic of democracy and historical sociopolitical kyriarchal practices has produced the kyriocentric (master-centered) logic of identity as the assertion of "natural differences" between elite men and wo/men, freeborn and slaves, property owners and farmers or artisans, Athenian-born citizens and other residents, Greeks and barbarians, the civilized and uncivilized world. A similar process of ideological kyriocentrism is inscribed in Christian Scriptures in and through the so-called (household) codes of submission.

The Focus of a Kyriarchal Analytic

To sum up my argument, kyriarchal power and kyriocentric ideology operate not only along the axis of the gender system but also along the axes of race, class, heterosexual culture, and religion. These axes of power function to structure the more general system of domination in a matrix, or better, patrix-like fashion. Hence, the fourth paradigm needs to adopt a discursive analytic that can analyze the axes of power inscribed both in the biblical text and in its contemporary interpretations, including biblical studies as a discipline that shapes graduate biblical education.

Modern liberal democracy perpetrates many of the ideological practices found in ancient democratic kyriarchy, insofar as it claims that its citizens "are created equal" and are entitled to "liberty and the pursuit of happiness," yet at the same time it retains "natural" kyriarchal, economic, sociopolitical stratifications. Emancipatory biblical studies such as postcolonial studies or liberation the*logies, which have developed their analytic without explicitly taking into account the status position of multiply-oppressed wo/men, perpetuate the ideologies of kyriocentrism although they do not intend to do so.

In light of this analysis, it becomes clear that the universalist kyriocentric rhetoric of Euro-American elite men does not simply reinforce the dominance of the male sex; it also legitimates the imperial "White Father" or, in black idiom, the enslaving "Boss-Man" as the universal subject. By implication, European American feminist theory or Marxist theory that articulates gender or class difference as primary and originary difference mask the complex interstructuring of kyriarchal dominations inscribed *in* the subject positions of individual wo/men and in the status positions of dominance and subordination *between* wo/men. They also mask the participation of white elite wo/men—or better, "ladies"—and of Christian religion in kyriarchal oppression, insofar as both have served as the civilizing colonialist conduits of kyriarchal knowledges, values, religion, and culture.

Since modern liberal democracies are modeled after the classical ideal of kyriarchal democracy, they continue the contradiction between kyriarchal practices and democratic self-understandings inscribed in the discourses of democracy in antiquity. It must not be overlooked, however, that this institutionalized contradiction between the ideals of radical emancipatory democracy and their historical kyriarchal actualizations has also engendered movements for emancipation seeking full self-determining citizenship.

In the past centuries the emancipatory struggles for equal rights as citizens have gained voting and civil rights for all adult citizens. Since these movements, however, could not completely overcome the kyriarchal stratifications that continue to determine modern liberal representative democracies, they seem to have made the democratic circle merely coextensive with the kyriarchal pyramid, thereby reinscribing the contradiction between democratic vision and political kyriarchal practice, and thereby spawning new movements of emancipation. Such an analysis helps us to understand the work of emancipatory scholarship and education as an integral part of social radical democratic movements for change.

Hence, biblical scholarship in the fourth paradigm of biblical studies needs to equip its practitioners to become skilled in analyzing the kyriarchal and kyriocentric inscriptions of today as well as those at work in the biblical text. We need to learn how to produce and teach knowledge of the biblical text not simply for knowledge's sake or just for mediating understanding, but rather also for engaging the intersectional analytic of kyriarchy and kyriocentrism, for the sake of conscientization and critical knowledge production.

If the fourth paradigm of biblical scholarship were to adopt as its shared analytic an intersectional, multiplicative analysis of the kyriarchal structures of domination, marginalization, racism, heterosexism, class conflict, and imperialism or colonialism—then the discourses of the paradigm would be able to create a common theoretical space that allows for the articulation of differences, while at the same time focusing research on the power structures of domination, subordination, and the ideological legitimizations they engender as hegemonic "common sense." To focus on the diverse struggles for justice, this paradigm needs to articulate, for all four paradigms of biblical studies, an ideology critique and ethics of interpretation that is able not only to *read*, but also to critically *evaluate* the kyriarchal structures of injustice and the kyriocentric ideologies that are inscribed in biblical texts, which continue to inculcate and legitimate those structures and ideologies today.

Such a development and adoption of a shared multiaxial analytic framework, however, is only possible if the different theoretical voices inhabiting the fourth paradigm are not essentialized[54] in an add-and-stir fashion, as is the case, for instance, with regard to "feminist postcolo-

---

54. See the very important discussion of Chakravorty Spivak's concept of "strategic essentialism" by Roland Boer, "Green Ants and Gibeonites: B. Wongar, Joshua 9 and Some Problems of Postcolonialism," in *Semeia* 75 (special issue), *Postcolonialism and Scriptural Reading*, ed. Laura E. Donaldson (Atlanta: Scholars Press, 1996), 129–52.

nialism" or "postcolonial race theory." Instead, the different approaches need to be conceptualized and understood as analytic strategies or practices seeking to transform kyriarchal relations of domination. They are all necessary if such a transformation should be possible. Instead of conceptualizing the different analytic approaches in terms of identity—such as, for instance, feminism, black criticism, postcolonialism, and so forth—we have to see them as varying, shifting, and diverging subject positions that operate within a common space determined by struggles for justice and transformation.

I have called this space of struggles the *ekklēsia* of wo/men, conceptualized as a radical democratic emancipatory space of possibility and vision.[55] In such an emancipatory imaginary, the different voices of the fourth paradigm, like those of all four paradigms of biblical studies, are then best imagined as constituting a *forum*, a public space of critical-constructive debate, ethical evaluation, and interpretive practices. Graduate biblical education in this paradigm of radical equality would, I suggest, be able to fundamentally change academic practices of biblical interpretation. It also would require a rethinking of the pedagogical hermeneutical practices of the fourth paradigm of biblical studies. A critical pedagogy in the tradition of Paulo Freire, I propose, would be appropriate for imagining and inhabiting such a radical democratic emancipatory space.

According to Adriana Hernández, who draws on the work of Giroux, the following key categories structure a critical pedagogy and—in my view—are equally significant for an emancipatory pedagogy of biblical studies:

—Critical pedagogy understands the notion of the political as permeating the social order, understanding power not only in negative terms but also in its capacity to create a different social order.

—By combining the discourse of critique with one of possibility, critical pedagogy seeks to empower subjects to become agents in a process of social transformation.

—Critical pedagogy understands the teacher as a transformative intellectual who moves beyond mere technical concerns or elitist professional interests.

55. Elizabeth Castelli, "The *Ekklēsia* of Women and Feminist Utopia: Locating the Work of Elisabeth Schüssler Fiorenza in North American Feminist Thought," in *On the Cutting Edge: The Study of Women in Biblical Worlds*, ed. Jane Schaberg, Alice Bach, and Esther Fuchs (New York: Continuum, 2003), 36–52.

—Critical pedagogy does not see education as a neutral space but recognizes it "as a site of struggle among dominant and subordinate cultural practices along diverse axes of power such as race, gender, class, sexual orientation."[56]

In short, in Hernández's view, critical pedagogy "refers to a necessary dynamic of theory and practice with political and ethical concerns leading the process of reflection and reorganization. These concerns should be structured around a fundamental emancipatory discourse of equality, freedom and justice, and should aim at democratic vision."[57]

A PEDAGOGICAL MODEL OF AGENCY
AND CONSCIENTIZATION

Following the lead of Hernández, I argue that the fourth, emancipatory paradigm of biblical studies has as its task not just to interpret biblical texts and traditions but *also* to articulate a critical pedagogy for transforming Western malestream epistemological frameworks, individualistic apolitical practices, and sociopolitical relations of cultural colonization. By analyzing the Bible's kyriocentric power of persuasion, an emancipatory pedagogy seeks to foster biblical interpretation as a critical emancipative praxis of struggle against all forms of domination.

Liberation pedagogies of all stripes have not only pointed to the perspectival and contextual nature of scientific knowledge and biblical interpretation, but also asserted that biblical scholarship and theology are—knowingly or not—always engaged for or against the oppressed. Hence, multiplex emancipatory hermeneutical practices are needed that allow the "nonpersons"—to use an expression of Gustavo Gutiérrez— to become subjects of interpretation and historical agents of change. Since the fourth, rhetorical-emancipatory paradigm understands biblical studies as public discourse, it needs to engender a pedagogy of critical conscientization and systemic ethicopolitical analysis.

Religious biblical identity that is shaped by Scripture must in evernew readings be deconstructed and reconstructed in terms of a global praxis for the liberation of all wo/men. Equally, cultural identity that is shaped by biblical discourses must be critically interrogated and trans-

56. Adriana Hernández, *Pedagogy, Democracy, and Feminism: Rethinking the Public Sphere* (Albany: State University of New York Press, 1997), 11.
57. Ibid., 12.

formed. Hence, it is necessary to reconceptualize the pedagogy of biblical studies as a critical ethical-political practice. Interpreting subjects need to learn to reclaim their authority for assessing both the oppressive and the liberating imagination of particular biblical texts and their interpretations in a critical spiraling dance of interpretation. Interpreters must reject the epistemological blueprints and methodological rules of the "master," which marginalize and trivialize wo/men.

As I have elaborated elsewhere, crucial hermeneutical moves in such a critical pedagogy of interpretation and emancipatory analytic are as follows: experience and conscientization, recognition of social location and critical analysis of domination, suspicion and critical analysis, assessment and evaluation in terms of a scale of values, (re)imagination, reconstruction or re-membering, and transformative action for change.[58] These practices are not just hermeneutical but also pedagogical. They should not be construed simply as successive independent methodological steps of inquiry or as discrete methodological rules or recipes. Rather, they must be understood as interpretive moves and pedagogical strategies that interact with each other simultaneously in the process of making meaning out of a particular biblical text—or any other cultural text—in the context of the globalization of inequality.

By deconstructing the kyriarchal rhetoric and politics of inequality and subordination inscribed in the Bible and in present-day contexts, both general and professional interpreters are able to generate ever-fresh articulations of radical democratic religious visions and emancipatory practices. Such an emancipatory process of biblical interpretation has as its "doubled" reference point both the interpreter's contemporary presence and the biblical past. In other words, this process of interpretation investigates both the language systems, ideological frameworks, and sociopolitical-religious locations of *contemporary interpreters* who are living in kyriarchal systems of domination; and also the linguistic and sociohistorical kyriarchal systems and ideologies inscribed in *biblical texts* and their effective histories of interpretation.

An ethics of interpretation strategically engages these hermeneutical moves as pedagogical discursive practices in order to *displace* literalist doctrinal, positivist-scientific, and relativist practices of knowledge

---

58. See my book *Wisdom Ways: Introducing Feminist Biblical Interpretation* (Maryknoll, NY: Orbis Press, 2001), 165–205; and my article "Invitation to Dance in the Open House of Wisdom: Feminist Study of the Bible," in *Engaging the Bible: Critical Readings from Contemporary Women*, ed. Choi Hee An and Katheryn Pfister Darr (Minneapolis: Fortress Press, 2006), 81–104.

production that operate both in the depoliticized academy as well as in popular hegemonic forms of interpretation. Most importantly, this pedagogical process and hermeneutical dance commences not by focusing on malestream texts and traditions, but by placing wo/men as biblical interpreters in the center of its attention. It seeks to recast interpretation not in positivist but in rhetorical terms; it does not compel interpreters to deny, but rather to recognize that biblical texts and interpretations are rhetorical, produced in and by particular historical debates and struggles.

An emancipatory pedagogical process of biblical interpretation argues for the integrity and indivisibility of the interpretive process as well as for the primacy of the contemporary starting point of interpretation. To that end, it engages in a hermeneutical dance of deconstruction and reconstruction, or of critique and retrieval, and applies itself both to the level of text and of interpretation. Thereby, this pedagogy seeks to overcome the hermeneutical splits between sense and meaning, explanation and understanding, critique and consent, and distanciation and empathy; between reading behind the text and in front of the text, between the present and the past, interpretation and application, and realism and imagination.

Such a pedagogical emancipatory process of biblical studies continually moves between the present and the past, between interpretation and application, between realism and imagination. It moves, spirals, turns, and dances in the places found in "the white spaces between the black letters" of Scripture—to use a metaphor of Jewish interpretation. Hence, it is very difficult to boil such a dynamic process of interpretation down to a logical consecutive description. If I try to do so here, I hope readers will see my attempt not as a transcript of a process, but more as a basic instruction in dance steps that they must execute in their own manner in order to keep dancing.

In academic courses and seminars as well as in the context of workshops, participants need to engage both levels of interpretation at one and the same time. General interpreters will tend to focus on the level of contemporary meaning-making, utilizing—when appropriate—the resources of professional interpretation; professional interpreters need to be trained to operate equally on both levels of meaning-making. If these interpretive practices were to be incorporated into academic biblical pedagogy, they would enable participants to move between the paradigms of biblical studies by using the analytic of the fourth paradigm as a hermeneutical lens and optic.

A *hermeneutics of experience and socioreligious location*, for example, compels interpreters to look at their own experience and the social location from where they interpret a biblical text, as well as trace the experience and social location inscribed in the biblical text. The meaning of a text emerges from the creative interplay between critical reflection on experience and social location today, and on those that are inscribed in biblical texts.

A *hermeneutics of domination* in turn analyzes the kyriarchal structures of domination and investigates how they are inscribed in the text by the author, and how contemporary professional readings reinscribe them.

A *hermeneutics of suspicion* is necessary not only because of the kyriarchal structures of domination inscribed in the biblical text and legitimated today by the text's authority, but especially because of the grammatically kyriocentric language of biblical texts, which erase wo/men from history or are the*logically claimed to be the Word of G*d.

A *hermeneutics of critical evaluation and ethics of inquiry* explores the ideological mechanisms identified by a hermeneutics of suspicion and assesses them in terms of an emancipatory scale of values. It asks how much a text contributes to or diminishes the emancipation and well-being of every wo/man and of the planet.

A *hermeneutics of creative imagination* compels both general and professional interpreters to imagine and "dream" an alternate world of justice and well-being, one different from the present one of kyriarchal domination. It also traces the utopias, dreams, and visions of such an envisioned different "world" inscribed in biblical writings.

A *hermeneutics of historical reconstruction and memory*[59] uses the tools of historiography to reconstruct the struggles of colonialized, slave, and freeborn wo/men against kyriarchal domination inscribed in early Christian literature in order to contribute to a historical consciousness and identity different from that of kyriarchal domination. It does so by placing, for instance, slave wo/men in the center of its attention. In so doing, it changes our image of early Christianity, of church and world today, and of ourselves.

Thus the dance of interpretation always has as its goal a *hermeneutics of change and transformation*. When seeking future visions and transformations, we can only extrapolate from present-day experience, which

---

59. See Elisabeth Schüssler Fiorenza, "Re-Visioning Christian Origins: *In Memory of Her* Revisited," in *Christian Beginnings: Worship, Belief and Society*, ed. Kieran O'Mahony (London: Continuum International, 2003), 225–50.

is always already determined by past experience. Hence, biblical interpreters need to become skilled in analyzing the past and the present—biblical texts and contemporary worlds—in order to articulate creative visions and transcending imaginations for a new humanity, global ecology, and religious community.

Patricia Hill Collins has dubbed such a pedagogical praxis of change and transformation "visionary pragmatism." Visionary pragmatism points to an alternative vision of the world but does not prescribe a fixed goal and end point for which it then claims universal truth.[60] The process of "visionary pragmatism" reveals how current actions are part of a larger, meaningful struggle. It demonstrates that ethical and truthful visions of self-affirmation and community cannot be separated from the struggles on their behalf. One takes a stand by constructing new knowledge and new interpretations.

While vision can be conjured up in historical imagination, pragmatic action requires that one remain responsive to the injustices of everyday life. If biblical religion and scholarship are worth anything, they must inspire such "visionary pragmatism" in the everyday struggles for justice and the well-being of all. General and professional interpreters in the space of the fourth paradigm thus are able to contribute substantively to democratic societal and religious discourses.

Religious biblical identity that is shaped by the Scriptures must be deconstructed and reconstructed in ever-new readings toward a global praxis for the liberation of all wo/men. Hence, it is necessary to reconceptualize the traditional spiritual practice of "discerning the spirits" (1 Cor. 12:10) as a critical ethical-political practice. Equally, cultural-political identity that is shaped by biblical discourses must be critically interrogated and transformed. In short, in such a critical pedagogical process, interpreters learn to engage in a critical spiraling dance of interpretation in order to reclaim their own intellectual and spiritual authority for assessing both the oppressive and the liberating imagination of particular biblical texts and their interpretations. Hence, an emancipatory pedagogy cannot do other than reject the epistemological blueprints and methodological rules of the "master," those that marginalize and trivialize wo/men.

Such a critical rhetorical-emancipative process of interpretation challenges both scientific practitioners of biblical studies and general

---

60. Patricia Hill Collins, *Fighting Words: Black Wo/men and the Search for Justice* (Minneapolis: University of Minnesota Press, 1998).

interpreters of the Bible to become more theoethically sophisticated interpreters. It does so by problematizing both the modernist ethos of biblical studies and interpreters' own sociopolitical locations and functions in global structures of domination. At the same time, it enables biblical scholars to struggle for a more just and radical democratic articulation of religion in the global *cosmopolis*.

To conclude my argument: I propose that a critical rhetorical emancipative method and hermeneutical process-pedagogy situated in the space of the fourth paradigm of biblical studies is best understood as wisdom-praxis. The spiraling dance of interpretation seeks to engender public the*logical deliberation and religious transformation. It is not restricted to Christian canonical texts, but it can be and has been explored successfully by scholars of other religious traditions and Scriptures of other religions.

Moreover, it is not restricted to the biblical scholar as expert reader. Rather, it calls for transformative and engaged biblical interpreters who may or may not be professional readers. This pedagogical process of conscientization has been used in graduate education, in parish discussions, in college classes, and in work with illiterate wo/men. This process of conscientization and emancipatory knowledge production is not specific to biblical studies. Rather, it can be deployed in all areas of the*logical studies and the study of religion.[61] I thus am articulating a shared analytic and interdisciplinary method of interpretation that is engendered by the radical democratic space of the fourth paradigm. In the next chapter I will explore the pedagogical and didactic practices that facilitate such a radical democratic space of collaboration.

---

61. For instance, Professor Lieve Troch, a systematic feminist liberation theologian, and I have conducted workshops in Brazil and Ecuador. These workshops have analyzed various topical areas such as Christology, Mary, power, and interreligious dialogue, creating a feminist study center in terms of a kyriarchal analysis and fashioning a radical democratic educational space through the "dance of interpretation."

4

Changing Biblical Studies

Toward a Radical Democratic Pedagogy and Ethos

The preceding chapters have discussed the paradigmatic constitution of biblical studies and argued that paradigms of interpretation provide frames of meaning and "regimes of truth" that organize the relations between text, contexts, and interpreters. Whenever we read/hear/interpret a biblical text, or any text, we read/hear/interpret it by engaging one or more of the established paradigms of interpretation. But whereas malestream paradigms of interpretation generally do not call for a critical hermeneutical self-consciousness, the fourth emancipatory paradigm makes explicit not only the theoretical and hermeneutical lenses with which it approaches the biblical text, but also the specific discursive space and ethos that shape biblical studies.

Writing from within the fourth paradigm of biblical studies, I have thus far explicitly focused on epistemology and pedagogy, looking only implicitly at didactics and communication. In this chapter, the question of how to envision and constitute a radical democratic learning space takes center stage. Hence, I will pursue questions such as the following: What educational practices and procedures are advocated by traditional educational models, and how can they be changed? What kind of educational and communicative practices does biblical studies need to develop in order to fashion an emancipatory democratizing rhetorical space, a "citizen council"[1] and forum of many voices, who envision, articulate, debate, and practice a radical democratic ethos of biblical studies?

Hegemonic paradigms neglect or refuse to critically reflect on their sociopolitical contexts and ethos. They tend to conceal the fact that they operate from a sociopolitical and religious analytic standpoint. In contrast, the fourth radical democratic emancipatory paradigm, as I have described it, openly states that it engages in biblical interpretation with the purpose of both producing transformative knowledge and fostering conscientization. By explicitly reflecting on its analytic lenses, its theoretical frameworks, and the pedagogy that it deploys in the process of interpretation, it challenges the hegemonic paradigms of biblical studies to understand their educational work as contributing to a biblically inspired radical democratic citizenry. The following question then arises: How can graduate education be articulated so that it engenders a radical democratic ethos and scholarly practice?

In order to understand the epistemological change that needs to take place for such a radical democratic space of graduate education to take form, it is necessary to articulate a critical theory of education. Such a theory, academic and otherwise, engenders four distinct but overlapping theoretical practices:

1. *Epistemology*—the theory of knowledge, of what we know, and how we can know what we know
2. *Pedagogy*—the critical articulation of educational theory
3. *Didactics*[2]—the critical reflection on the "how to" of educational practices in and outside the classroom
4. *Communication*—the critical mode of how we make known what we know and how we exchange ideas

In this chapter I focus on constructing a pedagogical didactic model that informs a radical democratic learning space for graduate biblical education. To explore the epistemic change necessary for generating an emancipatory pedagogy and didactics for biblical studies, I begin with a discussion of the attempts to transform malestream models of teaching.

---

1. See, e.g., Tom Atlee with Rosa Zubizaretta, *The Tao of Democracy: Using Co-Intelligence to Create a World That Works for All* (Cranston, RI: Writers' Collective, 2003), 105–217; Frances Moore Lappé, *Democracy's Edge: Choosing to Save Our Country by Bringing Democracy to Life* (San Francisco: Jossey-Bass, 2006); Robert W. Fuller, *All Rise: Somebodies, Nobodies, and the Politics of Dignity* (San Francisco: Berrett-Koehler Publishers, 2006).

2. The Greek root of "didactics" is *didaktikos*, meaning someone who is apt at teaching. Didactics has a somewhat different informal development in Anglo-American educational discourses, but it is a well-developed academic discipline in Northern European and German-speaking countries.

Despite the rich literature and research on collaborative teaching and learning,[3] the educational practices of malestream pedagogical paradigms have not been changed, and this, I contend, is because the attempts to change them have not sought to transform the Didactic Triangle.[4]

The standard didactic triangle consists of three components: (1) knowledge; (2) teacher; and (3) learners, or students. The legend of the didactic triangle reads as follows: teachers teach knowledge, which students learn and give back to teachers in their exams in order for teachers to evaluate and assess whether learning has taken place and knowledge has been acquired. This process gives the impression that knowledge is a given power to which teachers as well as learners are subject. Both have to serve knowledge, one by teaching and the other by learning. Yet by casting knowledge as abstract power that is not contingent upon its practitioners and social-political contexts, the epistemology of the didactic triangle is not able to critically articulate the ideological functions of knowledge.

In the second section, I discuss four proposals for a transformative didactics. Two of them stress agency and context, and two emphasize cultural and religious differences. The third section explores the interactive psychotherapeutic model of Theme-Centered Interaction (TCI), developed by Ruth Cohn, which has been taken up in the*logical studies in Germany[5] and is now also emerging in the United States.[6] Here, I have found Silvia Hagleitner's comparison of Paulo Freire's pedagogical model with the TCI model especially helpful.[7] When it is translated into

3. For references, see, e.g., Elizabeth F. Berkeley, Patricia K. Cross, and Claire Howell Major, *Collaborative Learning Techniques: A Handbook for College Faculty* (San Francisco: Jossey-Bass, 2005); Barbara J. Mills and Philip G. Cottell Jr., *Cooperative Learning for Higher Education Faculty* (Phoenix, AZ: Oryx Press, 1998); Maryellen Weimer, *Learner-Centered Teaching: Five Key Changes to Practice* (San Francisco: Jossey-Bass, 2002); Marjorie Mayo, *Imagining Tomorrow: Adult Education for Transformation* (Leicester: National Institute of Adult Continuing Education, 1997); C. Roland Christensen, David A. Garvin, and Ann Sweet, eds., *Education for Judgment: The Artistry of Discussion Leadership* (Boston: Harvard Business School Press, 1991); Marcia B. Baxter Magolda, ed., *Teaching to Promote Intellectual and Personal Maturity: Incorporating Student's Worldviews and Identities into the Learning Process* (San Francisco: Jossey-Bass, 2000).

4. L. Klingberg, *Einführung in die allgemeine Didaktik* (Frankfurt: Fischer, 1982); L. Klingberg, *Lehren und Lernen—Inhalt und Methode: Zur Systematik und Problemgeschichte didaktischer Kategorien* (Oldenburg: Universität Oldenburg, 1995); I. Westbury, S. Hopman, and K. Riquarts, eds., *Teaching as a Reflective Practice: The German Didactic Tradition* (Mahwah, NJ: L. Erlbaum Associates, 2000); W. Klafki, *Neue Studien zur Bildungstheorie und Didaktik: Zeitgemässe Allgemeinbildung und kritisch-konstruktive Didaktik* (Weinheim: Beltz, 1996).

5. Cf., e.g., Karl Josef Ludwig, ed., *Im Ursprung ist Beziehung: Theologisches Lernen als Themenzentrierte Interaktion* (Mainz: Matthias-Grünewald-Verlag, 1997); see especially the series by Hilberath Bernd Jochen and Matthias Scharer, eds., Kommunikative Theologie, vols. 1–7 (Mainz: Matthias-Grünewald-Verlag, 2002–5). The University of Innsbruck has a five-semester MA program in Kommunikative Theologie.

6. See the bilingual volume of the Forschungskreis Kommunikative Theologie / Communicative Theology Research Group, *Kommunikative Theologie / Communicative Theology* (Berlin: LIT Verlag; New Brunswick, NJ: Transaction Publishers, 2007); Matthias Scharer and Bernd Jochen Hilberath, *The Practice of Communicative Theology: An Introduction to a New Theological Culture* (New York: Crossroad, 2008). I am grateful to Professor Mary Ann Hinsdale for having drawn my attention to this work.

7. Silvia Hagleitner, *Mit Lust an der Welt—in Sorge um sie: Feministisch-politische Bildungsarbeit nach Paulo Freire und Ruth Cohn* (Mainz: Matthias-Grünewald-Verlag, 1996).

epistemological-rhetorical terms, Hagleitner's feminist-political pedagogical model can be seen as a crucial step toward a radical democratic
pedagogical model and space.

The fourth and last section of the chapter seeks to articulate the
rhetorical contours of such a radical democratic space in terms of ethos.
I argue that the didactic models developed in the fourth paradigm
engender a reconceptualization of malestream pedagogical theory. They
change the hegemonic knowledge-teacher-student didactic triangle in
such a way that it becomes adequate to a radical democratic paradigm
of education. This reformulation of the didactic triangle in feminist
political terms seeks to articulate a shared radical democratic ethos able
to be inhabited by the different voices and directions in biblical studies. Such a transformation seeks to foster communicative agency for
participation in imagined citizen councils that debate the meaning and
use of Scripture on the grounds of emancipatory biblical studies.

TRANSFORMING MALESTREAM PEDAGOGICAL MODELS

In my book *Wisdom Ways*,[8] I sketched three hegemonic models of pedagogy that correspond roughly to the four paradigms of biblical studies: the banking model, the master-disciple model, and the consumer
model. These three malestream modes of learning, I suggested, need
to be either complemented or replaced by a radical democratic pedagogical model. Since the critical feminist biblical inquiry of the fourth
paradigm of interpretation has as its goal not just to produce specialists,
but also to empower or enable "citizens" for actively participating in
biblical deliberations and self-determining decision-making processes,
such inquiry needs to break down the walls between the biblical spe-
cialist and the general reader.

The Banking Model

The banking model of learning and acquiring knowledge, which is the
traditional, dominant model of education, is a descriptive, factual accumulation and absorption model. The Brazilian educator Paulo Freire

8. Elisabeth Schüssler Fiorenza, *Wisdom Ways: Introducing Feminist Biblical Interpretation* (Maryknoll, NY: Orbis Books, 2001).

has dubbed this traditional lecture-and-examination model of education the "banking" model because it treats knowledge like monetary funds.[9] The teacher owns the assets and deposits knowledge. Students are passive receptacles of the knowledge. Knowledge is packaged and transmitted by textbooks taught by the teacher and can be owned, sold, or stored as capital. In this educational model, teachers are the experts who collect and deposit all the available knowledge and facts in their lectures and assigned readings. Students are expected to absorb this knowledge by internalizing and memorizing it in order to be able to repeat it accurately in exams or assigned topic papers.

This hegemonic model presupposes that there is a finite amount of knowledge that determines a field of study. The teacher, as the authority, guarantees the value of the knowledge that readers/students receive and bank in their memory. Examinations make sure that students can accurately repeat the knowledge stored in textbooks or lecture notes in order to become competent in their field of studies. Study plans and curricular requirements ensure that all the knowledge that is deemed essential and necessary to master a discipline is transmitted by the teacher and replicated by the student.

The banking model is a top-down model. The university model of lecturing has its roots in that of preaching, and this model is closely aligned with the religious-the*logical paradigm. Just as preachers are understood to proclaim the authoritative word of G*d, so also teachers are expected to transmit a preexisting body of authoritative knowledge that must be internalized and reproduced by students in exams or papers.

This pedagogical model works through traditional curricular requirements, lectures, testing, and assigned paper topics. In short, it presupposes an understanding of the discipline or field of study that can be delineated, controlled, and replicated. In this model, all power rests with the teacher, thus engendering a nondemocratic educational environment predicated upon objectivism and a limitable body of knowledge. Standards of excellence are measurements that determine how much a candidate or student has acquired aptitude in "controlling" and replicating a field of study.

For instance, the introductory course in biblical studies resorts most often to the banking model of education, adopting its traditional lecture and testing style since it is often the only biblical course taken by students majoring in other fields, either at the college or master's level.

9. Paulo Freire, *Pedagogy of the Oppressed* (New York: Continuum, 1970).

Yet, since educational theory has more and more emphasized that a learner-centered pedagogy is much more effective in knowledge acquisition than a passive replication mode, it is important to abandon the banking model and to change the introductory course in such a way that it allows a learner-centered style.

Freire sought to replace the pedagogical banking model with a critical pedagogy that engenders a form of active learning, in which traditional notions of what constitutes knowledge and its pedagogical transmission are problematized, questioned, evaluated, and displaced. In his model, students and teachers cooperate and dialogue with each other as opposed to interacting hierarchically and competitively. The result is a democratic environment in which students and teachers are seen as each having the power of knowledge—albeit in different ways—and the individual voices, knowledge, and talents of each are articulated, owned, and recognized.

Such an active learning approach fosters critical engagement with knowledge and sociocultural contexts. For it to be successful, however, it needs to clearly articulate the institutional power structures that condition such an egalitarian attempt at interaction. For instance, in all my courses I utilize a contract grading system that allows students to decide on the amount of work they want to do. I also seek to involve them in self-evaluation of their work, and I use the first couple of classes to engage in a discussion of the power structures of the university in general and the divinity school in particular. I do so in order to engender critical awareness of kyriarchal structures and how they affect our work.

Paul Aspan and Faith Kirkham Hawkins have elaborated how alternative modes of student evaluation contribute to a democratic classroom that is attentive to "the diverse identities, gifts, and concerns of students." Intent on modifying the banking model of education, they require undergraduate students to engage in variegated learning strategies and self-evaluations.[10] In the first two weeks, they ask students to reflect on "how they learn best, what their special talents or needs are, and how those might be melded with the study of the syllabus" in order to develop a plan or portfolio for "a personal course of study."[11]

Such a portfolio can contain written essays on suggested topics, interpretive modules of texts, visual art, or artistic performances with

10. Paul F. Aspan and Faith Kirkham Hawkins, "After the Facts: Alternative Student Evaluation for Active Learning Pedagogies in the Undergraduate Biblical Studies Classroom," *Teaching Theology and Religion* 3 (2000): 133–51, here 135.

11. Ibid., 144.

written explications, classroom presentations, and group, partner, or individual projects. If students submit work during the semester, they receive feedback from the instructor. The final portfolio also contains self-evaluations of their work and suggestions for grades according to the guidelines of evaluation given. The goal of this course design is for students, by using all their talents and intelligences, to master the course content as defined by the syllabus. However, even with these efforts, it seems that the banking model remains operative insofar as it is not the students but the faculty who determine the materials to be studied.

The Master-Disciple Model

The second malestream pedagogical model is the master-apprentice pedagogical method, which is implemented primarily in graduate courses and in advanced seminars. The master-disciple model is a top-down model, even if the *Doktorvater*, as the dissertation director is called in German, is very benevolent. In this model of learning, the teacher is the expert who serves as a model to be imitated by his[12] students. Students are supposed to learn the skills of interpretation by imitating the "master." In this pedagogical model, unlike in the banking model, students are not expected to focus only on the content delineated in the syllabus and lectures. Rather, they are trained in the skills of exegesis and explanation by imitating the "masters," or leading scholars in the field whose methods are often understood to be rules and norms that, if followed, guarantee that the true meaning of a biblical text is found. The teacher is the "master" or expert who controls the methods and knows the solutions to questions. Students are led to believe that the truth can be nailed down if one knows the right methods and is trained to use them cleanly and skillfully. If one is working in this mode of learning, then one will expect a course or seminar to teach methods of biblical interpretation in the "correct" way, so that the true meaning of the text can be established.

In 1924, Joachim Wach, a sociologist of religion, wrote a classic article on "Master and Disciple" in German, which was translated and published in English in 1962.[13] Wach distinguishes between the

---

12. Since this model has been developed in and through the exclusion of wo/men and other marginalized people, the male pronoun is appropriate here.

13. Joachim Wach, "Master and Disciple: Two Religio-Sociological Studies," trans. Susanne Heigel-Wach and Fred Streng, in *Journal of Religion* 42, no. 1 (1962): 1–21; full text available through http://www.wabashcenter .wabash.edu. See also Frederick M. Denny, ed., "Joachim Wach's 'Master and Disciple' Revisited: A Contemporary Symposium," *Teaching Theology and Religion* 1, no. 1 (1998): 13–19.

following two types of master-disciple relationships: the teacher-student, and the more personal master-follower. The teacher-student relationship is a learning and teaching relationship where the teacher and the student come together to explore an object of study or a body of knowledge that is of common interest to both, one that they pursue with devotion. In the master-follower relationship, the relationship between master and disciple is profoundly close. Here the student is called to a deeply personal and intimate relationship with the master. "The beloved master must be an essential part of his own existence."[14] If other students follow the beloved master, rivalries may develop; but each student has a unique and essentially different personal relationship with the master. Furthermore, Wach's master-follower model, clearly not a model of equal relationships, is often taken up in the mentorship model. Historically significant systems of mentorship include, for instance, traditional Greek pederasty, the guru-disciple tradition practiced in Hinduism and Buddhism, the discipleship system practiced by rabbinical Judaism and the Christian church, and apprenticing under the medieval guild system. It is obvious that in both of Wach's senses, the master-disciple model of education has religious roots. In the teacher-student relationship, devotion to the subject matter figures prominently, whereas in the personal master-follower relationship, it is discipleship that does so.

Margaret Miles has responded to Wach's models by pointing out that both are inadequate insofar as education presupposes both a community of learners and a culture of education. It is not a simple individualistic transmission from teacher to learner, or from master to disciple. Moreover, she notes, Wach's models are deeply gendered and outdated.[15] I would add that his proposal reinforces not only gender but also race, class, and cultural differences. The work of Janice Hocker Rushing has elucidated how dangerous such master-disciple relationships and pairings between an older male professor and a younger woman can be because they often engender a loss of voice and of self.[16]

How this master-disciple model is usually modified today can be seen from the following example. In a very interesting discussion of the question "What Is a Seminar?" Carl Holladay and Luke Johnson[17] elucidate

    14. Wach, "Master and Disciple," 2.
    15. Margaret Miles, "Are Wach's Models of Student and Disciple Adequate for the Nineties?" in "Joachim Wach's 'Master and Disciple' Revisited: A Contemporary Symposium," ed. Frederick M. Denny, *Teaching Theology and Religion* 1, no. 1 (1998): 13–19, here 14–15.
    16. Janice Hocker Rushing, *Erotic Mentoring: Women's Transformations in the University* (Walnut Creek, CA: Left Coast Press, 2006)
    17. Carl R. Holladay and Luke T. Johnson, "What Is a Seminar? Two Views of the Same Course," *Teaching Theology and Religion* 1, no. 1 (1998): 27–30.

their different approaches to their jointly taught graduate seminar on "Graeco-Roman Backgrounds to the New Testament." They agree on the following: a seminar generally has a small number of participants, all of whom are advanced in their field and equally share in the work of the seminar. The seminar discussions should "genuinely be open and of significance to a particular field." However, they also recognize the different types of knowledge that even advanced students bring to the table. Hence, both conduct their seminar differently since each adopts distinct pedagogical methods that formulate teacher-student or master-follower relations differently. Their description of their separate approaches seems to indicate that one is drawn to Wach's first model, and the other to the second. In one form, students and faculty participate equally in the discussion of a subject matter and prepare equally for the sessions. In the other, the faculty leader of the seminar prepares each seminar session with the student who will lead the seminar discussion in the following week. In the first form both students and teacher are focused on the subject matter under discussion; the second form encourages the master to teach the disciple to follow in his footsteps.

As with Wach, both of these modified master-disciple seminar models are focused on the ancient text and its contexts but seem not to take into account the wider cultures and communities in which they work or the different questions raised by feminist/gender, race-ethnicity, or postcolonial studies. The contemporary contexts of interpretation and their ideological pressures are eclipsed. Moreover, they do not overcome the tendency of the master to form the disciple into "his own image and likeness."

Page duBois[18] has warned that such a master-disciple model subscribes to a form of reasoning that is competitive and combative. The preferred mode for ascertaining truth is adversarial debate and the honing of arguments that can withstand the most acerbic assault. Hence, this form of reasoning and argument can be likened to the practice of forensic interrogation, to the method of arrest and discipline, to an understanding of methods as "police arts," to "a dividing, a splitting, a fracturing of the logical body, a process that resembles torture."

The Socratic dialogue (presented via Plato) that is prevalent in this mode of education locates truth in the mind of the master, who controls question and answer. The search for truth requires hard labor, compelled by the assumption that truth must be hunted down and

---

18. Page duBois, *Torture and Truth* (New York: Routledge, 1991).

coerced through persistent questioning. However, this forensic-combative context of the Platonic dialogue is not intrinsic to it, as Martha Nussbaum[19] has shown. If situated in a deliberative rhetorical context, such critical questioning and debate are not oriented toward winning an argument but toward weighing and evaluating arguments; in this way, they are able to envision and articulate a biblical reading that seeks to foster the well-being of everyone.

The Consumer Model of Education

The third pedagogical model is the consumer model, which offers two distinct but interrelated learning approaches: the smorgasbord and the therapeutic. In the *smorgasbord approach*, students pick and choose what they think is useful. They buy books or subscribe to courses as they would buy cars or clothing, either for utility or entertainment. At Harvard Divinity School, for instance, we start every semester with a "shopping period," during which students move from class to class as buyers move from shelf to shelf in a supermarket, to select the most informative, the most cutting-edge, the easiest, or the most palatable fare.

In this didactic model, teachers act not only as experts or masters but also as salespersons who are skilled at advertising their wares. Just as the semester begins with a shopping period, so it ends with students filling out product evaluation forms detailing how well the teacher performed, whether the reading material was adequate, or whether the demands were too high. Just as books are judged on how much they have sold or how long they have been on the *New York Times* bestseller list, so also conferences and workshops or Bible study groups are judged by the numbers they have attracted.

In the second form of the didactic consumer model—*the therapeutic approach*—lectures, courses, books, or workshops are selected and evaluated according to whether they make one "feel good." Books, courses, or workshops should not be too demanding but should satisfy the needs of their readers, students, or attendees. The success of religious books or classes is often judged according to whether they are spiritually edifying or esthetically pleasing. Hence, courses and books on all kinds of forms of spirituality abound.

---

19. See, e.g., Martha Nussbaum, *Cultivating Humanity: A Classical Defense of Reform in Liberal Education* (Cambridge, MA: Harvard University Press, 1998); as well as Martha Nussbaum, *The Fragility of Goodness: Luck and Ethics in Greek Tragedy and Philosophy* (Cambridge: Cambridge University Press, 2001).

Biblical texts and courses are expected to address individuals and gratify their spiritual wants and longings. They are to give security and certainty in an ever-changing world and alienating society. Books and courses on how to pray and meditate with the Bible are much preferred over those that seek to foster a critical engagement with it. The Bible becomes an oracle for spiritual guidance that helps its readers to accept and submit to the demands of everyday life and the powers that be. This third pedagogical model allows for choice and takes emotions into account while at the same time depriving students of a critical education.

Tina Pippin, in her reflections on "Liberatory Pedagogies in the Religious Studies Classroom,"[20] offers one example of how this pedagogical model can be transformed by critical pedagogy. In the organization of her upper-level course on the "Life and Letters of Paul," she "wanted to experiment more completely with a liberatory and feminist pedagogy that involves the students in the creation of the syllabus and in determining what they wanted and needed to know." On the first day of classes they drafted together their "class covenant," which articulated the expectations of the class. Pippin brought to class a tool kit with which to construct the syllabus and articulate student expectations. In her tool kit was "an outline syllabus to get us started, some sample course objectives from which to work, the list of textbooks . . . that we would choose from," a list of topics that are "too big for one semester," topics that "one should consider learning in a 'Life and Letters of Paul' class," and a list of suggestions "for on-site educational experiences."[21]

Pippin also paid careful attention to dynamics and emotional undercurrents in the class. When two first-year students insisted that the course methods were not liberatory for them, and "their experiences (traditional education and conservative Christian) formed the base for their resistance to the class,"[22] the participants searched actively for new ways to work with and learn from each other. Positive feedback was given to those who were unhappy about and questioned the class pedagogy. The feedback included statements such as "You hold us accountable for what we say we're about," or "I want to thank you for expressing my thoughts and feelings about the class when I don't have words," and this made it possible for the class to continue its work.[23]

---

20. Tina Pippin, "Liberatory Pedagogies in the Religious Studies Classroom," in *Teaching Theology and Religion* 1, no. 3 (1998): 177–82.
21. Ibid., 178.
22. Ibid., 179.
23. Ibid.

Pippin does not reflect on the extent to which a didactic that seeks to placate students who are not happy with a course remains caught up in the "feel good" tendencies of the consumer model. As Zygmunt Bauman so succinctly observes in *Does Ethics Have a Chance in a World of Consumers?*

> More than any other society, the society of consumers stands and falls by the happiness of its members. The answers they give to the question, "Are you happy?", may be viewed as the ultimate test of the consumer society's success and failure.[24]

To transform the consumer model of education, it will be necessary to engage a process of critical consciousness-raising rather than to seek to please consumers who are dissatisfied.

To sum up my argument: All three malestream pedagogical models and learning approaches can also be analyzed in terms of gender. In the first two models—the banker and the master-disciple—knowledge production is coded in culturally masculine terms insofar as the models stress mastery, expertise, and control of knowledge. Both approaches are at home in the malestream academy and church, two sites that until very recently have excluded wo/men and subordinated minority peoples from their authoritative knowledge production. These first two models not only construct the author/master in masculine terms, but also construe students in culturally feminine terms.

In contrast, the third model—the consumer model—with its consumer and psychological approaches, is coded in feminine terms. Both versions construe agency in a culturally feminine mode that acts to privatize knowledge, making knowledge in general and biblical knowledge in particular a readily available commodity. They construct students as consumers or patients who purchase religious knowledge for their own private use, enjoyment, and edification. None of these approaches, however, qualify as an emancipatory, liberating model of education adequate to the fourth paradigm.

While students are compelled to engage in these three pedagogical models at one time or another, the fourth emancipative paradigm needs to develop a different pedagogical model capable of integrating the positive aspects of all three of malestream pedagogical models without falling victim to their self-alienating and distorting powers.

24. Zygmunt Bauman, *Does Ethics Have a Chance in a World of Consumers?* (Cambridge, MA: Harvard University Press, 2008), 167.

TOWARD A RADICAL DEMOCRATIC
EMANCIPATORY PEDAGOGY

In the following section, I therefore will sketch four examples, each of which attempts to articulate a pedagogical model of agency, contextuality, interaction, and difference. These four examples have been developed within the circumference of the fourth paradigm, and all four provide crucial steps toward a full radical democratic emancipatory model.

A Feminist Pedagogical Model

I begin by discussing the development of a feminist pedagogical model that laid important groundwork toward the democratization of biblical interpretation, since it claimed full citizenship for wo/men who had been excluded for centuries from academic biblical studies. In the first book dedicated to feminist pedagogy in the*logical studies, titled *Your Daughters Shall Prophesy: Feminist Alternatives in Theological Education*, the Cornwall Collective discusses seven alternative experiments developed in the 1970s and early 1980s: The Center for Women and Religion of the Graduate Theological Union in Berkeley, the Women's Theological Coalition of the Boston Theological Institute, Black Women in Ministry, the Research and Resource Associate Program at Harvard Divinity School, the Seminary Quarter at Grailville, Training Women for Ministry at Andover Newton Theological School, and the Women Counseling Team at Union Theological Seminary in New York.[25]

According to the book's introduction, it is the fruit of a collaborative effort to develop a feminist understanding of the*logical education. Since members of the Collective were convinced that "collective reflection on shared experience" is crucial for a the*logy "appropriate to a pluralistic world," the Collective chose these seven programs as their "experiential base" and invited nineteen wo/men "to reflect together on the insights drawn from such experiences."[26] The group was eager to discuss "how what we learn is shaped by the person with whom we learn"; to explore "racism and the responsibility of white women in theological education"; to inquire as to "how marginality engenders

---

25. The Cornwall Collective, *Your Daughters Shall Prophesy: Feminist Alternatives in Theological Education* (New York: Pilgrim Press, 1980).
26. Ibid., xiv.

alternative leadership styles"; to investigate "the forms of power and the possibility of institutional change." The group also articulated the following eight tenets that inspire and shape feminist movements for liberation:

—Reflection on experience is an essential starting point for learning . . . and for acting toward systemic change.

—Naming and transforming the images and symbols of the spiritual dimensions of our lives is integral to seeking wholeness.

—Shared and collective styles of leadership act to affirm equality within relationships in institutions and overcome the dominant/ subordinate styles of hierarchical decision making.

—Equity in access to power and decision making requires the redistribution of power as well as new images of power.

—The personal is political and the political is personal.

—Women have the right to determine their own lives, including their bodies.

—Feminists share a commitment to developing a worldview through a collective process that is inclusive of persons of differing race, class, age, sexual preference, nationality, and faith.

—Hope becomes present, manifesting itself in empowerment now, rather than projected into a future vision.[27]

In sum, the Cornwall Collective emphasized that their reflections are part of a "journey" of feminists in the*logical education, "a journey of many women engaged in a collaborative struggle to confront sexism and racism in theological education."[28] Hence, the Collective stressed struggle and discussed the sites of struggle (sexuality, race, and gender domination) at length. In so doing it sought to articulate "a worldview through a collective process."[29] The Collective's emphasis that educational structures must be changed so that wo/men can become equal academic citizens has become the sine qua non of feminist the*logical analysis and practice.

In subsequent years, identity politics and social location have shaped feminist discourses. A rich feminist debate and literature ensued that articulated feminist the*logy and biblical studies in terms of social location, cultural identity, and religious perspective. Since hegemonic biblical studies and education do not specifically address the hermeneutical

27. Ibid., 106–18.
28. Ibid., 113.
29. Ibid., 111 n. 7.

problems that arise when the sociopolitical locations of teachers and students are taken into account, feminist biblical studies focused not just on the exegesis of text but especially also on hermeneutical questions that the discipline had not critically considered.

To address these issues, I have sought to develop a pedagogical model that can affirm the diversity, the common vision, and the agency of all biblical interpreters. This model has two educational components: (1) a systemic analysis of the structures and mind-sets of domination, and (2) stress on the agency and struggle of the marginalized and excluded voices of the fourth paradigm. Both seek to foster responsible diversity, while at the same time seeking to articulate a critique and vision common to all the different directions and struggles in the fourth paradigm.

Hegemonic scholarship denies students the tools for investigating the ideologies, discourses, and knowledges that shape their self-identity and determine their lives. Instead of empowering students as critical thinkers, education in general and biblical education in particular often contributes to their self-alienation and conformity to the values and mores of hegemonic kyriarchal societies and religions. Hence, a feminist emancipatory, radical democratic model of education is not so much interested in inculcating traditional biblical teachings and malestream scientific knowledges as it is in fostering critical thinking on sociopolitical contexts and locations, and motivating the power to envision a different world. Its basic assumption is that knowledge is publicly available to all who can think and that everyone has something to contribute to knowledge. Radical democracy is sustained by the quality of vision and civic imagination of its citizens.

Such a mode of a critical feminist analysis does not emphasize diversity, fluidity, and indecidability as much as it stresses agency, struggle, and transformation. Its focus is not text, but interpreters, authors, recipients, and interpretive communities in their sociopolitical contexts. Such a focus on agency and praxis goes against the grain of conservative neoliberal postmodern fluidity, indeterminacy, and the deconstruction of the subject. From its very beginnings, feminist pedagogy has insisted on the analysis of structures of domination, paying attention to how they shape access to educational resources, regulate and limit decision making, enforce decisions, shape the "hidden curriculum," and formulate standards of excellence that serve as criteria of inclusion or exclusion concerning what constitutes academic competence, who is admitted to graduate studies, or who is hired by specifying the needs of programs.

A Contextual Pedagogical Model

Although not explicitly feminist, many of the essays collected by Fernando Segovia and Mary Ann Tolbert in *Reading from This Place*,[30] as well as by Gerald West in *Reading Other-Wise: Socially Engaged Biblical Scholars Reading with Their Local Communities*,[31] reflect the feminist work of the years since *Your Daughters Shall Prophesy* was published. Whereas *Reading from This Place* mirrors the dazzling pluralism of social locations and raises the difficulty of communication between individuals whose identity is constituted by such different sociopolitical-cultural locations, *Reading Other-Wise* insists that communities of faith, especially the poor and disenfranchised, must become actively involved in biblical interpretation.[32] What is therefore necessary is that biblical scholars become skilled in interpretation "with" the poor.[33]

Following the lead of Gerald West and Bob Ekblad,[34] Robert Williamson Jr. of Emory University shares his experience of developing a course titled "Reading Job from the Margins." This course sought to investigate four reading sites where students in groups of two or three explored the book of Job and its questions about suffering and G*d. One group read Job with inmates at a wo/men's prison, another with senior citizens, a third group read with people in a homeless shelter, and a fourth with a truly transient and unhoused population. The class also met together once a week to discuss the book of Job and their experience at these different sites of reading.[35]

In critically reflecting on the course process, Williamson points out that the workload was not only heavy and students did not have sufficient time for an exegesis of Job, but also that "the problem inherent in courses of this nature is the possibility of exploiting or exoticizing our

30. Fernando Segovia and Mary Ann Tolbert, eds., *Reading from This Place: Social Location and Biblical Interpretation*, 2 vols. (Minneapolis: Fortress Press, 1995–2000).

31. Gerald West, ed., *Reading Other-Wise: Socially Engaged Biblical Scholars Reading with Their Local Communities*, Semeia Studies 62 (Atlanta: Society of Biblical Literature, 2007).

32. See also James R. Cochrane, *Circles of Dignity: Community Wisdom and Theological Reflection* (Minneapolis: Fortress Press, 1999).

33. Whereas West has developed such a reading with the poor in South Africa, the Centro de Estudos Bíblicos has developed a popular Bible reading in Brazil, which is grounded in the reality of the poor and has social and political relevance. It presupposes that the Bible is liberative and transformative without subjecting it first to a hermeneutics of suspicion. In her forthcoming dissertation, Isabel Félix will compare this approach with my own.

34. Bob Ekblad, *Reading the Bible with the Damned* (Louisville, KY: Westminster John Knox Press, 2005); see also Miguel A. De La Torre, *Reading the Bible from the Margins* (Maryknoll, NY: Orbis Books, 2002).

35. Robert Williamson Jr., "Reading Job from the Margins: Dialogical Exegesis and Theological Education," *Society of Biblical Literature Forum* (n.p.: cited June 2008), http://www.sbl-site.org/publications/article.aspx?articleId=777 (accessed April 9, 2009).

reading partners." This observation indicates that "Dialogical Exegesis" or "Reading With" is not a radical democratic endeavor as long as it does not engage in a critical analysis of oppressive social structures and understand itself as a process of conscientization. Moreover, it reinscribes the dichotomy between the professional and the general reader insofar as it does not equally problematize the social-institutional location of the professional reader.

This contextual pedagogical model is heavily influenced by Latin American Liberation The*logy. It is thus situated within the fourth emancipatory paradigm of biblical studies. But like liberation the*logy, its primary location has been the first the*logical paradigm of biblical studies. It is based on the assumption that the Bible is a liberating book that has first been addressed as "glad tidings" to the poor and marginalized, and so the poor and disenfranchised are those who best understand the liberating biblical Word. Since it is heavily rooted in a social class analytic, it does not problematize kyriocentric language and rhetoric in a hermeneutics of suspicion as a critical feminist model does.

A Didactic Model of Interreligious Communication

In my view, the pedagogical model of Scriptural Reasoning can be situated within the perimeter of the fourth paradigm, although it is heavily indebted to the first the*logical paradigm and does not make explicit emancipatory claims. Scriptural Reasoning is a pedagogical model that stresses differences and communication between persons coming from different religious locations. Although this model advocates an interactive model of interpretation with reference to the sacredness of Scriptures, it nevertheless has gained some purchase in the academy: it has created its own journal, *The Journal of Scriptural Reasoning*, and has even developed a doctoral concentration at the University of Virginia.[36] These are accomplishments that the critical feminist, contextual, intercultural, and postcolonial models lack.

Scriptural Reasoning brings Jews, Christians, and Muslims together in groups to discuss the meaning of their sacred texts. According to the Jewish scholar Peter Ochs, Scriptural Reasoning is an academic practice

---

36. For a bibliography on Scriptural Reasoning, see http://etext.lib.virginia.edu/journals/jsrforum/biblio.html (accessed April 9, 2009).

as well as a religious or the*logical practice. As academic practice, it insists that

—Study is a group as well as an individual activity.
—The primary intellectual virtue is reading the sources well.
—Group study should address at least two different scriptural sources and scriptural traditions.
—Comparative interpretations should be stimulated by a range of interests and should draw out the implications of scriptural studies for addressing contemporary intellectual and societal debates.

Ochs also lines out specific aspects of the the*logical practice of Scriptural Reasoning:

—The English term *Scripture* connotes the sanctified writing and reading of the records of a tradition.
—People turn to Scripture for guidance on how to understand and act in the world.
—*Scriptural Reasoning* presupposes both that G*d's instruction is revealed in Scripture and that what is revealed cannot be immediately seen in the plain sense of the words. Rather the grammar, the historical contexts, and the semantic fields are the pathways deep into Scripture.
—The plain sense "speaks for eternity," but the deeper meaning is disclosed only for the time and place of the interpreter.
—Seeking the deeper sense of Scripture is a form of prayer.
—The process of understanding is dialogical. It is assumed that the interpreter addresses G*d and believes that G*d answers, at which point the interpreter asks a deeper question and G*d answers back; this process continues and repeats itself.
—Scriptural Reasoning seeks to bring the eschatological future into the present.
—Individual words generate not single meanings but broad fields of meaning.
—To search for Scripture's deeper meaning involves not only prayer and the traditions but also conversations in the study fellow groups.
—Each member of a study fellowship, however, is a member first of a distinct religious tradition of study and practice.

—Scriptural Reasoning prevents participants from generalizing about the way a Scripture will be named and maintained within a tradition.

—However, Scriptural Reasoning challenges the presupposition that there is only one scripture we can call "scripture."[37]

David Ford, in turn, advocates Scriptural Reasoning as a model for high-quality debate and a practice modeling twentieth-century citizenship. Unlike the rhetoric of pluralist religious dialogue, scriptural reasoning does not conceal disagreements and conflicts but seeks to make them public in a nonviolent way. Ford stresses the priority of group study "to which everyone brings their own scripture or internal libraries."[38] He outlines the following maxims for participants:

—Acknowledge *the sacredness* of the others' scriptures to them.
—The "native speakers" hosting a scripture and its tradition must acknowledge that they do not exclusively own their scriptures.
—The aim is not consensus but the recognition of deep differences.
—Do not be afraid of *argument*.
—Draw on *shared academic resources* to build understanding.
—Allow time to read and reread, to ask many questions and entertain alternative possibilities of understanding.
—Read, interpret, and discuss scripture with a view toward the fulfillment of G*d's purpose of peace between all.
—Be open to mutual hospitality turning into friendship.[39]

Ford sums up the purpose of Scriptural Reasoning in this way:

The picture of a collegiality of intensive study and conversation that emerges from such description might be seen as boundary-crossing liturgy. This gathers in hospitality and friendship members of academic institutions whose primary communities are synagogue, church and mosque. Its quasi-liturgical character is appropriate, since it is likely that study of scripture which acknowledges the presence of G*d (variously identified) comes as close to worshipping together as faithful members of these three traditions can come with integrity.[40]

37. See http://etext.lib.virginia.edu/journals/jsrforum/writings/OchFeat.html (accessed April 9, 2009).

38. See reference to Arif Ali Nayed, "Reading Scripture Together: Towards a Sacred Hermeneutic of Togetherness," presented at a Scriptural Reasoning Conference in Cambridge, UK, June 2003, and published in *The Promise of Scriptural Reasoning*, ed. David Ford and C. C. Pecknold (Malden, MA: Blackwell Publishing, 2006), 4 n. 12.

39. David Ford, "An Interfaith Wisdom: Scriptural Reasoning between Jews, Christians and Muslims," in Ford and Pecknold, *The Promise of Scriptural Reasoning*, 1–22, here 57.

40. Ibid., 7.

While this pedagogical model of Scriptural Reasoning has one foot in the fourth emancipative paradigm of interpretation insofar as it enables dialogue and fosters respect between different religions that have often interpreted their Scriptures as divine weapons against each other, it does not seek to transform the first the*logical paradigm of interpretation in terms of the methodological approach of the fourth paradigm. However, it does articulate radical equality and respect for differences as the basis for interreligious interpretation and thereby contributes a significant element to the pedagogy of the fourth emancipatory paradigm.

A Postcolonial Pedagogical Model

A postcolonial pedagogical model of difference and indeterminacy has been developed by Fernando Segovia. Segovia underscores the importance of recognizing difference and diversity as central to the pedagogy of the fourth paradigm of biblical studies and has proposed this comprehensive pedagogical program within a postcolonial framework. Yet as Segovia himself points out, the model is of a theoretical rather than a practical nature.[41] His proposal deals with pedagogical discourse in the abstract rather than with concrete proposals for curriculum structure and teaching approaches.

Segovia's pedagogical model envisions diversity in methods, emphasizes context and perspective, calls readers to become agents of the process of interpretation, and abandons the model of passive reception in favor of self-conscious, highly critical, and global dialogue that is multicultural and multilingual and includes many different voices. He points to the profoundly Western character of biblical studies and the deleterious consequences of that focus for those living outside Western culture and for minorities within the West. In light of this, he argues for the basic principle of taking into account the lives of the Other and urges the discipline to become less Western, more global, and more inclusive. Segovia's proposal not only stresses diversity but also underscores the reality of empire, imperialism, and colonialism. Hence, Segovia's proposal advances a postcolonial and intercultural pedagogy. The goal of his model is not to satisfy intellectual curiosity but to bring a critical engagement with texts and readings. This postcolonial model stresses

---

41. Fernando F. Segovia, "Pedagogical Discourse and Practices in Cultural Studies," in *Decolonizing Biblical Studies: A View from the Margins* (Maryknoll, NY: Orbis Books, 2000), 87–115, here 111.

a fourfold diversity: diversity in text, diversity in readings, diversity in paradigm, and diversity in readers.

1. *Diversity in text* assumes that there are many different voices inscribed in the text. It also encompasses a diversity of text that includes all extant early Christian writings and radically throws into question any canonical approach. The diversity of voices within texts and within cultures places texts within the overall sociocultural framework of the period under consideration. Such a diversity of voices calls for a combination of formalist, practical, and cultural methods in terms of intercultural criticism, with the goal of discovering the reality of texts as Others in their own right. Since Segovia attempts to prevent any overriding of texts by positing texts as Others, he comes close to historical criticism's stress on the "rights of the text," but in distinction to it he insists on a polyglot, polyvalent, and fluid view of meaning and text. No final and finite determination of text is possible.

2. Segovia stresses *diversity in readings* on three different levels, which encompass the diversity of reading traditions. These levels are as follows:

—academic disciplinary readings, which need to be distinguished from
—religious institutional, devotional, spiritual, and from
—popular modes of reading.

The pedagogical goal of diversity in readings is to take seriously the sociocultural context of Western colonialism and imperialism of the past four hundred years. It seeks to recover the subjugated voices of those dominated and silenced in history. Though I agree with Segovia in this goal, I need to point out that wo/men's dehumanization and oppression is much older than Western colonialism; hence, a postcolonial reading needs to team up with a critical feminist one. Moreover, for both to achieve the pedagogical goal of diversity in readings and to fashion a "text" of one's own that is not imperial-colonial, an ethics of interpretation needs to be developed.

3. The *diversity of disciplinary paradigms* requires an analysis of the beginnings of the discipline and of historical criticism as its dominant mode for a century. Moreover, the diversity within each of the disciplinary paradigms of interpretation asks for an expansive knowledge of the major lines of interpretation: an articulation of a metatheory that underlies different interpretive strategies and models within each paradigm and explains their relationship with each other. It requires

sophisticated knowledge and education that enables one to interact with a variety of interpretive models. Graduate students need to have knowledge of all the paradigms, but in the process of specialization they have to make a choice as to which paradigm they will work within since they cannot master all of them. Hence, it is important that they learn to speak the different theoretical languages of the disciplinary paradigms as well as to theorize their own social location and standpoint in one of them.

4. With *diversity in readers*, Segovia distinguishes between diverse intratextual readers and diverse extratextual readers—the real flesh-and-blood readers. This distinction encompasses the dichotomies of individual and social readers, of compliant and resisting readers.

This diversity results in a multilingual, multicultural, and multi-centered cacophony of voices in the contemporary marketplace. In this process, "the flesh and blood readers come to be looked upon as 'texts' themselves—constantly engaged as they are, whether implicitly or explicitly, in a process of 'self' construction."[42] Consequently, they must be studied as "texts." This theory, understanding readers as "constructs," creates an incredible din of readers. It asserts that all readers are textual constructions and hence, like texts, are undecidable and multivalent.

Yet the intercultural model of reading the imperial-colonial framework has as its goal critical engagement with other readers in dialogue and struggle, since sooner or later there is always resistance to the imperial center from those who are a part of the politically, economically, culturally, and religiously subordinated margins. Such resistance has occurred in biblical studies within the last quarter of the twentieth century. At the same time, however, these disciplinary changes have taken place in the age of neocolonialism, which has engendered two groups of readers: those associated with the imperial traditions of the West, and those associated with the colonies of the empires. Such colonial dualism is not able to get hold of the complexity of either struggles or transformations.

In a concluding section, Segovia not only stresses the theoretical character of his pedagogical proposal over the practical; he also recognizes that it is restricted to academic readers who are highly privileged, whose work reaches only a very limited audience, and who are ever tempted by competition and superiority toward others who are less

42. Ibid., 109.

educated. Nevertheless, his sketch does amply document the rich diversity of the fourth paradigm and its interpretations or readings.

However, such rich diversity of texts and readings also raises the practical question as to how competence can be achieved in all these different areas, approaches, and methods. What educational practices would achieve basic competence, not only in the fourth paradigm, but also with respect to scholars' ability to dialogue with the other three? Moreover, how can general interpreters or readers gain basic knowledge of the interpretive process so that they can benefit from the work of the professional interpreter? Is the difference between scholarly and general readers only a difference of degree, or is it one of dependency?

Furthermore, many of the differences celebrated in the fourth paradigm are constructed in a dualistic fashion of "over-and-againstness": wo/men over and against men, blacks over and against whites, colonialized over and against colonizer, Asians over and against Westerners, third world over and against first world, and so on. The consequence is that each group develops and stresses its own analysis of domination independently from each other rather than interstructurally. Sexuality-, gender-, race-, class-, imperial-, religious-, and cultural-analyses are deployed independently of each other, although the situations and lives of wo/men are determined by all these intersecting structures of domination. Hence, it is important to create a radical democratic pedagogical model that is dialogical and deliberative, able to critically reflect on identity formation and on cultural-religious location, socialization, and education.

TRANSFORMING THE DIDACTIC TRIANGLE

To change biblical studies, according to my argument here, those of us who have situated our work in the emancipatory space of the fourth paradigm need to articulate a *different*, cointentional, radical democratic pedagogy of biblical reflection/learning/reading. This pedagogy would allow scholars and general readers to become collaborators in the creation as well as in the critical communication of the contents and methods of biblical knowledge. Rather than continue the dualistic rhetoric of over-and-againstness, we need to envision and negotiate differences and diversity within a common analytic space of an intersectional ethics of interpretation and create institutional structures that can invigorate and sustain the work of the fourth paradigm.

A Radical Democratic Pedagogy

Such a political, radical egalitarian pedagogical model is situated in the public space of the cosmopolis[43] or the *ekklēsia* of wo/men. In a radical democratic pedagogical model, both scholars and general readers recognize that biblical knowledge is power, which can serve either domination or liberation. Power can be understood in two very different ways: either in kyriocentric terms as control and power over, or in radical democratic terms as energy that moves us and invigorates life. Hence, it is important to critically investigate the power relations of malestream pedagogy and didactics.

To articulate and practice an emancipatory democratic ethos, I argue that in the process of interpretation, the fourth paradigm—positioned within the radical democratic space opened up by the liberation struggles of marginalized wo/men for freedom and autonomy—needs to integrate experience and imagination, emotion and feelings, valuation and vision, critical inquiry, scientific accuracy, intellectual clarity, and responsible persuasion. Moreover, such a radical democratic ethos must assert the subjectivity and agency of wo/men in kyriarchal texts, cultures, and religions. With Alicia Suskin Ostriker, we must insist that such a radical democratic educational approach be

> engaged both theoretically and practically in the question of what will happen when the spiritual imagination of women, women who may call themselves Jews or Christians, pagans or atheists, witches or worshippers of the Great Goddess, is released into language and into history.[44]

Because of the all-too-human need to use the Bible to bolster our identity over and against that of others, because of the need for using the Bible as a security blanket—as an avenue for controlling the divine, or as a means for possessing revelatory knowledge as an exclusive privilege—biblical interpreters are ever tempted to build up securing walls and to keep out those who are not like us. Thus the fourth emancipatory paradigm of biblical studies is best understood in a radical democratic key, insisting that all wo/men are competent biblical interpreters. It seeks to facilitate wo/men's critical readings by fostering examination of our own presuppositions and social locations.

43. See Kwame Anthony Appiah, *Cosmopolitanism: Ethics in a World of Strangers* (New York: W. W. Norton, 2006).
44. Alicia Suskin Ostriker, *Feminist Revision and the Bible* (Cambridge, MA: Blackwell Publishers, 1993), 30.

According to Frances Moore Lappé, democracy begins with the creation of a "culture of connection" that fosters "relationships of mutual respect": relationships that emerge only if participants feel like decision-making citizens rather than victims or spectators. One of the most important "arts of democracy" is the ability to use disagreement and conflict creatively, since a democratic process and culture is all about change.[45] Hence, emancipatory Bible study needs to seek freedom from cultural centricity or bias and religious prejudice and try to replace them with critical arguments that appeal to reason *and* to the emotions. If such Bible study wants to further self-scrutiny and the ability to imagine what it would be like to be in the shoes of someone different from oneself, what it would be like to see the world from the point of view of another who is not like oneself but still much like oneself—then it needs to develop pedagogical practices that foster such difference in equality. It requires us to make sure that books—even Bibles—and authors/teachers do not become unquestioned "authorities."

Instead of using the Bible as a religious or cultural security blanket, a radical democratic model of biblical education has to equip its practitioners for critical questioning and debate in order to be able to arrive at deliberative judgments about the Bible's contributions to the "good life," to democratic self-determination and self-esteem. It is about choice and deliberation and the power to take charge of our own life and thought, rather than about control, dependence, obedience, and passive reception. Its style of reasoning is not combative-competitive but deliberative, engaging in conversations about values and beliefs that are most important to us rather than retreating into positivism, dogmatism, or relativism, which avoids engagement with differences.[46]

In such an emancipatory pedagogical model, thought and study are problem oriented rather than positivistic or dogmatic—perspectival rather than relativistic. They are contextual-collaborative, recognizing that our own perspective and knowledge are limited by our social-religious location and that differences enrich our thought and life. Truth and meaning are not a given fact or hidden revelation but are achieved in critical practices of deliberation. In short, to be able to

---

45. Frances Moore Lappé, *Democracy's Edge: Choosing to Save Our Country by Bringing Democracy Alive* (San Francisco: Jossey-Bass, 2006), 251–76.

46. See Victor J. Klimoski, Kevin O'Neil, and Katarina M. Schuth, *Educating Leaders for Ministry: Issues and Responses* (Collegeville, MN: Liturgical Press, 2005), who point to four overarching challenges that faculty and administrators face today in theological education: theological differences, learning differences, integration, and assessment. However, they do not elaborate contextual differences and education for a radical democratic ministry.

achieve a constructive engagement with the difference and diversity inscribed in the Bible and in our contexts, we need to become aware of the pitfalls of one-dimensional thinking that strives to use the Bible to find definite answers and "final solutions."[47]

The ethos of a value-free scientific pedagogy abstracted from any social context, in turn, is articulated within the value system of kyriarchal authority, where students/readers silently absorb the materials on which the professor/author lectures. In contrast, a radical democratic model of education seeks to foster a style of biblical learning/teaching that does not undermine democratic thinking. Instead, it seeks to support and strengthen democratic modes of reasoning by recognizing the importance of experience, plural voices, emotions, and values in the educational process.

In contrast to a radical democratic pedagogical model, the educational process of a value-free scientific pedagogy is usually diagrammed in the Didactic Triangle, an articulation of the relations between teacher, knowledge, and students in terms of a pyramid in which either knowledge or the teacher can be on top. If knowledge is on the top of the didactic triangle—often expressed in terms of the curriculum—then the body of knowledge studied determines the relationship between teacher and students. If the teacher is on top, s/he determines the relationship between knowledge and students. In the first case, curricular knowledge is understood as a given to be transmitted from teacher to student; in the second case, the teacher is the subject of the process and selects knowledge to transmit to the students.

In both instances, the didactic relations are diagrammed in kyriarchal terms as relations of ruling and submitting. For the first arrangement, both teachers and students have to submit to and accept scientific knowledge in whose production they have not been involved; in the second arrangement, students have to internalize the scientific knowledge presented by the teacher either in terms of the lecture within the banking model or in terms of the seminar model of master/apprentice relations. Both forms of the pyramidal didactic triangle are operating in kyriarchal terms.

47. See Ostriker, *Feminist Revision and the Bible*, 122–23: "Human civilization has a stake in plural readings. We've seen this at least since the eighteenth century when the notion of religious tolerance was invented to keep the Christian sects from killing each other. The notion of racial tolerance came later. . . . Most people need 'right' answers, just as they need 'superior' races. . . . At this particular moment it happens to be feminists and other socially marginal types who are battling for cultural pluralism. Still, this is an activity we're undertaking on behalf of humanity, all of whom would be the happier, I believe, were they to give up their addiction to final solutions."

A radical democratic didactic model would need to diagram the didactic relationship between teacher, learner, and knowledge in a way that could articulate a radical equality of mutual respect between teacher, students, and knowledge. The image that comes to mind is that of a spiraling circle in which both teachers and students work to deconstruct and reconstruct scientific knowledge. Such radical equality does not mean that teacher and students are the same. Rather, it means that both teacher and students bring their different capabilities and knowledges to the task of creating new knowledge in a way that is critically interactive with the body of knowledge and scholarship already available.

Equalizing the Didactic Process:
Theme-Centered Interaction (TCI)

Theme-Centered Interaction (TCI)[48] spells out a method for working with groups that seeks to engender an active, creative, and discovering process of "living learning." This approach was developed by Ruth C. Cohn, a humanistic psychoanalyst and a Jewish émigré from Berlin, who was also trained in the Gestalt therapy of Fritz Perls.[49] Ruth Cohn's development of TCI was politically motivated. She wanted to create a pedagogy that could oppose the Nazi mind-set of the time and compel people to become engaged in politics. In her work *Gelebte Geschichte der Psychotherapie*, she writes:

> I want to encourage people who do not want all this suffering, not to resign themselves to it and to feel powerless, but to use their powers of imagination and of action to express and practice solidarity as long as we still feel autonomous power in ourselves. This is in essence what I want to achieve with TCI. (my translation)[50]

Cohn is convinced that persons are neither omnipotent nor powerless but rather are all partially powerful.[51] She insists on the autonomy of

---

48. See Mary Anne Kübel, ed., *Living Learning: A Reader in Theme-Centered Interaction* (Delhi: Media House, 2002).

49. Ruth Cohn's work has been very influential in the German-speaking parts of Europe because, in 1966, she founded the "Workshop for Living Learning" (WILL) and, in 1987, WILL International, to train group leaders in her method.

50. Ruth C. Cohn and Alfred Farau, *Gelebte Geschichte der Psychotherapie: Zwei Perspektiven*, 2nd ed. (Stuttgart: Klett-Cotta, 1993), 374.

51. Ibid., 359.

persons but relativizes it in terms of interdependence and with reference to the world.

> I want to do what I am doing. I am I.
> You want to do what you are doing. You are you.
> The world is our task. It does not meet our expectations.
> However, if we commit ourselves to it, it will become beautiful.
> If we don't, it won't.[52]

According to Cohn, every learning situation consists of four factors: (1) the individual (the I) who articulates the motivations, interests, personal histories, and levels of involvement of the individual participants—that is, the baggage and contributions they bring to (2) the group (the WE). The WE connotes the dynamics and types of relationships that form in the group. (3) The problem, topic, or theme (the IT) represents the subject and content of the training. (4) The GLOBE is the organizational environment of the training and the wider context of the participants. Cohn's approach and goal can be succinctly expressed and diagrammed (see the diagram).

From an ethical position, the four factors mean the following:

—We perceive and respect ourselves as persons; that as a part of our responsibility for ourselves and for others we can become more aware of our own wishes, abilities, and possibilities along with their brighter and darker aspects in order to decide and act more personally and with more integrity (factor: I).

—We respect this same importance in self-leadership in every other person and try to behave appropriately (factor: WE).

—We see the community experience in a group as the attention to our common relevant task (factor: IT).

—Our ability to be conscious and responsible is capable of expansion and can be applied, beyond a particular interactional group, on the levels of our local community, the nation, humankind, all life on this planet. This is a transpersonal and transcendental factor: the GLOBE. The Globe is thus comprised of a series of concentric circles that range from nearby to far away.[53]

It is important that participants identify and consider on which of the four levels the discussion is moving: whether it is on the I-level,

---

52. Ruth C. Cohn, "Die Selbsterfahrungsbewegung: Autismus oder Autonomy?" *Gruppendynamik* 5 (1974): 160–71, here 164.
53. Kübel, *Living Learning*, 399–402.

Theme-Centered Interaction

(Ruth C. Cohn)

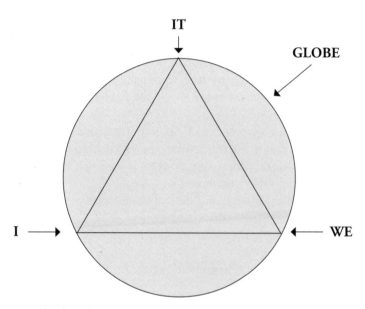

Figure 1: The four factors are depicted in the model of a triangle within a circle. This image signifies the foundation of a humanistic ethics.

the WE-level, the It-level, or the Globe-level. The goal is the dialogical integration of all four levels of speaking so that the whole group can engage in a fruitful and constructive discussion. If the group does not manage to do this, the discussion becomes trapped and cannot move on. Conversely, if participants speak only on the I-level or the WE-level, the group is caught in group-process debates. Hence, it is important to hold all four factors in creative tension and to notice on which level the discussion moves.

For instance, someone could raise the question of theoretical differences in biblical studies on the IT-level, but another participant of the group may understand the question on the I-level and think he is criticizing her; the result will be a misunderstanding. Or one participant might raise a critical question about how to deal with the differences in biblical studies on the Globe(context)-level. However, if all participants understand her question on the WE-level rather than on the Globe-level, they might think that she wants to underscore the conflicts in the group and may react negatively to her intervention.

To help groups to get unstuck, Ruth Cohn has formulated specific discussion rules that focus on the I- and WE- level of group exchanges. These are as follows:

1. Speak in the I-form and not as "we" or "one." Be your own chair wo/man, which means take responsibility for yourself. Decide when and what you want to say, and select what is important for you.
2. Pay attention to your and other participants' body language. Articulate and make transparent the motivation and background of your own reactions, questions, and feelings, and refrain from interpreting other's statements.
3. Choose what you say, and do and be selective in your communication.
4. Don't interpret the statement of others but instead express your personal reactions.
5. Don't generalize ("Everybody says . . . ") but be specific ("I think . . . ").
6. Mark your statements as personal impressions and not as judgments.
7. Individual discussions between a few members of the group rather than the whole group require that attention be paid to these members, not so much because they are "interruptions" but because they signal problems to be attended to.
8. Only one person can speak at a time.
9. If several persons make suggestions at the same time, stop and identify and number the suggestions so they can be discussed one after the other. Here it is good to nominate a moderator for the session.

This TCI process can be applied in different contexts and situations. For instance, in a Roman Catholic context and on the basis of TCI, Matthias Scharer has coedited the series on Kommunikative Theologie and also developed a five-semester MA program in Kommunikative Theologie at the University of Innsbruck.[54] Leony Renk, who is a Protestant minister and adult educator, has integrated TCI and Bibliodrama: a form of role-playing that enacts scenarios involv-

---

54. I am grateful to Professor Mary Ann Hinsdale for drawing my attention to this work.

ing characters—read literally or creatively imagined—from the biblical worlds. Over the years in workshops with women, she has used TCI to develop an approach to Bibliodrama that differs from other approaches insofar as she has defined Bibliodrama in feminist terms and explicated the significance of the political context of the "Globe." Bibliodrama on the basis of TCI allows for feminist transformation. Each dramatized biblical text is approached with a hermeneutic of suspicion and critically interrogated in light of the experience of the participants. In a hermeneutics of creative imagination, the text is re-visioned in and through the process of Bibliodrama.[55]

The method of TCI lends itself to bringing together wo/men from different religions and cultures. Scharer has done so by organizing international conferences of scholars, whereas Renk has used TCI especially for dialogues between Jewish and Christian wo/men, but also for conversations between Jewish, Christian, secular, and Muslim wo/men. For instance, the story of Hagar (Gen. 21) plays a significant role in all three Abrahamic religions. Participants can thus connect with Hagar on different levels of engagement and dramatically explore the themes of the story in many ways, examining how these have been used to deepen misunderstandings between the religions. Renk sums up this experience:

> The more we interrogate our faith-experiences anew in the context of our knowledge and experience, as to how they have been misused in the past, the more helpful becomes such knowledge for us and hence for our society. As members of the different religions we— everyone for herself and everyone for one to another—must unlearn to be the sole owner of the truth. Therefore interreligious and intercultural meetings are significant and further the work of peace. (my translation)[56]

To sum up my argument: The TCI approach has a radically democratic potential insofar as it insists on the fundamental equality and responsibility of the I's that form the WE. Thus TCI replaces the slot of "teacher" in the didactic triangle with that of the I who is its own chairperson, leader, and teacher. True, TCI still trains group leaders who are charged with the task of keeping the four TCI factors in creative balance, but they are

55. Antje Röckemann, "In Spiralen Fliegen: Bibliodrama and TZI interkulturell," in *In Spiralen Fliegen: Bibliodrama and TZI [Themenzentrierte Interaktion] interkulturell*, ed. Margarete Pauschert and Antje Röckemann (Münster: Schlangenbrut, 1999), 7–13, here 11.

56. Leony Renk, "Interkulturelles Lernen mit dem Globe: Interreligiöse und interkulturelle Begegnungen im Bibliodrama," in *Interreligiöses Bibliodrama: Bibliodrama als neuer Weg zur christlich-jüdischen Begegnung*, ed. Leony Renk, Bibliodrama-Kontexte 6 (Schenefeld [Hamburg]: EB-Verlag, 2005), 69–84, here 83.

integrated in the group process as part of the WE.[57] Hence, TCI seeks to constitute the WE as an interactive congregation of different-but-equal I's who are focused on a common problem or task. Thereby TCI intends to foster a culture of mutual recognition and autonomy in interdependence. Moreover, it contextualizes the four TCI factors—the I, the WE and the IT—with the GLOBE, the world and all its beings. However, it is not able to sociopolitically locate the I and the WE because TCI has not developed a critical systemic analysis of the GLOBE.

Such an analysis is necessary because the structures and ideologies of domination, as we saw in chapter 3, provide sociocultural, religious, and political identity slots that prioritize how people learn to understand themselves and how they treat and are treated by others. Focusing only on one or two of the discourses of domination rather than on the way in which all of them interact and contribute to the production of domination and exclusion—such limited focusing leads at best to a dual-system analysis that reproduces differences in terms of structural divisions. Such analysis uncovers the dynamics underlying—for instance—either a gender or imperialist structural location, either a race or a class one, but does not lead to a comprehensive analysis of all the intersecting multiplicative structures of domination. It often leads to a confessional stance of fixed identity rather than to a careful analysis of socio-religious contextual structural location and critical reflection on one's own subject location. Hence, it is important to develop a didactic process that compels its participants to carefully reflect on their socioreligious contextualization as individuals, as group, and with regard to the subject matter under discussion.

Developing a Critical Analysis of the Globe

Although Ruth C. Cohn sought to enable people to make the world a better place with her method, in the development of her method, the factor Globe has not been sufficiently articulated and integrated. Since her model and method have been developed primarily in psychotherapeutic terms, TCI has not paid sufficient attention to explicating the Globe and making this explication central to the TCI process.[58] Hence, Silvia

---

57. I have not, however, found much reflection on this tension in the literature.
58. Hartmut Raguse, "Kritische Bestandaufnahme der TZI," in *TZI [Themen Zentrierte Interaktion]: Pädagogisch-therapeutische Gruppenarbeit nach Ruth C. Cohn*, ed. Cornelia Löhmer und Rüdiger Standhardt (Stuttgart: Kletta-Cotta, 1992), 264–77, here 273.

Hagleitner has sought to integrate the political-liberationist approach of Paulo Freire with Ruth C. Cohn's psychotherapeutic approach in order to develop a feminist political educational framework, one for which the Globe is central.

Hagleitner argues that the approach of Paulo Freire is necessary for political educational work with TCI, and that political educational work with Paulo Freire's theory needs the approach of TCI.[59] Such an integration of the two approaches is possible because both Cohn and Freire see suffering and oppression in the world not as given and unchangeable, but as produced by people and therefore changeable. They both underscore the dialectics between social situations and the possibility to change them. The recognition of human capabilities to act and decide as well as conviction of the changeability and transformability of sociohistorical situations is the starting point for both in the development of their different sociopedagogical theories of action. Both have as their pedagogical goal the activation of people to sympathetic engagement (Cohn) and to revolutionary praxis (Freire).[60]

Hagleitner sees the fact that the "Globe" is not defined clearly and is understood in universalistic, generalizing, and nonspecific terms as a lacuna in the TCI model. Since TCI lacks a critical sociopolitical analysis of the Globe, groups often focus merely on personal problems, which are more immediate and pressing. Hence, it is necessary that TCI develop a sociopolitical, critical analysis of global situations of domination and focus its group analysis and interaction on the attempt to articulate the intertwinement of the I, WE, and IT with the structures of domination and exploitation that determine the Globe. The work in groups therefore needs to engage questions like this: What are the points of contact between the chosen theme and the global structures of domination? How am I determined by such global structures? How are WE as a group embedded in such global structures? And how can WE act to change them? How are our group differences and conflicts determined by such structures of inequality and exploitation?[61]

In short, TCI needs to adopt a critical feminist political analytics of domination in order to explore the political, social, religious, and economic global structures in which its group work takes place. In addition, focused observations of everyday life are important for elaborating the Globe. Finally, TCI needs to ask how the individual and the group

59. Hagleitner, *Mit Lust an der Welt*, 163.
60. Ibid., 162.
61. Ibid., 164–65.

are determined by sociopolitical Globe-factors in order to empower group participants to recognize the structures and ideologies of domination, to critically analyze them, and to change them. The radical democratic approach of TCI needs to be critically developed to create radical democratic self- and world-understandings that can transform kyriarchal relations of exploitation and educational spaces of domination. Such a transformed TCI method and approach could change the educational practices of biblical studies.

TOWARD A RADICAL DEMOCRATIC
EMANCIPATORY ETHOS-SPACE

I have surveyed the didactic possibilities of the fourth emancipatory paradigm of biblical studies to articulate not only a common analytic but also a common didactic model of dialogue and deliberation, initiative and self-affirmation. Such didactic articulations are indebted to the insights of cooperative teaching and learning theories as well as to critical pedagogy in general and feminist critical pedagogy in particular. Rather than attempting to give a comprehensive review of all such attempts, I have chosen examples that seek to develop a collaborative radical democratic didactics, or learning approach.[62] However, such theoretical and practical proposals require the transformation of the didactic triangle in order to theoretically articulate a generative space for the development of interactive pedagogical models within the bounds of the fourth emancipatory radical democratic paradigm.

As I have argued above, the approach of Theme-Centered Interaction (TCI) has radically transformed the didactic triangle by replacing the "teacher" with the "I" of the individual, and the "students" with the "WE" of the group. It has not, however, replaced the top of the triangle—"knowledge"—but only particularized it as the "theme" on which the group has chosen to focus its work. Moreover, it has collapsed the didactic circle, which is focused on explicating the didactic triangle, and has replaced it with the "GLOBE": the diverse contexts and settings of group interaction.

Academic science fosters an attitude of value-neutrality and disinterestedness; on the other hand, TCI insists that the process of knowl-

---

62. Cf. Johannes Wildt, "Theologie lehren: Ein Weiterbildungskonzept in Kooperation zwischen Fach- und Hochschuldidaktik," in *Theologie lehren: Hochschuldidaktik und die Reform der Theologie*, ed. Monika Scheidler, Bernd Jochen Hilberath, and Johannes Wildt (Freiburg: Herder, 2002), 27–56.

edge production is situated, framed, and affected by the Globe, the social-political-religious worlds in which we think, speak, and know. However, as Hagleitner has argued, because of TCI's psychoanalytic orientation, the Globe has remained underdeveloped. Hence, it is important to modify TCI by resorting to feminist contextual, post-colonial, and liberation the*logical insights.

The didactic changes needed by the TCI model are best intensi-fied or corrected by the didactic models engendered within the fourth emancipatory paradigm. By replacing the teacher and learner/student with the I, the individual, TCI engenders the radical equality of the WE. This is a revolutionary change when considered in light of the didactic triangle, since in this triangle, knowledge—or the IT—creates a kyriarchal relationship between teachers and students and instills the assumption that knowledge is transmitted rather than investigated and produced by both. West's *Reading-With* model of biblical interpreta-tion reinscribes this assumption with its distinction between the profes-sional and the ordinary reader.

However, it would be a misreading of a feminist radical democratic didactics if one were to assume that the equality of the WE assumes the same power and knowledge as the I—the individuals. Teachers, mod-erators, learners, and all participants bring different talents, experiences, and expertise to the table when debating, for instance, the meaning of a biblical text or the different paradigms of biblical studies. Such dif-ferences among participants can easily devolve into divisions if they are not recognized as shaped by the kyriarchal structures of race, gender, heterosexism, class, imperialism, age, and so on. Kyriarchal pedagogies have the tendency to reproduce these structures by denying agency to the subordinated—agency that is absolutely necessary for creating radi-cal democratic knowledges. Transforming the didactic triangle into a circle dance in which the I, the WE and the IT interact with each other creates an ever-increasing space of radical democratic equality in the midst of kyriarchy and transforming kyriarchy, a space that can be dia-grammed (see diagram).

This diagram replaces the pyramidal form of the didactic triangle and the TCI symbol of the globe with the global sociopolitical pyramid, which I have named as kyriarchy, and which is determined by struc-tures of domination and exploitation. The circle within the globe—determined by its structures—symbolizes the radical democratic ethos and space that is created by the constructive interactions of the I, the WE, and the IT. Participants in such a radical democratic discourse are

A Critical Feminist Didactic Model

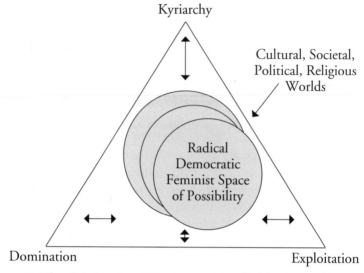

Figure 2: The global sociopolitical pyramid, called kyriarchy.[63]

active moral agents who deliberate, urge, validate, and argue meanings and actions with each other. The arrows indicate the pressures of transformation that are exercised both by the kyriarchal pyramid on the I, the WE, the IT, and the GLOBE, as well as by the transformative radical egalitarian actions and discourses on the kyriarchal sociopolitical pyramid. These discursive actions create a radical democratic rhetorical space insofar as rhetoric is an intersubjective-democratic process that

> is doubly ethical: it is the result of a choice on the part of the rhetor as to the reality advocated and the method of doing so, and it urges choice rather than complete and necessary acceptance on the part of the audience. Truth that is rhetorically made encourages choice and awareness of alternative realities.[64]

63. I have developed and tested this didactic feminist model as the FSR, Inc./WATER (Feminist Studies in Religion, Inc./Women's Alliance for Theology, Ethics and Ritual) Summer Forum, "Making the Connections: Claiming Our Past—Envisioning Our Future Together," which took place in June 2008 and brought 30 international and interreligious feminist scholars in religion to Washington for a week of exchange and collaboration.
64. Barry Brummett, "Some Implications of 'Process' or 'Intersubjectivity' in Postmodern Rhetoric," in *Contemporary Rhetorical Theory: A Reader*, ed. John Lois Lucaites, Celeste Michelle Condit, and Sally Caudill (New York: Guilford Press, 1999), 166. However, a purely intersubjective conceptualization is still too privatized and individualist. Hence, I have qualified it with "democratic."

The rhetorical interplay between the I, WE, and IT creates the ethos of biblical studies. The meaning of "ethos," just like that of rhetoric,[65] changes over time, and its definition is different in different cultures. According to Baumlin, the definition of "ethos" in antiquity articulates the "problematic relation between human character and discourse. More specifically, it raises questions concerning the inclusion of the speaker's character as an aspect of discourse, the representation of that character in discourse, and the role of that character in persuasion.[66] In modernity, Peter Ramus greatly influenced the ethos of the discipline[67] insofar as he held sway among Protestant interpreters of the sixteenth century. Since he sought to sever logic from rhetoric and then to retain logic as the only valid component for generating a mode of "pure reasoning," he introduced the split of rhetoric from logic that demoted rhetoric to mere style, decoration, manipulation, and eloquence in oral performance.

Etymologically, the meaning of "ethos" can be derived either from the Greek *ethos*—meaning custom, habit, usage, folkways—or from the Greek *ēthos*—meaning character formation as the totality of all characteristic traits rather than mere custom or morally approved habits. A third etymological root, suggested by Susan Jarratt and Nedra Reynolds, is *ēthea*, a plural noun that is the original root of both terms and means "hunts" or "hangouts." This etymology understands ethos as a pedagogical space where customs and character are formed, "where one is accustomed to being."[68] Ethos as a disciplinary space determines the professional character of individuals and expresses the way one lives. In

65. For a history of rhetoric, see, e.g., Thomas M. Conley, *Rhetoric in the European Tradition* (Chicago: University of Chicago Press, 1990); for a feminist history of rhetoric, see Cheryl Glenn, *Rhetoric Retold: Regendering the Tradition from Antiquity through the Renaissance* (Carbondale: Southern Illinois University Press, 1997).

66. James S. Baumlin, "Positioning Ethos in Historical and Contemporary Theory," in *Ethos: New Essays in Rhetorical and Critical Theory*, ed. James S. Baumlin and Tita French Baumlin (Dallas: Southern Methodist University Press, 1994), xi–xxxi, here xiii. See also William W. Fortenbaugh, "Aristotle's Accounts of Persuasion through Character," in *Theory, Text, Context: Issues in Greek Rhetoric and Oratory*, ed. Christopher Lyle Johnstone (Albany: State University of New York Press, 1996), 147–68; George A. Kennedy, "Reworking Aristotle's Rhetoric," in ibid., 169–84; and especially Nan Johnson, "Ethos and the Aims of Rhetoric," in *Essays on Classical Rhetoric and Modern Discourse*, ed. R. J. Connors, L. S. Ede, and A. A. Lunsford (Carbondale: Southern Illinois University Press, 1984), 98–114. See also the contributions of Manfred Kraus, Anders Eriksson, Thomas H. Olbricht, Todd Penner and Caroline Vander Stichele, and J. David Hester (Amador) in *Rhetoric, Ethic, and Moral Persuasion in Biblical Discourse*, ed. Thomas H. Olbricht and Anders Eriksson (New York: T&T Clark International, 2005).

67. See Thomas H. Olbricht, "The Flowering of Rhetorical Criticism in America," in *The Rhetorical Analysis of Scripture: Essays from the 1995 Conference*, ed. Stanley E. Porter and Thomas H. Olbricht (Sheffield: Sheffield Academic Press, 1997), 79–102, here 80: "Studies in rhetoric were not unfamiliar to our Puritan forefathers. Puritan scholars embraced particularly the grammar, rhetoric and logic of Peter Ramus (1515–1572) and Omer Talon. . . . The biblical scholars of the era borrowed from these insights, structuring commentaries according to dictates of the Ramian logical divisions and subdivisions."

68. Susan C. Jarratt and Nedra Reynolds, "The Splitting Image: Contemporary Feminisms and the Ethics of ēthos," in J. S. Baumlin and T. F. Baumlin, *Ethos: New Essays in Rhetorical and Critical Theory*, 37–64, here 48; see also Tobin Siebers, *Morals and Stories* (New York: Columbia University Press, 1992), 63.

this spatial sense, ethos theorizes the "positionality" inherent in rhetoric. This notion of ethos is, for instance, typical of Hannah Arendt's political philosophy, as John McGowan has pointed out:

> By extension, ethics can thus be understood not simply to encompass the formation and judgment of character, but also to include the production of a place that character can inhabit. To put it in even more strongly Arendtian terms, ethics must build on the intimate connection between character to place. Only where we create a certain kind of place can a certain kind of person emerge.[69]

Habit, custom, and education always form character in a social space and locate the speaker in the practices and experiences of the group to which s/he belongs or speaks. "Ethos," like experience, can then be understood in terms of "positionality," as the "place from which values are interpreted and constructed rather than as a locus of an already-determined set of values."[70] "Ethos," understood as positioning, is "the awareness that one always speaks from a particular place in a social structure."[71] The willingness of the audience to step into the space occupied (temporarily) by the speaker is crucial in establishing the ethics of ethos while acknowledging the differences rather than the sameness between speaker and audience.

Read through a feminist optic, "ethos" can be understood "as an ethical and political tool, as a way of claiming and taking responsibility for our positions in the world, for the ways we see, the places from where we speak."[72] Understanding ethos in terms of "rhetorical space" elucidates why voice and position are central to rhetorical inquiry and scholarly authority. According to Lorraine Code, rhetorical spaces

> are fictive but not fanciful or fixed locations whose tacit (rarely spoken) territorial imperatives structure and limit the kind of utterances that can be voiced within them with a reasonable expectation of uptake and choral support, an expectation of being heard, understood, taken seriously. They are the sites where the very possibility of an utterance counting as "true-or-false," or of a discussion yielding insight, is made manifest.[73]

69. John McGowan, *Hannah Arendt: An Introduction* (Minneapolis: University of Minnesota Press, 1998), 167.

70. Linda Alcoff, "Cultural Feminism versus Post-Structuralism: The Identity Crisis in Feminist Theory," *Signs* 13 (1988): 405–36, here 434.

71. Susan C. Jarratt and Nedra Reynolds, "The Splitting Image," 47–49.

72. Ibid., 52.

73. Lorraine Code, *Rhetorical Spaces: Essays on Gendered Locations* (New York: Routledge, 1995), ix–x. For the discussion of feminist epistemology, see also Nancy Tuana and Sandra Morgan, eds., *Engendering Rationalities* (Albany:

To understand biblical studies as an epistemological[74] rhetorical space would mean first of all examining the conditions for the possibility of constructing and using biblical knowledge in such a way that does not reinforce the structural violence of the status quo in society, church, and academy. It would entail the investigation of the kyriarchal (gendered, raced, classed, and colonized) structures and circumstances in which wo/men and subaltern men "occupy positions of minimal epistemic authority and where questions of differential power and privilege figure centrally."[75]

Such a rhetorical reconceptualization of the disciplinary ethos of biblical studies is necessary to overcome the false dichotomy between engaged, socially located scholarship (e.g., feminist, postcolonial, African American, queer, and other subdisciplines) and value-neutral "scientific" (malestream) biblical interpretation. While the former allegedly utilizes ethical criteria, the latter is said to live up to a scientific ethos by making use of cognitive criteria. Instead, I would argue that a scientific ethos demands both ethical and cognitive criteria, which must be reasoned out in terms of intersubjectively understandable and communicable knowledge.

In short, ethos is a habit or a pattern of social practices that are inseparable from social location and are always shaped by relations of power. Hence, it becomes important to explore the notion of ethos not just in terms of the ethos of the individual biblical scholar, but also in terms of the WE, the professional ethos of the discipline that determines the social self-identity, positioning, and socialization of the emerging biblical scholar. Ethos as a radical democratic disciplinary space is best expressed for me in the image of the open House of Divine Wisdom. Wisdom/wisdom[76] holds out as a promise the fullness and possibility of the "good life" and encourages a search for justice and order in the world, which can be discerned by experience. Wisdom/wisdom teaching does not keep faith and knowledge apart—it does not divide the world into religious and secular—but provides a model for living a "mysticism of everyday things." In short, the educational spaces of Wisdom/

State University of New York Press, 2001); and Liz Stanley, ed., *Knowing Feminisms: On Academic Borders, Territories and Tribes* (Thousand Oaks, CA: Sage Publications, 1997).

74. See the essays in part 2, "Rhetoric and Epistemology," in Lucaites, Condit, and Caudill, *Contemporary Rhetorical Theory*, 137–247; Richard A. Cherwitz and James W. Hikins, *Communication and Knowledge: An Investigation in Rhetorical Epistemology* (Columbia: University of South Carolina Press, 1986); see also Richard Harvey Brown, *Society as Text: Essays on Rhetoric, Reason, and Reality* (Chicago: University of Chicago Press, 1987).

75. Code, *Rhetorical Spaces*, viii.

76. This way of writing Wisdom/wisdom seeks to refer to Wisdom as a personified divine figure *and* to wisdom as a state of mind characterized by a deep understanding and profound insight.

wisdom are roads and journeys, public places and open borders, nourishment and celebration. Divine Wisdom provides sustenance in the struggles for justice and cultivates creation and life in fullness. The open cosmic House of Divine Wisdom needs no exclusive walls or boundaries, no fortifications or barricades to separate and shut up the insiders from the outsiders, or the Bible from its surrounding world.

To approach biblical studies as the space of Wisdom/wisdom's dwelling as envisioned in Proverbs 9:1–5 means to acknowledge the multivalence of the Bible and its openness to change. It means to give up using it as a security blanket and to recognize that the free spaces between its seven pillars invite the Spirit to blow where it wills. This image of Wisdom/wisdom's open space seeks to replace the understanding of canonical and scholarly authority as limiting, controlling, and exclusive authority and "power over," which demands subordination. Instead it understands the power of the Bible and of biblical scholarship in the original Latin meaning of authority (*augere/auctoritas*) as enhancing, nurturing, and enriching creativity. Biblical authority and biblical studies renewed in the paradigm of Divine Wisdom will be able to foster such creativity, strength, self-affirmation, and freedom of the sacred.

INSTEAD OF A CONCLUSION

In his book *We Scholars*, David Damrosch proposes a new framework for scholarly academic work, one of collaboration instead of isolation and competition. Since he realizes how difficult it is to change the monologic culture of the university and to transform it into the place of collaborative work, he insists, "Any proposal for reform must locate itself between two poles: a change should be as substantial as possible while realizable in a significant number of situations."[77]

In this book I have sought to analyze the culture of biblical studies as a disciplinary institution and an intellectual-religious practice in order to argue for substantial change in graduate biblical education. I thereby sought to create a radical democratic imaginative space for envisioning such substantial change. The question remains whether such a proposal can do justice to the second pole mentioned by Damrosch, which requires that it be "realizable in a significant number of situations."

---

77. David Damrosch, *We Scholars: Changing the Culture of the University* (Cambridge, MA: Harvard University Press, 1995), 164.

Throughout the book I have sought to mention a number of situations where such change can be realized. I am confident that readers who have followed my arguments in these pages—whether WE are students in colleges and graduate schools, faculty and teachers, pastors or rabbis, librarians or journalists, Bible readers or social activists who value the Bible and are looking for new ways to engage with it—will work for changing the ethos of biblical studies from a kyriarchal to a radical democratic emancipatory one. By articulating the struggles within the discipline, by elaborating the central but often marginalized contributions of the fourth paradigm, and by searching for a new didactic model—I have sought to create a space for the WE which can inhabit the transformative radical democratic Wisdom space that engenders new visions and practices for changing society, culture, and biblical religion. In the next and final chapter, I want to present one practical example of how we can transform biblical studies.

Metalogue

From Theory to Practice

Rather than calling this last chapter an "epilogue," which usually consists of a summary and conclusion, I have decided to characterize it instead with the title "metalogue." This is appropriate since a metalogue means a conversation *about* a theoretical subject, a communication about communication. This chapter is thus a communication about the communications that have taken place in the seminar. Although the term "metalogue" seems not to be in the dictionary, it nevertheless has a foothold in scholarly discourses. According to Karen Staller, metalogues are sites or locations where boundaries of acceptable scholarship are negotiated and standards of good scientific practices are articulated.[1]

In the preceding chapters I have critically explored the changes that intercultural, democratizing, and emancipatory criticism, as a new approach, seeks to engender in biblical studies. African, Asian, Indigenous, Latin American, Aboriginal, and Hispanic studies, along with feminist, Latina, black, queer, liberation the*logical, postcolonial, and third-world studies, have begun to decenter the hegemonic paradigms of biblical studies. The theoretical and methodological challenges brought by these voices from the margins to the field of Christian[2] Testament/Early Christian Studies are shaping a new exciting approach

---

1. Cf. Karen Staller, "Metalogue as Methodology," *Qualitative Social Work* 6, no. 2 (2007): 137–57.
2. I use "Christian Testament" and "Hebrew Bible" rather than "New Testament" and "Old Testament" in order to avoid Christian supersessionism.

in biblical criticism, one that points toward different didactic methods within the framework of the fourth paradigm of interpretation.

In this chapter, I want to move from pedagogical theory to concrete educational experiences and practices. Hence, I present a collaborative effort to reflect on the dialogues and discussions from my seminar on "Democratizing/Emancipatory Biblical Studies" at Harvard Divinity School, which brought us together in the fall semester of 2008. Eight participants gathered with me around the seminar table: one MTS student from Harvard, one MA student from Andover Newton, two MDiv students from Harvard Divinity School, and four doctoral students—three from Harvard and one from Boston College. I will outline the seminar description and process in short, then form a virtual roundtable, in which participants reflect on their learning experiences during the semester.

As a metalogue, this chapter is an attempt to stage a conversation about our seminar conversations and dialogues on biblical studies as a disciplinary field of inquiry. It also seeks to move from theory to practice by reflecting on the pedagogical practices and habits developed in the seminar. In short, this chapter was conceived as a metalogue about the content of the chapters of this book, as well as on the work of the seminar and of each participant in it.

CREATING A RADICAL DEMOCRATIC SPACE: FORUM

In the summer of 2008 I was in the process of finishing a first draft of the chapters of this book and was acutely aware that its theoretical elaborations needed a didactic "gravity" that would ground the theoretical reflections in pedagogical praxis. To achieve this, I planned to adopt the Theme-Centered Interaction (TCI) didactic model discussed in the previous chapter and to modify it in terms of a critical feminist approach. I decided to test out this didactic model, which I had developed, at a feminist workshop site and in a graduate seminar at Harvard Divinity School.

The Summer Forum "Making the Connections: Claiming Our Past—Envisioning Our Future Together" took place in June 2008 and was sponsored by Feminist Studies in Religion (FSR, Inc.) and Women's Alliance for Theology, Ethics and Ritual (WATER). The Forum was interreligious and brought thirty young feminist scholars in religion from around the world to Washington for a week of exchange and collaboration.[3] This gave me the opportunity to develop the Forum as a radical egalitarian interactive space.

I introduced the ethos of the Summer Forum as follows: This forum is envisioned as a radical democratic space, an assembly of equals who explore and debate the central questions of feminist the*logy and studies in religion for imagining a vibrant feminist future. As a pilot project it seeks to articulate a radical communal and intellectual space that enables us as sociocultural and religious subjects to speak as equals and to forge feminist alliances. Hence, we do not divide participants in terms of the academy into faculty and students. Rather, we understand ourselves both as colleagues, as participants who bring their rich and diverse experience and research to the table, and as resource persons who seek not only to have the responsibility to facilitate our conversations, debates, inquiries, and discussions but also to learn from each other.

The methods we have chosen are not those of the academy, lecture, seminar, and mentorship but those that enable us as cultural, social, and religious intellectual subjects to speak as equals, to forge alliances, and to create knowledge that fosters the well-being of wo/men. The primary methods we will use are group conversations and forum discussions. They seek to foster

—substantial conversations across generations, disciplines, religions, and cultures to develop feminist theologies and studies in religion as a common project;
—critical analysis and communication across theoretical and spiritual dividing lines;
—accountability to wo/men on the bottom of the kyriarchal pyramid and engagement in feminist movements for change and transformation; and
—strategies for fostering academic survival, intellectual flourishing, forging alliances and friendships.

In order to enable each of us to share our variegated experiences and competencies and to work closely together, we have constructed two different group venues. The morning groups are selected on the principle of diversity, the diversity of social-cultural-geographical-religious locations, and the diversity of interests and competencies. Their task is to explore the site of feminist theologies/studies in religion from such

---

3. Resource persons were professors Judith Plaskow, Kwok Pui-lan, Mary E. Hunt, Deborah Whitehead, and myself. Unfortunately Professor Katie Geneva Cannon had to cancel at the last minute for family reasons.

different perspectives with the goal to articulate differences and at the same time to chart common ground. They are to articulate a group project envisioning how to articulate and institutionalize feminist the-*logies/studies in religion as "a radical space of possibility" (bell hooks), where feminist knowledge can be articulated for sociopolitical and religious change and transformation. We will share these projects with each other on Friday morning.

The afternoon groups are self-selected around important issues and problems that determine wo/men's lives. The task is to explore the radical democratic space of feminist studies in religion/the*logies in terms of our own work and research as well as in terms of questions and issues that are central to wo/men's well-being. In this way we want to become conscious that our community of accountability is not just the academy or institutionalized religion, but also and especially wo/men in society and religion. Finally, the themes or *topoi* that are defining each day seek to focus our discussions in the mornings and afternoons in terms of history, institutionalization, resources, and futures of Feminist Studies in Religion. As a richly gifted group of intellectuals, we bring our variegated experiences, socioreligious locations, theoretical approaches, and work for change to this radical democratic space of wisdom. In short, the program seeks to instantiate the *ekklēsia* of wo/men as such a radical democratic space so that all can contribute to this forum in different ways but with a common goal: to engender knowledge that is emancipatory and life-giving.

CREATING A RADICAL DEMOCRATIC SPACE: SEMINAR

In summer of 2008, I also needed to decide what I was going to teach after my study leave, which had been supported by a grant from the Wabash Center for Teaching and Learning. Hence, it seemed beneficial to plan a graduate seminar on the same topic as the emerging book. I decided to seize this fortuitous opportunity and to offer a seminar that would put the ideas of the book manuscript into critical practice. By designing a syllabus that sought to translate the practices of a radical democratic ethos, which the work advocates, into didactic language, I took the risk of never being able to publish this work if the pedagogical design would prove to be a failure because students could not work with it.

To achieve an equal playing level, I determined to adopt again the Theme-Centered Interaction (TCI) didactic model discussed in the previous chapter and to modify it in terms of a critical feminist approach. The TCI didactic model deconstructs the kyriarchal teacher-student relationship of the didactic triangle and replaces it with an equal-participant model. By allowing the rough drafts of my chapters to be seen as drafts of a seminar participant, rather than as authoritative chapters of a professor, my chapter drafts could thus function as a site for critical reflection and feedback.

Since Harvard Divinity School requires grading, I used the same method of contract grading that I have used for years in all my courses. I find that contract grading reduces competition and anxiety because students can decide for themselves toward which grade level they want to work. It also allows for constructive feedback since evaluation is based on the work done and not on a competitive grading scale. Finally, I asked participants to choose a study partner with whom to discuss their work. With their partner, they would give and receive evaluative feed-back on the draft of the paper as well as on the final paper.[4]

In the syllabus, I summed up the envisioned pedagogical process and the goals of the seminar as follows:

—The seminar seeks to engender a collaborative radical democratic process of teaching and learning. Hence, all participants are equally responsible for its work and success.

—In the beginning, participants should identify the knowledge and skills they bring to the seminar as well as the areas of inquiry they want to work in.

—The seminar process employs the pedagogical model of TCI (Theme-Centered Interaction), that was developed by Ruth C. Cohn. This model has four factors: The "I" of each participant, who needs to be her/his own "chairperson" or moderator; the "We" of all the seminar members, who have to come together to work on the "It," which encompasses the specific *topic* (e.g., historical paradigm) and the overall *theme* (democratizing biblical studies). Reflections and discussions have always to remain aware of the "Globe," the contextual world in which we do our work.

—The six reflection papers should be critical, constructive feedback papers. Hence, I have chosen to offer drafts of my manuscript for such feedback. Feedback should be given from the perspective of your chosen area and as advice either from your own perspective

---

4. After semester end we had two additional "editorial meetings" to prepare the papers for publication on the accompanying Web site.

or from the viewpoint of an editor persona, from that of a teaching facilitator, or from that of a consulting expert.

—At the second session, each participant will choose a partner with whom to do teamwork. The partner should be interested in the same grade level and research area in order to be able to give critical feedback.

—The syllabus will be completed after all participants who intend to write a paper have submitted their paper topics and these are accepted. Papers can be theoretical or practical papers and contribute to an academic or professional research area. Topics should be discussed with your partner and with me. After we have settled on the paper topics, we will schedule the second part of the semester.

The conversations engendered by the drafted chapters in the first part of the semester are intended to serve as a model for future discussions of the other participants' papers in the second part of the seminar. To that end, I propose the following instructions as a format for critical constructive feedback: "In your response papers, please address the following:

1. Formulate a concise abstract of the chapter.
2. Discuss what you think is important and why.
3. Indicate what you think needs to be changed and why.
4. Articulate what you would add in light of your focus. (Please remember, you can adopt a persona or write in your own name.)"

To this instruction, I added the following postscript: "If you want to try out your hand at editing, I would be grateful, but this is not required."

In the first seminar session during Harvard's shopping period, I tried to spell out the goal and approach of the seminar as follows:

—The seminar's object of inquiry is not the Bible but the discipline of biblical studies.

—The seminar is interdisciplinary and metadisciplinary in method. It seeks to transgress and transcend disciplinary boundaries.

—The seminar has as a practical goal to introduce future ministers, religious leaders, and professors of biblical studies into the professional ethos and practices of the discipline.

—The seminar looks at the field from the perspective of the margins and asks how marginalized people and emancipatory studies can become fully enfranchised.

—Our goal is not to seek knowledge for knowledge's sake but to articulate emancipatory and radical democratic biblical knowledges.

To that end I delineated four areas of inquiry:

1. The self-understanding of the discipline that emerged in the nineteenth and twentieth centuries, when theories of colonialism, racism, sexism, and class struggle were developed. Moreover, the discipline is characterized by a dualistic self-understanding as either accountable to the academy or to communities of faith. Academic study focuses on what the text meant, and the*logical/religious study focuses on what it means today. This dualistic self-understanding constitutes an embedded problem for graduate education.

2. Because of its location either in the academy or in religious communities, the discipline does not articulate any accountability to society either in its research programs or in its organization and pedagogy. The absence of research in the interest of democratic societies, however, is radically challenged by the discipline's "voices from the margins": feminist, black, Asian, postcolonial, queer, postmodern, intercultural, Latina, empire studies of the Bible, and many more. These studies insist that critical reflection on one's sociopolitical religious context and location is crucial for all emancipative knowledge. They have shown that because of a scientistic ethos, both academic and the*logical biblical studies are not able to educate biblical scholars, ministers, and religious leaders for work in a democratic society and global situation of domination and exploitation.

3. Hence, the voices from the margins seek to articulate knowledge that is emancipatory and transformative. However, insofar as they advocate a great array of differences but do not stress common strategies and goals, they are in danger of remaining fragmented, becoming embroiled in deconstructing each other, and competing for the few available resources. Hence, they cannot develop the intellectual power to change the discipline. Rather, they reinforce the malaise of a discipline that on the whole is fragmented into countless subdisciplines, with innumerable different analytics and methods. In short, this rich diversity of emancipatory biblical studies opens up great possibilities for the vitality of the field but also poses the problem of further fragmentation and the difficulty of collaboration and communication between its different directions.

4. This rich disciplinary diversity and fragmentation raises the question as to what constitutes basic competence and excellence in biblical studies, not only analytically but also pedagogically and professionally,

two areas that are widely discussed in the humanities but less so in religious and biblical studies. We are faced with an explosion not only of methods but also of knowledges, and graduate education becomes more and more functionalized. For this reason, we need to ask: What are essential requirements to achieve competence in biblical studies? What should a graduate program in emancipatory biblical studies look like if it is to foster the necessary abilities to do biblical studies in an ever more complex and globalizing world? What competence is needed to discuss and teach the Bible not only in the academy and communities of faith but also in the public square?

In order to stimulate a wide-ranging discussion on these critical points, I needed to decenter my own voice and open up a space of agency and collaboration. In a first assignment I therefore asked participants to post their reflections on the following questions:

—What are your goals and objectives for this seminar?
—How will you assess them?
—What expertise do you bring to the seminar process?
—Choose one site of exploration and research from the following four areas:

1. Academy/church/religion
2. Democracy/marginal voices
3. Communication in biblical studies
4. Pedagogy/professional education

As the reflection papers below and the posted research papers on the accompanying Web site indicate, the last point of this assignment was much too general. However, because of its unspecific character, it allowed participants to explore different possibilities throughout the semester.

At the end of the semester, participants were asked to reflect on their goals for the seminar, which they had formulated in the beginning of the semester. After the seminar had ended, we decided to add these reflection papers as a roundtable and discussed in an editorial session the following order.

A FORUM OF MANY VOICES / A KALEIDOSCOPE OF PERSONAL REFLECTIONS

To move from theory to practice, from the perspective of the instructor to that of the participants, I want to conclude this book with this

"Roundtable of Many Voices," which seeks to display the theoretical questions and reflective practices that embody democratizing biblical studies. Rather than summarizing each contribution, I want readers to listen carefully to all the voices. These reflections on experience envision a variegated praxis of emancipatory biblical studies and promise a rich future for the profession.

Roberto Mata

This "Democratizing Biblical Studies" seminar has been a challenging and transformative learning journey. In contrast to many other traditional courses, the purpose and pedagogy of the course encouraged me to speak from my own social location, to articulate my concerns, and to envision biblical studies as a democratic, welcoming, and liberating discipleship of equals. However, the seminar was challenging because I had to confront my own socialization into the hegemonic pedagogical models and the scientific-positivist ethos of biblical studies. Although I had taken similar courses before, I found myself at times fearful yet joyful, suspicious and yet hopeful.

After reflecting on these contrasting emotions, I realize that when one has been silenced for so long, even one's own voice sounds foreign. Therefore, we must cross the borders in order to envision a healthier understanding of one's self, the text, and the field. Thinking of biblical studies as borderlands and of its obstacles as borders—which can be crossed, subverted, and transformed—has helped me conceptualize the challenges and possibilities it holds for the marginalized. Hence, I have framed my experiences and engagement with the seminar in terms of the five stages of the border-crossing experience: critical awakening, journeying, crossing, negotiating, and transforming. Through these stages, I have also been able to envision biblical studies as truly democratic and inclusive, particularly of those voices that have been historically silenced.

Awakening

Critical awakening is actually a process of conscientization, since it involves naming one's reality and taking action to transcend the sources of oppression, which Paulo Freire refers to as limit-situations. Through discussions of four major paradigm models in biblical studies, this course has helped me map the impact of the scientific-positivist ethos and its socialization practices on minority students. Since the neutral and value-free ethos of the field can silence our voices and concerns, the questions we ask and the scholarship we produce has little to say to society, and much less to our communities. Considering these dynamics, the pursuit of a degree in this field can become meaningless. Such was my situation about three years ago, while completing the master of divinity program. Yet, on the brink of abandoning my studies, I encountered the work of Elisabeth Schüssler Fiorenza and other scholars, in whom I have found mentors and a community. With their invaluable assistance, I have been able to experience this critical awakening, which demands that I embark on a border-crossing journey to transform the field.

Journeying

Through the "Democratizing Biblical Studies" seminar, I have been able to move from naming the Eurocentric ethos of biblical studies, to mapping strategies for its transformation. Because the border-crossing journey contains several perils (ideological, methodological, and practical ones), the task demands that one travels with other potential border crossers, *compañeras* and *compañeros*. In this seminar, these companions have helped me stay on course. They have challenged me to speak with my own voice, have patiently read my various paper drafts, and have shared their respective strategies to cross the hegemonic and Eurocentric borders of the field. Most importantly, they have shared their own transformative vision for biblical studies. As a journey, this seminar has also been a process of detoxification, of debunking the various theoretical and methodological fallacies that others and I have internalized, and this can be painful at times, but nonetheless necessary.

Crossing

The seminar "Democratizing Biblical Studies" has also been a continuous border-crossing experience academically and socially. As framed by Elisabeth Schüssler Fiorenza, the fourth paradigm of biblical studies demands that we engage in dialogue with those situated in other paradigms. Dispensing of any trash-and-burn approach, we are encouraged to understand the ways other paradigms function and to assess their implications for society. Because every crossing, or paradigm shift in this case, is a risky enterprise, there is an element of vulnerability, looming chaos at times, and uncertainty due to our unfamiliarity with the terrain. However, here is where the work of intellectual coyotes—those who are familiar with the borderlands' terrain, perils, and safe places—comes into play. Apart from the work of Elisabeth Schüssler Fiorenza, I have found the work of Paulo Freire, Fernando Segovia, Henry A. Giroux, Gloria Anzaldua, and Frantz Fanon particularly illuminating for the purposes of this study. Their critical reflection on pedagogy, paradigms of interpretation, borderlands, and colonialism has enabled me, and others, to evade the traps of *La Migra* (the border patrol), those gatekeepers for whom there is only one proper way of doing biblical studies. The intellectual vigilantes for whom the "truth" or "single true meaning" of biblical texts can only be obtained through methodologies forged in the furnaces of the West. Considering our background as ethnic minorities, we are unwilling to simply adopt their portrait of the "true biblical scholar" in order to be deemed competent. We must negotiate throughout all the borders before us.

Negotiating

Crossing into the borderlands of biblical studies enabled me to see not only the possibilities, but also the extent of the marginalization of ethnic and racial minorities. Thus, as unacknowledged border crossers to this field, we must begin an arduous process of negotiation. In recent years, although racial and ethnic minorities have been granted admission into elite seminaries and divinity schools, the socialization practices of these institutions can either turn us into the idealized image of the Eurocentric scholar or drive us into academic attrition. These socialization practices are enforced through departmental requirements, hegemonic pedagogies, and formal interactions with our professors and peers. In order to gain agency, we negotiate the situation by deploying our bilingual and bicultural skills, for we must negotiate between the world of academia and our communities. Like other students, we are willing to meet program requirements, such as learning German or French, in order to assert our competence. Yet as we embrace the field, we gradually redefine its rules, develop new theoretical frameworks, and transform it into a space we can safely inhabit.

Transforming

Through the "Democratizing Biblical Studies" seminar, I have also been able to envision how the fourth paradigm can enact the transformation of the field and open up spaces for the voices in the margins. From this foundation, I have been able to frame ways to reconnect with my community of faith and to address issues that are relevant for the wider public as well. Furthermore, I have been able to devise ways to cross[5] the socialization practices of the field and to avoid attrition. Most importantly, I have had the privilege of embarking on this transformative journey under the guidance of an experienced border crosser, Elisabeth Schüssler Fiorenza, one of the leading biblical scholars in the field. For racial and ethnic minorities, her work and courses have served as both a map and compass, as a safe space, and as inspiration to remain in the struggle for the transformation of biblical studies.

Michelle Chaplin Sanchez

On the first day of class, Elisabeth Schüssler Fiorenza introduced us to the style of pedagogy she wanted to try out in her seminar "Democratizing Biblical Studies"—her own feminist adapted version of Ruth Cohn's Theme-Centered Interaction (TCI). She explained that everyone in the class should understand each other as a situated individual, an "I" first and foremost. As an "I," each person should speak from experience, training, and individual resources, but not be perceived as authoritative in any strong or fixed sense over any other "I"; nor should one "I" be pressured to conform to any other "I." The group of "I's" would work together to determine the "It," the focus of our mutual interest, and the interaction between the "It" and the "I" would be mutually constructive. We would come to understand ourselves in relation to the topic of our concern, with certain elements of our personal resources being especially called to the fore by that topic of concern. Out of this could potentially, though not necessarily, emerge a group identity, or a "We." Every week we returned explicitly to this model—discussing our "I," discussing the "It," determining whether or not a "We" had formed, and assessing what the impact would be on the "Globe." Schüssler Fiorenza's approach did amend Cohn's TCI in several ways, one of which was of particular significance for my own thinking. Instead of framing our pedagogy as a mere reconstruction of the didactic pyramid, one that simply replaces Teacher/Student/

---

5. Crossing refers to the decentering or disavowing of the borders, socialization practices in this case, established by Eurocentric academic elites in biblical studies.

Knowledge with I/We/It, she reformed it as a circle *inside* a pyramid. "The world," she told us, "is kyriarchal. It is shaped like a pyramid, with the powerful on the top and the powerless on the bottom. Our task is to create a democratic space inside of that pyramid."

This specific model and Schüssler Fiorenza's use of it was entirely new to me, though the idea of democratic education was something I had experienced before and found to be important. My undergraduate education took place at New College of Florida, a liberal arts college that practiced a radically alternative model of education. Grades were dropped in favor of detailed evaluations, and students were encouraged to take charge of their education, at times even designing their own majors and curriculum. This system worked exceptionally well for me and helped me to develop a sense that undergraduate and graduate education should not be about moving up a social ladder, not about simply bolstering one's CV or graduating with honors. It should be a central component of a life practice—something that emerges out of interest in the world and a desire to impact the world in a positive way. Working through the feminist adaptation of TCI helped to provide for me the language to describe what I had already experienced and now continue to pursue.

My particular area of study is Christian theology, focusing on the intersection of philosophy of religion and constructive theology. In the years that I have been pursuing this work, I have maintained a connection to Christian ministry. I have always been convinced that keeping these two sources in mind was important to the quality and scope of my work, but at times it has felt like existing in the Bermuda Triangle—in some kind of fuzzy space where the connection between the academy and the church is mysteriously lost. Still, most of us live and have connections in broader society; most of us are involved in religious institutions to some extent. There *must* be some kind of connection.

Perhaps lack of communication between the academy and society persists so strongly precisely because we are discouraged from taking up our "I" in both the church and the academy. There has always been enormous pressure to align oneself to the hegemonic power of either the church's tradition or the academy's standards of rigor that have been accepted and internalized as "obvious." Knowing myself, my "I," as existing in the messy overlap of these worlds, I have long felt that my work should and *can* be relevant to my society, but have been searching for ways to make this a reality. In this class and with this language, I was able to explore some of the reasons for the academy/church split that ordinary academic procedures fail to highlight. I was able to state my subject position explicitly, and use unusual resources to try to articulate an approach to both theology and the Bible that does not fit neatly in the division of academic subdisciplines.

Specifically, I came to this course as a theologian in training, concerned with the place of the Bible in my work. The Bible is, of course, the implicit or explicit interlocutor of much historic Christian theology, especially in my own broadly Protestant Reformed tradition. It has been my experience, however, that interaction with the Bible in the practice of theology is not only increasingly rare, but also difficult for a variety of reasons that are well documented in the "Democratizing Biblical Studies" discussion of the first, theological paradigm. This paradigm is in many ways a microcosm of the dual-discipline split between academy and church that plagues religious studies as a whole. As a theologian, this idea captured my attention by speaking to my experience of the difficulty of straddling such diverse commitments.

On the academic side, the positivist-scientific ethos of historical-criticism that has dominated scholarly engagement with the Bible for decades has pushed the first paradigm toward theology departments and away from biblical studies entirely. This in turn prevents theologians from engaging the Bible, because such engagement is too often seen as the proper task of the "disinterested" biblical scholar. Anything less, such an ethos suggests, will lack sufficient rigor. On the side of the community, however, the first paradigm has taken on a decidedly literalist-fundamentalist orientation in many public discourses, one that borrows much from the epistemological assumptions of positivism by insisting that the Bible proclaims univalent truth. This dichotomy has tragically suppressed many voices that would approach the Bible in a more creative, border-crossing manner, such as described by Roberto Mata (above).

In many ways, given this situation, the first paradigm is the most absent of all of the paradigms at work in biblical studies today. It is also perhaps most in need of being addressed if biblical studies is to have societal relevance and practice ethically responsible scholarship. While there are many ways to approach this area of lack and disjoint in biblical studies, it seems clear to me that one possible approach would be for theologians to again engage the Bible—and in so doing, engage directly in the discourses of *both* churches and biblical studies, providing a natural conversational link to break the dichotomy. This, however, requires theoretical and methodological rigor and an approach that looks for and affirms collaboration with the other paradigms and with religious communities, even (or especially) in struggle.

Exploring what would be required to strengthen the first paradigm in a way that is informed by the critical lens of Schüssler Fiorenza's vision for the fourth paradigm, as outlined in chapter 3, became my project in the course. It was a topic that I had been interested in exploring for a long time, but I had never discovered the appropriate setting. Most university courses fit neatly into disciplinary and paradigmatic parameters, obscuring opportunities for challenging those parameters and creating spaces for new, collaborative approaches. In this sense, the pedagogical method described above provided me with a unique opportunity, one that I felt was rare for a student. I used it to approach the controversial issue of biblical authority from a standpoint rooted in the first paradigm, because this seemed to me to be the core point of tension dividing the first paradigm from the other paradigms, and largely excluding the first paradigm from academic discourse. What if authority, and the notion of truth that implicitly legitimizes authority, is formed by kyriarchal society and is not merely "given"?

Employing the tools in "Democratizing Biblical Studies," I used a kyriarchal analytic to deconstruct the notions of truth that lend credence to a univalent understanding of biblical authority, and began to imagine how the first paradigm could function within the bounds of its theoretical commitments without using methods that reinscribe kyriarchy as if it were given, obvious, or natural. I found that becoming aware of the extent to which our notions of truth and authority derive from and reinscribe societal power structures could give us a way to look back at the Christian theological tradition and recognize divinity precisely in its tenuousness, its paradox, and its diversity. Much is at stake in our ability to face our conflicts without either artificially ignoring them or exacerbating them. By directly engaging with a kyriarchal critique, theologians can use the Bible, engage with the Bible, and discuss the Bible with fellow theologians as well as the public in a way that is wise to the way the Bible has been used, without feeling the pressure either to fully accept the Bible univalently or to reject it as a sacred text.

First, however, we must work to create an ethos where these problems, faced from our own individual situations, can be acknowledged with minimal pressure to conform or to deny our own experience. This is what this class allowed me to do, and I see in this kind of pedagogy the potential for an exciting step forward in thinking of creative solutions to old divisions, both inside and ultimately beyond the boundaries of biblical studies.

John Falcone

Protagonists of social change know how important it is to "think globally and act locally." I embarked upon my PhD program to help religious educators use the Bible as a liberative and sustaining resource in their communities of practice. But—as Michelle Chaplin Sanchez suggests—the intersections of different biblical paradigms in theory and practice can complicate this task. Our seminar helped me to construct my own critical map of contemporary biblical interpretation; and it challenged me to make my own theorizing, learning, and future teaching more genuinely transformative and democratic. By analyzing the current paradigms of biblical interpretation through a feminist-TCI didactic, we used the seminar experience itself to experiment with rhetorical concepts and democratizing practices. We tinkered with the tools of transformation, acquiring a feel for their heft, their finesse, and their unavoidable double edges.

To themes like "analyzing," "critiquing," "changing," and "fashioning" more democratic spaces for biblical education, I would add (with Roberto Mata), the idea of "negotiating." For me, negotiating means finding a way forward with integrity when we are confronted with conflicting forces and values. Implicit in much of this book, negotiation played a central role in our seminar, as instructor, Harvard students, and visiting students together made the decisions and built the trust that moved our inquiry forward. As many feminist social scientists insist, negotiation is an ever-present fact of life. We cannot eliminate the contradictions in our learning, our teaching, or our living, so long as power differentials, insider/outsider identities, and other unegalitarian realities structure our experience: so long as kyriarchy pervades our psyches and our globe. But we can negotiate these contradictions with greater (or lesser) integrity in the concrete realities of our classrooms and our lives. Biblical studies reformers face this challenge in at least two ways: negotiating the "circle dance" of shared leadership, and negotiating the give-and-take of interparadigm conversation.

In a democratizing biblical studies classroom, both the instructor and the students develop the capacity to bring our challenging and messy negotiations to consciousness and to voice. Negotiating the focus of our seminar is a case in point. On the first day of class, Elisabeth Schüssler Fiorenza invited us to offer our own ideas about formats and formulations for the "It" of our work. At the same time, she bravely and generously offered to let us collaborate on her book, as an entry point into our exploration of biblical studies. While TCI dynamics played an integral part in our learning, a full-fledged process for discussing and selecting the "It" of our seminar might have taken several class sessions of trust building and discernment to complete. Also, class rosters at Harvard are not settled until the second meeting of the semester, after a weeklong "shopping period" is done. Would it have been fair —or attractive to student shoppers—to put off specifying the very topic of our biblical studies class until we had completed a month of group dynamics? Would it have been more fair—or even feasible—to fix the roster four weeks early, so that a chosen set of students and an unpaid professor could develop their common theme more democratically? As educational reformers, we can negotiate, but not eliminate, these types of contradictions.

Similarly, as a student I have been deeply pleased with my learning and growth in this seminar. On the one hand, engaging an established scholar in her own writing, and generating a collegial product, has been the epitome of effective and egalitarian education. As "situated learning" theorists argue, learning works best in settings like this: substantive activities structured in transparent and teachable ways. On the other hand, like all who seek sustainable social transformation, I took the exigencies of my own strategic positioning into account in negotiating our common "It."

Whatever my particular intellectual interests at the inception of the seminar, I adapted to the developing foci of the group and to the offerings of the instructor. As a junior colleague who has not yet received his PhD, this negotiated process allowed me to collaborate with a senior scholar and thus to forward our group's common agenda of democratizing the way the Bible is interpreted. Whether as tenured instructors or hopeful professionals in training, we cannot escape the micropolitics of learning and knowledge production. To the contrary, integrity demands that we take them seriously and use them to leverage as much democratic transformation as possible.

Negotiation also plays a role at the interface between biblical paradigms. As academics, ministers, or religious activists, we must wrestle with the values and the exigencies of the communities to which we are accountable if we hope to move the project of participatory democracy forward. For example, as I compared Schüssler Fiorenza's paradigm analysis with the pastoral and political practices of people "on the ground," it became clear that grassroots Bible teachers and preachers often employ strategies of biblical interpretation in tangled and eclectic ways. Many committed religionists ground their preaching on historical-critical positivism; many liberationists appeal to norms of biblical theology; the combinations are easy to multiply. The danger of such "methodological promiscuity" is not so much its intellectual contradictions, but its blind spots—the ways it can mask oppression and consumerism in the very midst of our efforts to create more wholesome schools, churches, and social groups. By weaving back and forth in our discussions between theory and practical experience, our seminar helped me articulate all these dynamics in a much clearer way.

I came to biblical studies from an inner-city Catholic high school, a place of multiple negotiations. We taught our students the stories and symbols of their native cultures, their ties to family and history. We also taught them to read, write, and figure, to show up on time and to speak the dominant dialect of white American English. In a similar way, we taught biblical interpretation for both resistance and liberation, for both survival and transformation. For Catholic high school educators, framing our vision in this way underlines yet another tension to be negotiated—the one between community sustainability and critique. On the one hand, tradition and cultural cohesion can be powerful bulwarks against capitalist assimilation. Stubborn cultural particularities and unsubmissive memories can help us resist integration into the dominant consumer world. On the other hand, critical consciousness and a hermeneutics of suspicion are essential for unmasking and dismantling oppression. The Bible cannot be swallowed whole as an unproblematic text of liberation, but it must somehow remain a formative and normative text within Christian communities if those communities wish to draw on the cultural memory and sustainable practices of which that Bible is a part. Both liberation and the*logy, both tradition and suspicion, remain necessary in the living tension that defines a Catholic school as a *religious* community of survival and justice, rather than a purely political or secular one. This was the tension I brought to our seminar each week.

Catholic Bible educators need a pedagogy that directs this tension in a meaningful and practicable way, a pedagogy that helps learners find their own creative and liberating "voice" in and through their particular cultural heritage. In such a vision, I've come to believe, *liberationist* values and analysis must fix and focus the *theological* norm. Within this framework, the particularities of the biblical text—its symbols, gaps, indeterminacies, and preoccupations; its historical contradictions and narrative strangeness—can become sources for critique *and* cultural continuity. Through the coaching and healing of their teachers, students can learn to negotiate the intersections of tradition and critique, to transform their life settings with increasing integrity.

Schüssler Fiorenza's work deconstructs biblical studies in a way that helps religious workers, cultural workers, and their students to take up the pieces and build something liberative, something new. High school religion teachers and ministerial leaders deserve the kind of biblical studies education that will deepen their ability to "think globally and act locally" with the biblical text. Critically conscious professors in training deserve a similar kind of education in "negotiating" texts, learning spaces, and broader social contexts. Our seminar provided a setting for this type of work.

As any good teacher knows, the "explicit" curriculum of readings and assignments is only a small part of what really is taught and learned in a school. Just as important are the "implicit" and "null" curricula: what we teach through our methods and styles, through our prejudices, through our deafening silences. These curricula can be surprisingly powerful because they infiltrate our minds unnoticed, setting limits on what "can" be thought or discussed. In our seminar, professor and students together addressed the epistemological and academic challenges that the current clash of paradigms presents. By examining our pedagogies—our implicit and null curricula—we moved the conversation to an equally important but frequently neglected level. What, we asked, is the full range of "education" that is really transpiring in our efforts at biblical interpretation?

Arminta Fox

From the beginning, this seminar with Elisabeth Schüssler Fiorenza challenged me to actively engage my own learning. I was expected to read, reflect on the reading, formulate my own thoughts, and then contribute those thoughts to group discussions and ultimately to the larger project of the seminar: to democratize biblical studies. These expectations may seem fairly straightforward, but in reality trusting in one's own voice can be difficult when one is accustomed to the aggressive ripping apart of arguments that is standard in the field. Fear of such attacks keeps scholars from taking risks with ideas and scholarship. In such a stifling of creativity, the kyriarchal system undermines the field of biblical studies, and perhaps the broader educational system, as my colleague John Falcone suggests. The privileged professional lives of a few scholars are maintained through the oppression of many others.

Both in our class together and in this book, Schüssler Fiorenza pushed the limits of biblical studies scholarship by calling attention to the ways in which kyriarchy rears its ugly head in graduate education. The previous chapters are a testament to the work that needs to be done to democratize biblical studies. Schüssler Fiorenza works toward this goal in several ways: she names the problems, describes their contexts, envisions solutions, and works toward those solutions in a collaborative model. I was fortunate to be a part of such a collaborative effort as a student in her course. In this capacity, I also had to recognize the problems in the educational system and find ways to be a fully engaged, democratic participant in the field, beginning with our class. Experiencing Schüssler Fiorenza's theories in the classroom environment allowed me to see the impacts of this kyriarchal system on my own academic work.

Our first written assignment for the seminar was a reflection on our goals and the ways we envisioned our background knowledge contributing to our discussions. For the latter, I listed my background in psychology and trauma studies, which I thought might be helpful in facilitating discussions. Realistically, I was not sure how this background could be of any real use in a course on biblical studies education. However, I would soon realize that this previous work and knowledge was important in large part because it was *not* a reproduction of the skills acquired in biblical studies. Additionally, rather than trusting in my own thoughts, I searched the work of my classmates for clues in formulating my own goals. Once again I was drawing from a system that promotes the reproduction of previous scholarship. Thus one of my first projects became learning to rely on myself and formulate my own voice, which could then contribute to the community.

One way in which Schüssler Fiorenza encouraged us to be self-reflective was by asking us to keep a portfolio of our experiences with the course. This portfolio would include the first assignment of our individual learning goals, our responses to each chapter of the book, the ways in which each reading and class session helped us to think about our final papers, and our final reflections. I decided that I would also keep notes regarding my class preparation and participation. These notes reflect my initial difficulty in relying on my own ideas. During a particularly difficult night when I was attempting to write a response, I typed out my anxieties in the hopes of moving past them and later learning from them. Most of my thoughts involved fears that my posting on the Web site would not meet the standards set by my fellow classmates. I was worried about what they would think of me if I failed to understand part of the reading, or if the language I used was not as technical or theoretical as the language of others. After recording my frustrations and fears, I wrote out thoughts to encourage myself again and to get through the assignment. By focusing on the knowledge and skills I knew I possessed, I was able to recognize that my contribution was unique and important. This was true even when I had to be vulnerable by showing that I did not know everything, or when I needed to encourage myself to overcome my fears that I knew nothing.

In this seminar, I had to trust that it was OK to engage the material and contribute my voice. In other words, I had to form the "I" from the feminist TCI model for myself. Once I had done so, I was able to concentrate on the group, the "We." As a group, we were not as effective at the beginning of the semester, when many of us were still learning to formulate and trust in our own voices. The twofold nature of responses—first, posting responses on the course Web site, and second, discussing materials in class—allowed time for us to reflect on the course materials; we formulated both the "I" and the "We" as we responded individually and together. Because of our various backgrounds, we had different strengths and weaknesses. In working together, we had the opportunity to learn from the experiential knowledge of each class member rather than replicate the same knowledge separately in order to be judged and graded on our ability to fit a mold. By the second half of the semester, I found that as a group we were able to accomplish much more than we could have accomplished individually.

Coming from a background in psychology and counseling, my reflections and contributions often centered on the formation and maintenance of the communities of our classroom, our field, and our world. In my final paper, I explored the ways in which an understanding of the traumatic aspects of biblical studies can provide new avenues for envisioning the transformation/healing process of democratizing biblical studies. In addition to drawing on my experiential knowledge, this paper came out of my reflections on the course materials and class discussions. Drawing from Schüssler Fiorenza's analysis of kyriarchy in biblical studies education and her proposed "I," "WE," "IT," "Globe" pedagogical model, I explored these concepts in terms of the trauma and recovery processes that impact our learning communities. I found that many people in the field of biblical studies suffer from institutionalized trauma, which must be addressed proactively in the classroom.

Continuing the idea of collaborative learning, Schüssler Fiorenza paired us together, based on our interests. My partner and I frequently met over coffee and lunch to discuss the course materials and our final papers. This partnership was another way in which we explored the use of our own voices in working toward the goals of the course. It was helpful to have honest feedback, which gave me encouragement and constructive criticism. Additionally, I enjoyed the opportunity to engage the materials of the course and my own voice in my encouragement and critiques of my partner's work. Once we had written our first drafts, our partners and other classmates offered their responses. This editing process enabled us to engage the material in nine different ways rather than simply through the professor, or the teaching fellow, as in other classes.

By organizing this seminar in such a way, Schüssler Fiorenza allowed us to experience many of the arguments she makes in this book. In my struggle to write, I realized that I was afraid to express myself and to fully engage the material because of the competitive nature that I had observed in the academic setting. Contrasting my experiences of this seminar with others I have taken, I learned that the current system is constructed in a way that does not encourage students to learn from each other. This is a great loss to the field.

Through my own and others' papers, I saw firsthand the importance of interdisciplinary work and diverse interests that can expand our understanding of course materials. For example, by allowing my previous work with trauma, recovery processes, and Quaker pedagogical principles to inform my experience of the course, I was able to see the trauma present in biblical studies education and to envision ways for a healing transformation. By challenging me to engage my own learning, this course has encouraged me to produce meaningful scholarship that has power in its interdisciplinary and diverse character. Articulating this project with my own background ensures that it is both personally meaningful and bears integrity. Most importantly, learning about the need to democratize biblical studies in such an experiential and hands-on way equipped me with the tools and motivations to democratize biblical studies in my future work.

Jason Bachand

Reflecting upon my initial learning goals and the knowledge I hoped to acquire from this course, it is clear that much has changed. In formulating my learning plan, I began with a distinctively third-paradigm perspective, drawing on a recent field study experience in India and, specifically, encounters with Dalit (oppressed) Christians. I spoke of what liberation theology does for the Dalits, using the language of James Cone in citing the "preferential option for the poor." Yet even without much foreknowledge of the emerging fourth paradigm, I stated that "no system of belief operates beyond the influence of context, and every category of faith begins with an emotional (and to a much lesser extent, intellectual) assent to preconditioned assumptions." At the time I had only this vague understanding of location with which to engage the hermeneutical task. I would soon see what progress has been made in the fourth paradigm toward raising consciousness about how sociopolitical location forms the biases and presumptions of biblical and academic study.

At the onset it was my intention to seek a hermeneutic of biblical studies derived from Dalit liberation theology and the Hindu concept of *darśan* (seeing the divine image). Now, I understand how such a hermeneutic, while perhaps intellectually or spiritual interesting, could have become yet another piece of an already fragmented field of study. My own presuppositions and biases would be manifested as a paradigm seeking legitimacy through kyriarchy. Whether or not I would have avoided the pitfalls of imperialist thinking—hoping to show that my paradigm was more humane, compassionate, logical, or "true" than others—cannot be certain. What I believe to be true now, however, is that a radical democratic space in biblical studies will not be created via the introduction of additional, competing hermeneutics. As Elisabeth Schüssler Fiorenza has demonstrated in this book, new voices and old voices engaging in equal dialogue toward genuine understanding are the means needed to arrive at that end. Ultimately the gradual realization of my own imperialist modes of thought dramatically altered my learning goals, which were, I must concede in hindsight, decidedly biased toward justifying my own views at the expense of others. After all, it is this "critical" pedagogy that dominates in the academy, not just in divinity schools and seminaries, but also in many fields of inquiry across public and private institutions. Prior to this course, the "banking model" or the "master-disciple" models were the only pedagogies I had encountered in any teaching environment.

I came into class feeling very comfortable as self-identified liberationist with a disdain for the fundamentalist variety of first-paradigm
thinking. I introduced myself in class as a "proud enemy of the religious right." To say that I was oblivious to my own location is a bit of
an understatement. I hadn't previously turned the hermeneutical lens
inward, to become aware that the "value-free" knowledge I proudly
claimed from the second-paradigm, and liberationist convictions
drawn from the third, had become a tool of self-repeating dominance.
In claiming a superior or "better" perspective, I was fully engaged in the
perpetuation of kyriarchy.

At the close of the semester, I still believed in liberation theology's
objectives, and my beliefs about the Bible remain greatly informed by
the historical-critical perspective. But I'm also reminded, even as I seek
to flourish in my space and be guided by my own understanding of the
divine, to be self-aware and articulate about why I believe as I do. The
realization that no perspective on the Bible is value-free tempers my
theological thinking and humbles my sometimes zealous passion for
justice. My respect for different epistemologies runs deeper, and I am
fully convinced that complex thought is defined in part by the ability to
hold many ways of knowing in an appreciative, uncritical light.

Progressing through this seminar, together, I have been compelled
to consider the sociological and political history that formed my paradigmatic prejudice. I began the class ready to stake out my place in the
landscape of biblical studies, and discovered instead that I never really
knew where I was in the first place—or why. It was rather like the story
from the Upanishads of ten students, out on a walk in the forest, who
in the course of their promenade had to cross a river. The leader of
the students attempted to count to make sure all were present after the
crossing, only to repeatedly come up one short. Several students helpfully counted and each in turn came up one person short. At length, the
group came to the sad conclusion that one of them must have been lost
in the current during the crossing, until a wise man passing by pointed
out to the group that each counter had failed to include oneself in the
reckoning! This, perhaps, is the folly of any reductionist epistemology of
biblical studies, that in seeking to create a more pure, a more accurate,
or even a more sacred reading of Scripture, we invariably fail to count
ourselves, and our ancillary prejudices, in the theologies we create.

Thus, I have acquired a sense of urgency regarding the need to
engage all paradigms from time to time as I journey through life academically and as a spiritual seeker. I'm moving forward, too, with an

appreciation for the fourth paradigm's hermeneutic of location, that it is indeed OK to proudly locate oneself in a paradigm of choice within biblical studies, provided that determination is made honestly and with a critical self-regard (always making sure, you could say, to include oneself in the count!).

In addition to stating some learning objectives for the seminar, we were asked at the onset to develop an analytical self-matrix. I stated that my analytic would "hopefully come from participation and mutual seeking with all of the members of this class. We bring a wealth of experience, joys, pain, knowledge, and wisdom to this seminar, and from that tapestry I hope to draw inspiration and personal/professional development." Perhaps again reflecting a third paradigm perspective, I wanted my analytic to be a hermeneutic of the collective stories of our class, and I remain committed to this idea. The Theme-Centered Interaction model of didactics that we used as a class brought out, at least for me, a little bit of the *trauma* that comes with graduate studies, in biblical studies specifically.

My colleague, Arminta Fox, discussed trauma in her paper and a bit in the previous reflection, and I want to thank her for giving me that word and a broader vocabulary to speak of one product of kyriarchy in academic study. We wrestled with our own pain in our sessions and in doing so understood, in a real way, why biblical studies and educational theory are in need of a new democratic vision. For me, faith and the study of it are ultimately about people and what their convictions do for them. How does belief help or harm? How is it used for both healing and abuse? For others, of course, it's about discerning the other way: out of the self, through the Bible, and toward God. I am less convinced that the Bible has as much to say about God as it does about our own profound fears and needs. I'm willing to own that as one bias I have in biblical studies. Yet I also believe, as Elisabeth Schüssler Fiorenza does, that biblical studies needs a department of "public health" to examine how our beliefs about the Bible are formed, sustained, and—hopefully—challenged from time to time.

From the point of view of my own self-analytic, I feel that the class was an unqualified success. The work we've done together pushed me outside of my own narrow vision. Though I'm sure I originally envisioned a dialogue that would edify my profession and spiritual identity, the rhetorical-emancipatory analytic put to use in class worked as it should work, and my beliefs were problematized rather than justified. I learned to think differently about both knowledge itself and the way it is disseminated. I had to step outside of my own confidence. My experience, though by no means normative, might speak to other aspirants of a democratic space in biblical studies or other fields of inquiry, and sincerely wish that others might be blessed with the same opportunities for self-awareness and growth that Schüssler Fiorenza has proposed in this book.

I have to confess, however, that this class made me very anxious from the onset. Try as I might to be "cool" about taking a class at Harvard with Schüssler Fiorenza, it took me several weeks to get over the sheer terror of, well, taking a class at Harvard with Schüssler Fiorenza. Coming from Andover-Newton to Harvard Divinity School each week felt like an astronomical shift in worlds. The ethos of Harvard—its history, its reputation—is weighty, to say the least, and I felt that pressure each week. I was unsure: Would I be accepted here? Would I be viewed as inferior since I come from an institution with nowhere near the renown of Harvard? I wanted to be valued and respected, to know that my academic experience and personal history mattered. Every week I felt the terror of operating under kyriarchy: What if I got a poor grade in a course at Harvard? Wouldn't that surely be a blow to my professional aspirations? What would my classmates think of me?

This subjective experience of trauma helped me to quickly appreciate what Elisabeth is calling for in this book. My initial fears were allayed with time and the gradual understanding that our class sought to be different. Yet that anxiety gave me an appreciation of *why* we need a radical democratic space in biblical studies—in the academy, church, and public. I'm a very privileged white, male, middle-class student pursuing graduate education, and in a wider perspective my trauma is quite negligible. How much more urgent is a democratic space for those more severely impacted by biblical texts, the traditions and prejudices around them, and the very practical way they are often implemented? How much more urgent is radical democratic space for voices long silenced, for those whose abuse and terror is legitimized by biblical authority?

And yet how important, too, is a radical space for the voices of peace and compassion given poetry and grace by the Bible. How important the democratic space for the millions who call it life's instruction book, and their stories of faith and joy. We need to hear them, too.

I hope this exercise in self-analysis helps convey why democratizing biblical studies is a matter of healing and hope. Far from just a flourish for my CV, this seminar and Elisabeth's book have informed my faith and theology in ways I did not anticipate, and it is my hope that the vision of a democratic space will go with me into whatever personal and professional context I move. I imagine now what I was once unable to see: the discursive space that can create emancipation and peace not only in biblical studies but also wherever complex, integrated knowledge is sought. Thus I feel compelled to offer the prayer that Meister Eckhart wrote would be enough even if it were the only one ever spoken: "Thank you."

Tyler Schwaller

The seminar's exploration of paradigms provided sites for struggle that led to intellectual and, dare I say, spiritual growth. While Jason Bachand discovered that wrestling with his position within the paradigms of biblical studies deepened his faith and theology, tussling with the notion of paradigms more generally allowed me to better articulate the variegated spaces of the discipline and the authority of the methods located therein. My prior experiences in biblical studies had tinted much of my reading and interpretation in terms of the fourth paradigm, but over the course of the semester, I came to realize that locating the specific paradigm out of which scholarship functions—recognizing the assumptions invested in the frameworks employed—is important if one is to understand the particular disciplinary language being spoken. With competence in the various paradigms, we scholars and scholars-in-training can engage one another with sensitivity toward and understanding of one another's terms, and only then can we find meaningful points of contact for creative collaboration.

In my sophomore year as an undergraduate student, I had the rare and exciting opportunity to participate in a biblical studies class that was fashioned as a radically democratic space along the lines of that envisioned in *Democratizing Biblical Studies*. This class did not depend upon attendance requirements to enforce presence or regular examinations to ensure that students had read the materials; instead, the pedagogy of collaboration encouraged and facilitated full engagement on the part of all participants. A variety of creative educational tools were employed; yet on some days conversations would begin with the professor simply asking, "So what did you think of the readings?" Students were called upon to take responsibility for drawing out the arguments of those scholars whose work had been presented, to address the topic at hand. Through regular reflections and discussion, class members were trained to think critically, using their learning as well as their own experiences to respond to the key issues raised in the class. Still today I can recall with specificity the readings, conversations, debates, and presentations from that semester of study; I had engaged with the material and with my colleagues so fully that the personal and academic growth was permanent. I had never learned so much or retained it so completely.

Once I had experienced just how effective collaborative education could be, I began to wonder why all professors did not employ such pedagogy. Why didn't instructors expect students to take greater responsibility for their learning? Why were students not encouraged to participate as experts—in training but still capable of critical thought and significant intellectual contribution? Interested in biblical studies and passionate about education, I started to imagine how I might, in my own future classrooms, follow the example of the radically democratic model for learning that I had come to appreciate. Now as a master of divinity student at Harvard Divinity School, I have been in a small but noteworthy number of classes in which the professors have explicitly identified their pedagogical approach as informed by frameworks and methodologies that decenter traditional hegemonic methods of education. However, I am not convinced that many ever realize the radical notion of a democratic space; discussion sections, at their best, theoretically establish a forum of many voices, but most often the master-disciple model is the reality. Why is it that graduate education in biblical studies remains essentially unchanged even with increasing recognition that the dominant pedagogical practices are problematic and not necessarily the best?

With these questions in mind, I was thrilled when I saw that Elisabeth Schüssler Fiorenza was offering a seminar titled "Democratizing Biblical Studies" to explore these very pedagogical issues pertinent to the field. The seminar provided an opportunity to once again experience a collaborative classroom, and the insights into the discipline, explored through the diverse perspectives within the group, provided the tools to more fully understand and reflect upon the field so as to better consider its transformation. In my initial seminar reflection paper, I stated my hope "to better articulate the malestream history of biblical studies that has excluded voices from the margins, and to more thoroughly understand the rhetoric that has functioned in both institutions to maintain dominance of the elite." Most helpful in this regard was Schüssler Fiorenza's delineation of the paradigms that constitute biblical studies.

I found this particularly useful since it allowed me personally to more specifically consider what is at stake in scholarly work.

I have had the benefit of learning with scholars who have primarily located themselves within the third and fourth paradigms, and so my default assumption is to read texts with multiple meanings that can lend themselves toward the work of justice. I recall one time in an undergraduate class when the professor asked if a certain reading would be considered feminist. I answered affirmatively because I had read the ends to which the argument could be taken as supporting feminist claims. However, the author himself never identified as a feminist, nor did he state that he had feminist interests in mind; his work on its own did not seek to achieve the kind of feminist vision of equality that I had pushed it toward. Through the work of the seminar, I now would be able to name the scholarship as a third-paradigm effort at destabilizing traditional interpretations.

Over the course of the semester, I wrestled with the question "Does it really matter if one is able to locate the paradigm out of which scholarship functions?" In light of previous experience and the competence gained through this seminar, I ultimately came away answering affirmatively. I find myself invested in the fourth paradigm's struggle for justice, but not every scholarship that can be employed in efforts for equality works toward justice on its own. Though it is possible to use what is produced within another paradigm in fourth-paradigm efforts, it would be a mistake to conflate paradigms. By thinking explicitly about the frameworks and methods behind scholarship, it is possible to recognize where different approaches lead to distinct results. While third-paradigm work might helpfully destabilize traditional assumptions and create space for new meanings to occur, it does not necessarily seek justice. In fact, a problem encountered in the seminar is that the third paradigm's proliferation of interpretive possibilities denies the opportunity for subjugated peoples to name themselves as subjects and envision the truth of an alternative reality. An understanding of the paradigms prepares scholars to ask specific questions that can draw out the frameworks and approaches of particular work. In recognizing the starting points of scholarship, it is possible to acknowledge and appreciate parallels and to challenge and engage in the spaces where divergence occurs. For those in the fourth paradigm, only with the realization that work stops short of justice can there be a call forward.

Some of the most challenging and yet profound moments of the seminar came in the recognition that people were approaching a question or issue out of divergent paradigms. Through these experiences, I realized that even when the goals are similar, the authority invested in a particular paradigm can unintentionally lead to exclusion of other thoughts and ideas. Exclusivity comes in that paradigms are generally conceived as able to replace other competing approaches; their methods are constructed as authoritative. The trouble in communicating across different paradigms is that what is authoritative for some is not necessarily authoritative for others. Failure to recognize foundational differences results in an inability to address people on terms that are meaningful to them. Within the seminar, there was often a shared commitment to justice, and the spirit of collaboration meant giving full consideration to different voices. We learned, though, that the methods toward justice sometimes differed, and understanding the paradigm from which a person worked was necessary in order to know what was authoritative to that person. By identifying individual frameworks and approaches, we could pinpoint commonalities, as well as respect the values at the heart of another's work without being immediately dismissive or ultimately exclusive.

I imagine that a question that arose at times during the seminar will be asked in response to the book: "What does a transformed biblical studies look like? How *exactly* can collaboration occur?" This is the unspoken challenge of Schüssler Fiorenza's work. Deconstruction is the easy part. Reconstruction requires imagination. Though we envisioned possible manifestations of a radical democratic space, the seminar realized that for any scholar to singularly establish concrete steps and to paint a clear picture of the destination would be to re-create a kind of hegemony. To realize a collaborative discipline, the field must actually practice organic, spontaneous, dynamic, thoughtful, *creative* collaboration. The United States educational system—from primary to graduate school—teaches that pedagogy is a road map to be followed. Passage from one point to the next depends upon ability to prove that one has acquired the prescribed skills for moving forward. Even when desiring to imagine something different, it is an ingrained instinct to expect clear expectations. This is why some professors state that their pedagogy is informed by a nontraditional philosophy, and yet their classes look only vaguely nontraditional. To transform biblical studies, scholars will have to resist the urge to seek or develop concrete answers and instead harness their imaginative energies, being wildly creative as they produce new approaches to graduate education. The operative word in fashioning a radical democratic space for biblical studies is *practice*. The seminar was a practice in collaboration, in identifying different frameworks and valuing different approaches while working together around a common set of issues and questions. The result was a proliferation of ideas for transforming biblical studies, some reflected upon in this metalogue, others presented in papers posted online, and more spoken and still unspoken. What was practiced for a semester in the seminar, this book seeks to inspire in order that even more alternatives to malestream educational approaches might spring up. With its thorough explication of the problems, resources for reconceptualizing the discipline, and clear call to take up the dynamic forces of imagination and creativity, *Democratizing Biblical Studies* makes a significant contribution to the field and has the potential to move conversation forward and inspire pedagogical innovation.

Elizabeth Gish

I was drawn into biblical studies because I saw how much the Bible matters to people, and how profoundly biblical interpretation shapes our world today. Biblical stories and verses bring comfort to us in our darkest moments, inspire us to do better, and urge us to live a life filled with love and hope. As John Falcone notes in his roundtable contribution, biblical interpretation has the potential to support communities in "resistance and liberation, for both survival and transformation." At the same time, the Bible has been used to do great harm, and it continues to be used to justify violence and oppression. Its stories are used to condemn and judge; its verses are wielded like swords. I am intrigued by a collection of texts that hold such different meanings for such a wide range of people across cultures, continents, and centuries— intrigued that these texts have been and remain the source of much good, and at the same time, immense harm. Ultimately, my interest in biblical studies comes not from the perspective of a detached observer or curious interloper, but rather from my position as a feminist, scholar, and ordination candidate committed to the ways that we might transform our faith communities and, ultimately, our world. How can we bend the arc of history toward justice and equality? And what can we discern from ancient texts about the ways that faith communities have negotiated the challenges of living together with difficult questions, conflicting theologies and ideologies, and structures of kyriarchy over many centuries?

While these questions seem so pressing to me, and as I have learned from our class, also drive others' interests in biblical studies, Schüssler Fiorenza eloquently outlines for her readers the ways that the dominant approaches to biblical studies rarely attend to the role that biblical texts continue to play in shaping our world. Rather, the discipline is typically understood and practiced as a "value-neutral" science, where the emphasis is on acquiring the proper knowledge and language skills, and arriving at the best determination of *the* right theological or historical meaning of the text. Attention to the ways that the Bible is understood and used today is often, at best, left for footnotes. At worst (and most typically), it is not addressed at all.

Thus, our seminar, "Democratizing Biblical Studies," and engagement with Schüssler Fiorenza's book with the same title, presented a unique opportunity not only to think about the ways that biblical studies might be transformed as a discipline, but also to begin to frame research questions that might be possible within a transformed field. How might we begin to think about and enact biblical studies as a republic of many voices where scholars, students, the public, and faithful people can reflect together about the public and personal meanings of the biblical texts?

My goals for the class centered on exploring the ways to invite conservative communities situated in the first paradigm into new ways of reading the Bible that are more radically democratic and emancipatory. Although my religious background and experiences are rather heterogeneous, an important part of my childhood and adolescent years was influenced by conservative parts of the religious-theological-scriptural paradigm. This is no longer my spiritual or academic home, but I have remained committed to thinking about ways that biblical studies, as an academic discipline, can speak to the concerns of those who understand the Bible as sacred Scripture and believe that biblical texts represent the revealed, authoritative Word of G*d. How can we shape a republic of many voices that is truly democratic, creating safe space at the table for a range of voices across all of the paradigms?

Throughout our time together in class, some key themes emerged that helped me to better clarify my approach to this question. One of central issues we returned to repeatedly was David Damrosch's reminder in *We Scholars* that "any proposal for reform must locate itself between two poles: a change should be as substantial as possible while realizable in a significant number of situations." While taking time to think about how things *should be* is central to any reform project, another important part of our work focused on *how* to get there. What is possible in both the short and long term? Or as Tyler Schwaller asks in his roundtable contribution, "How *exactly* can collaboration occur?"

Through our discussions in class and in reading and providing feedback on the research of my classmates, three themes emerged that helped me to move closer to my goal of articulating realizable approaches to inviting more conservative parts of the first paradigm into ways of reading the Bible that are radically democratic and emancipatory.

First, I came to better appreciate the need to articulate the current challenges that biblical studies faces as a field, particularly from the perspective of the fourth paradigm, which understands biblical studies in ethical, rhetorical, political, cultural, emancipatory terms and biblical studies scholars as transformative, public intellectuals working toward a more just and equal world. In my own desire for change and action, grounded in the fourth paradigm, I can be too hasty in wanting to move from thinking and discussing to taking action. Yet it was very helpful for me to take the time, with the class, to discuss further and better articulate the issues at hand before making suggestions about what should be *done*. This ultimately helped to shape my class project, which emphasized the value of conversation and critical engagement around difficult questions as a key part of reform.

Following this, our work together throughout the class helped to clarify the ways that change and reform do not hinge only on better explaining our own perspective well enough to others or making the case for our position clearly enough. We must also be engaged more holistically: with our bodily presence and our emotions. Many inhabit the place in their particular biblical studies paradigm not only intellectually or cognitively, but also emotionally and bodily, and in seeking change we must find ways to better take this into account.

Finally, while much of my focus remains on opening up space for change within the conservative parts of the religious-theological-scriptural paradigm, our work in this class helped me to better recognize the way that both liberal and conservative parts of all the paradigms struggle (or rather, should struggle) with the ways that they perpetuate kyriarchal structures. The manifestation of kyriarchy is perhaps most overt in conservative parts of the first paradigm, but in some senses, it makes such kyriarchal structures easier to identify and, thus, address. In the other paradigms, particularly liberal parts, the kyriarchal structures are often more covert. So while lip service may be given to equality or feminism, and while overtly racist language may not be used, the structures of marginalization and oppression are still quite present. It seems to me that often it is more difficult to address manifestations of kyriarchy in contexts where people fancy themselves liberal, and somehow immune to sexism, racism, heterosexism, and classism. Thus I have been challenged to broaden my perspective in thinking about the ways that kyriarchal structures can be addressed throughout the various paradigms in biblical studies, and to remain attentive to the ways that I am implicated in the perpetuation of such structures. I have been moved to better address how we might dismantle the kyriarchal pyramid throughout biblical studies, which has, I believe, profound implications for the wider world that the discipline inevitably impacts.

Ultimately our work together in this course, and engagement with Schüssler Fiorenza's book, has helped me to be clearer about the ways that democratizing biblical studies is not "just" about reforming the way that biblical studies is taught to future scholars and future ministers, but that it has sweeping implications for the ways that we, as a society—as a democracy—live our lives, build our worlds, and nurture and create intellectual and faith communities.

Hannah Hofheinz

What would it be like to participate in a democratizing, emancipatory form of graduate education? How might this be envisioned? What would be the qualities of a radical democratic learning space? What pedagogical, personal, and intellectual benefits would be gained through a republic of many voices? What elements are required to achieve this liberative space? What persisting and transient systems and structures currently hinder, challenge, or simply refuse this type of inclusive learning? What systems and structures cry out for its realization? What practices draw together the learning communities in which I participate now and in the future? How, as a full person—thinking, heart-beating, interacting, learning, growing person—am I implicated, encouraged, challenged, and responsible for the transformative production of democratizing dynamic knowledge?

This course opened the door for me to step beyond the threshold of my assumed pedagogical practices and internalized educational experiences. With the seminar as my guide, I walked into a space shaped by these conscious and critical questions, a space that enveloped me in a rich, diverse, and deep collection of theoretical and human resources for life-affirming educational models. As demonstrated in the reflections above, this space, on the one hand, offered an intimate opportunity for self-reflection and coming to consciousness even as, on the other hand, it pushed us outward into the academy and world. It is a space that, as Elizabeth Gish stated, undeniably "has sweeping implications for the ways that we live our lives."

As a student in theology, I entered into this seminar, "Democratizing Biblical Studies," with a series of assumptions, questions, and curiosities. I assumed that I would engage with a substantive body of (hopefully) enlightening information that (hopefully) I would be expected to critically integrate into the toolbox of theory, experience, and methods that doctoral course work is supposed to provide. Instead, I engaged in a dynamic process of collaborative learning vastly broader than the original syllabus and more dynamic than any toolbox is equipped to handle. I questioned whether my more extensive background in theology and less extensive background in biblical studies would prove sufficient. I found that I was able to beneficially offer my unique background, my driving interests, and my full self to the pursuits of the course and the learning community. In addition, the similarly unique preparations, commitments, and resources of the other participants correspondingly expanded and challenged my own. Unlike my experience in other seminars, I leave this course convinced that *each* and *every* member of our learning community uniquely contributed, challenged, and furthered my education. Should even one person have been absent, our conversations and resources would have been fundamentally different, leading in turn to different educational results. For our particular experience, I thank each member of the seminar.

This course offered a collaborative and communal performance of democratizing biblical studies, a critical praxis far exceeding the text written into Elisabeth Schüssler Fiorenza's manuscript. As offered in the first chapter, this praxis recognizes that graduate biblical education (and graduate education in general) is accountable to (1) excellence within the academy, (2) a commitment to truth and justice within religious communities, and (3) the public ideals of human rights and democracy in society. As we progressed through the semester, I felt challenged individually and as a member of the learning community to successfully weave these three elements into a mutually informing dynamic. I attempted to meet this challenge (with variable success) by seeking to braid intellectual rigor, honesty, integrity, and accountability in the communal interactions inside the classroom and beyond—to braid them with a willingness to dream and imagine transformation transcending any kyriarchally determined boundaries of known reality. In inventorying this experience, I wonder whether, in order to be successfully internalized, an encounter with democratizing biblical studies requires the type of performance experienced in our classroom, or whether a text alone, such as this book, can sufficiently open the richness of transformative possibility.

Democratizing Biblical Studies recognizes that an essential element in re-envisioning and transforming biblical studies is the delineation of the ideologies and discourses shaping the four paradigms and thus endeavors to do just that. So also, this course supported and encouraged me to self-critically and self-reflectively question the ideologies and discourses that shape my intellectual and personal interactions. The third chapter's insistence on recognizing and maintaining the essential diversity of critical perspectives within the fourth paradigm exemplified an intimate challenge to my own ability to recognize and to hold within myself the diversity of elements informing my identity as a scholar, woman, and accountable community member. Because the course was fundamentally active rather than receptive or passive, this required not just thinking and reflecting internally but also *actively practicing* how I might seek to more transparently engage through the complexity of my identity in the community of learning.

In my experience, our version of Elisabeth Schüssler Fiorenza's "circle dance" did indeed create a flourishing space of radical democratic equality. While each of us brought unique and important resources into the room, it was through our community *together*—that is, our interaction and mutual engagement in imagining the possibility of a liberative, radical-democratic model of education—that I stepped across the threshold of the established and entered into the space of new possibility. Put differently, I gained a great deal as an "I" through the "We" that we formed in our mutual commitment to imagine democratizing biblical studies. I believe that as time continues, the value that I place on our relationships and interactions will only increase, even as I learn to critique and reevaluate some of the substantive material both constituting and constituted by this course experience. The sustaining value of meaningful relationships endures change, and I do believe ours is a meaningful relationship. This is not, however, to discount the depth, breadth, and importance of the substantive knowledge gained over the last four months.

Our discussions of sexuality challenged me to better understand not only the bodilyness of biblical interpretation and the educational enterprise, but also the ways in which the treatment of bodies in general and sexuality in particular illuminates a critical nexus of socially effective kyriarchal ideology, to be countered by a liberative model of cross-paradigm interaction in biblical studies. The insistent vocalization of experiences from the margins and of a continued silencing, dehumanizing, or ineffective inclusion of marginalized perspectives in the academy—all this required my focus on the importance of a transformed model of education for concrete and complicated lives. The seminar's direct confrontation with questions of trauma in the academy opened a space not only to weave these conceptual elements into my understanding of a re-envisioned biblical studies, but also to recognize my own position in the contexts of hurt and healing.

Throughout the semester, our work reinforced the importance of remembering the strength of theological authority and conservative, fundamentalist, and liberal religious conviction to either hinder or help with transformation through dialogue and interaction. I was pragmatically and consistently challenged to attend to forms of biblical studies outside of the academy, and to push the conversation into worldly precision, practicality, and clarity. These challenges illuminated how often I wrongly naturalize an imprecise generality about which I am myself unclear. When I was stuck and couldn't quite figure out how to formulate a question, a quiet yet strong voice would arise from somewhere in the room to pinpoint the issue. Collaboration was an essential element in my learning, and I am endlessly grateful. Most important, the learning facilitated by democratizing biblical studies is never simply for learning's sake. The dynamic and persistent passion for justice that overflowed in our seminar room rightly challenged me to ensure that my engagement with our materials moved beyond theory and intellectual engagement. No less than life itself is at stake in this pursuit. Desire and love are immediately and essentially involved in the re-envisioning of biblical studies.

Index